PERSONALITY TRAITS: THEORY, TESTING AND INFLUENCES

PSYCHOLOGY OF EMOTIONS, MOTIVATIONS AND ACTIONS

Additional books in this series can be found on Nova's website under the Series tab.

Additional E-books in this series can be found on Nova's website under the E-books tab.

PSYCHOLOGY OF EMOTIONS, MOTIVATIONS AND ACTIONS

PERSONALITY TRAITS:
THEORY, TESTING AND INFLUENCES

MELISSA E. JORDAN
EDITOR

Nova Science Publishers, Inc.

New York

NOTICE TO THE READER

The Publisher has taken reasonable care in the preparation of this book, but makes no expressed or implied warranty of any kind and assumes no responsibility for any errors or omissions. No liability is assumed for incidental or consequential damages in connection with or arising out of information contained in this book. The Publisher shall not be liable for any special, consequential, or exemplary damages resulting, in whole or in part, from the readers' use of, or reliance upon, this material. Any parts of this book based on government reports are so indicated and copyright is claimed for those parts to the extent applicable to compilations of such works.

Independent verification should be sought for any data, advice or recommendations contained in this book. In addition, no responsibility is assumed by the publisher for any injury and/or damage to persons or property arising from any methods, products, instructions, ideas or otherwise contained in this publication.

This publication is designed to provide accurate and authoritative information with regard to the subject matter covered herein. It is sold with the clear understanding that the Publisher is not engaged in rendering legal or any other professional services. If legal or any other expert assistance is required, the services of a competent person should be sought. FROM A DECLARATION OF PARTICIPANTS JOINTLY ADOPTED BY A COMMITTEE OF THE AMERICAN BAR ASSOCIATION AND A COMMITTEE OF PUBLISHERS.

Additional color graphics may be available in the e-book version of this book.

LIBRARY OF CONGRESS CATALOGING-IN-PUBLICATION DATA

Personality traits : theory, testing and influences / editor, Melissa E. Jordan.
      p. cm.
Includes index.
ISBN 978-1-61728-934-7 (hardcover)
1. Personality tests. 2. Personality assessment. 3. Personality disorders. I. Jordan, Melissa E.
BF698.5.P47 2010
155.2'32--dc22
                                        2010026177

Published by Nova Science Publishers, Inc. + New York

CONTENTS

PREFACE

Chapter 1 – A high prevalence of co-occurrence among addictive disorders and personality disorders has been documented. Studies have usually found between a 50 and 75 percent of addicted individuals with Axis II concurrent diagnosis. However, such diagnoses often do not take account of several changes related to the course of addiction that affect functioning of the frontal lobe and, consequently, the overall programming of behaviour. Simple diagnosis based on the ICD or DSM classifications, without regard to etiological factors, is just a still photograph reflecting a fractal of a long development process altered by addiction. Impairment of frontal cortical function due to direct effects of the substance or to mediators as stress factors, are the basis of most of the symptoms justifying the diagnosis of personality disorders. Miller's proposals on stable and induced-by-stress disorders, as well as new findings on executive dysfunction linked to addiction must be taken into consideration. Personality disorders, so understood, should be treated differently from the present, including cognitive stimulation techniques and attending to stress and coping, preventing symptomatic prescribing of drugs with dubious benefits and multiple side effects. New neurological and neuropsychological perspectives of addiction do not support concepts such as comorbidity as a priority intervention guide.

Chapter 2 - The aim of this chapter is to update the status of the art of the relationship between morningness-eveningness preference and personality. To this end, keeping in mind the wide number of personality models available in literature, this chapter discusses three of them: 1) Eysenck's model; 2) Big Five model; 3) Cloninger's model. On the basis of main data reported in papers, it is suggested that future studies should focus on the Cloninger's psychobiological model of personality because it takes into account both biological (temperament dimensions) and socio-cultural (character dimensions) aspects, being thus useful to address their respective importance linking circadian rhythms with personality characteristics. To this aim, cross-cultural comparisons are specifically needed. Implications of this chapter in several applied areas are also discussed.

Chapter 3 – Clinical and Forensic cases are reviewed regarding how an examiner should conceptualize the adult experience of having Imaginary Companions (IC). Some clinical and forensic research indicates that there is an overlap between adult IC and Dissociative experiences/disorders. However, other forensic case studies, a phenomenological perspective and expert opinion also indicate that the adult IC experience can occur in other clinical disorders, with personality disorders, and as the sole feature of one's clinical presentation. Also, research has identified that adult ICs can be linked to acts of violence, sex offending and self-harm. The diagnostic dilemma of how to conceptualize and diagnose these cases is most pertinent when ICs are involved and blamed for the commission of violent and criminal acts. Since the creation and dismissing of Adult ICs is a conscious and voluntary experience, the legal plea of Not Guilty by Reason of (Insanity) Mental Disease or Defect is not appropriate. Several different diagnostic possibilities are presented, consistent with DSM IV-TR. The Fantasy Prone Personality is also presented as another diagnostic classification possibility but with no current counterpart in the DSM IV-TR. The current gap in the authors knowledge in how to diagnose the presentation of ICs in adults, especially when they are involved in the commission of criminal acts should prompt more dialogue between clinicians, forensic examiners and researchers to develop a new diagnostic nomenclature.

The creation of Imaginary Companions (IC) that persist into adulthood can influence one's adult functioning and lead to clinical disorders and even forensic consequences. Currently, there exists a gap in our diagnostic nomenclature in how to regard, and diagnose the existence of ICs in the forensic evaluation. Cases were reviewed from the clinical and forensic literature regarding how to conceptualize the adult IC experience. A number of studies suggest an over-lap between the adult IC experience and dissociative and other clinical disorders. However, other studies, a phenomenological perspective and expert opinion describes them as different phenomena. Cases involving IC involvement and acts of violence will also be presented, and the difficulties of how to diagnose these cases is highlighted and suggestions are offered, including the Fantasy Prone Personality (Disorder). Although the Fantasy-Prone Personality is not regarded as a valid diagnostic category according to DSM IV-TR, the focus of this article is to highlight the current ambiguity in how to regard the adult IC phenomena, the personality type who continues to possess one into adulthood, and to suggest the Fantasy Prone Personality as one possible diagnostic alternative as well as other diagnostic options.

Chapter 4 – Individual differences in schizotypal personality traits (schizotypy), which might be the predisposition to schizophrenia, have commonly been explored as a means of examining the nature and structure of schizophrenia symptoms. Research on schizotypal personality in the general population may provide a particular opportunity to study the biological and cognitive markers of vulnerability to schizophrenia without the confounding effects of long-term hospitalization, medication, and severe psychotic symptoms.

A systematic review of general-population surveys indicated that the experiences associated with schizophrenia and related categories, such as paranoid delusional thinking and auditory hallucinations, are observed in an attenuated form in 5–8% of healthy people. These attenuated expressions could be regarded as the behavioral marker of an underlying risk for schizophrenia and related disorders, just as high blood pressure indicates high susceptibility for cardiovascular disease in a dose–response fashion.

Auditory hallucination (AH) refers to the perception that one's own inner speech originates outside the self. Patients with AH make external misattributions of the source of perceived speech. Recent studies have suggested that auditory hallucinations in patients with schizophrenia might occur in the right hemisphere, where they might produce irregular and unpredicted inner speech, which their auditory and sensory feedback processing system does not attribute to themselves.

In the present study, general participants judged self–other attribution in speech subjectively in response to on-line auditory feedback presented through their right, left, and both ears. People with high auditory-hallucination-like experiences made external misattributions more frequently under the right- and left-ear only conditions compared with the both-ears condition. The authorsinterpreted this result as suggesting that people with a high degree of proneness to AH might have disorders in both the right and left hemispheric language-related areas: speech perception deficit in the left hemisphere and prediction violation in speech processing in the right hemisphere.

A perspective that situates schizophrenia on a continuum with general personality variations implies that this disorder constitutes a potential risk for everyone and, thus, helps to promote understanding and correct misunderstandings that contribute to prejudice.

Chapter 5 – Talking about addiction genetics and its most common comorbid disorders, Personality Disorders (PD), one of the concepts that first should be clarified is the importance of the studies logic chronology on psychiatric genetics. Thus, it should be noted that for molecular genetic techniques to be justified in any study, a substantial role of genetics in the etiology of this disorder has to be demonstrated first by epidemiological data. Genetic epidemiological studies which here is referred to are mainly three: family, twin and adoption studies. So, if these studies do not raise doubts about whether or not one disorder is inherited, it is better to focus on the environmental causes and drop molecular studies determined to "grab" some related gene. Once the genetic implication has been demonstrated in some disorder's etiology, it is time to mathematical and molecular genetic studies. By means of these studies, detecting which gene or combination of genes causes the disorder is a matter of try. This is not easy, though, considering that only 2% of the 3 billion base pairs of DNA are genes.

Once in the field of molecular genetics, difficulties manifest. The first genes isolated and characterized are either Mendelian or monogenic characters, hereditary diseases or somatic malignancies mostly, in which there is a major gene involved. The Mendelian scheme fulfills the "one gene / one disease" rule. Thus, one single-locus mutations cause one specific disease, e.g. sickle cell anemia, cystic fibrosis, phenylketonuria and Huntington's disease. Non-Mendelian characters either depend on a small number of loci (oligogenic characters) or gene plots (polygenes), with each of them showing a small effect with an environmental factor varied contribution. All these possibilities are included within the term multifactorial character.

However, unlike one might suspect, monogenic characters are not exempt of complexity. Many of them either have "reduced penetrance", meaning that not all individuals with the conferring disease genotype develop it; "variable expression", meaning that there is a huge variability on disease's severity; or "pleiotropy", when the gene has more than a single appreciable effect on the body. On the other hand, different genes may promote a single phenotype in different families. In this case is called "genetic" or "locus heterogeneity". Even more, different mutations in the same gene can cause distinguishable clinical diseases. Hence, there is an enormous genetic complexity, even through simple Mendelian characters, which are only governed by one gene. This suggests that there is a few purely Mendelian biological characters, and that may be extend to purely polygenic also.

Studies on the role of genetic factors in biopsychosocial diseases in humans have to confront many problems. Among them, the polygenic and multifactorial nature of inheritance stands out by itself, so that multiple genes and environmental factors interact in each subject in very different ways and degrees.

Chapter 6 – Personality is a specific pattern of individual behavioral, emotional, and thought processesthatremain relatively stable throughout life. The pattern that is characterized by ready elicitation and maintenance of a high anxiety level is referred to as the "anxious personality". Although many researchers have proposed theoretical models of the anxious personality trait, the most influential have been "Neuroticism (vs. Emotional Stability)" developed by Eysenck, the "Behavioral Inhibition System" developed by Gray, "Neuroticism" developed by Costa and McCrae, and "Harm Avoidance" developed by Cloninger.

Research on personality can be originally traced back to the "personality trait theory", which attempted to account for human personality as several measurable "traits". Such studies have been based on factorial analysis in which many adjectival termswere adopted to describe individual behavioral, emotional, or thought characteristics,and converged into several fundamental components (i.e. traits). Although researchers in this field have not reached a consensus on the number of such personality traits, they have commonly found that one of themis closely related to an increased level of anxiety. In an attempt to settle this lingering controversy over the number of traits by proposing that human personality consists of five basic ones, mostly derivedfrom systematic factorial analysis, Costa and McCrae 985)adopted the term "Neuroticism" for that related to anxiety. They considered that individuals with a high Neuroticism (N) score tend to exhibit worry, nervousness, emotionality, insecurity, inadequacy, or hypochondria. The original adoption of N can be seen in "Neuroticism (vs. Emotional Stability)" proposed by Eysenck. Showing considerable similarity to N, this Neuroticism is associated with anxiety, depression, tension, feelingsof guilt, low self-esteem, lack of autonomy, moodiness, hypochondria, and obsession. However, Eysenck's theory was of distinct importance in the history of personality research because it specificallymentioned the biological basis of personality, whereas most traditional studies based on factorial analysis had made every endeavor to derive a minimum number of traitscapable of describing human personality. As with the anxiety-related personality trait, he explained that individual differences in Neuroticism are based on activation thresholds in the sympathetic nervous system or visceral brain, which is also referred to as the limbic system, including the amygdala, hippocampus, septum, and hypothalamus.

Chapter 7 – The 'mind-body connection' has become a new buzz phrase that has served a variety of purposes including validating the practice of clinical psychology amongst the medical professionals. The results from a myriad of studies within this century have provided empirical evidence for the relations between the mind and body. Central to this connection are personality differences in one's world view, specifically optimistic versus pessimistic dispositions. Featured prominently in this body of literature is the beneficial role of optimism in physical health outcomes. More careful examination of the relations between optimism and health has begun to differentiate between the benefits associated with physical health and those circumscribed to psychological health. Researchers have made several additional distinctions regarding research on optimism: some studies have elaborated on whether the relations between optimism and health are linear or curvilinear and others have highlighted the differences between optimism and pessimism.

Since personality differences account for the variation of emotional experiences from one person to the next, it shapes how one regulates their emotional experiences which in turn influence health. Emotion regulation, as defined by Gross is the process by which people influence the emotions they have and how they experience and express these emotions. These processes can be automatic or controlled and conscious or unconscious. These emotion processes are largely influenced by individual differences in personality. Personality differences in dispositional factors such as optimism have attracted the interest of researchers as well as lay persons. The culture is littered with the pursuit of happiness and ways of training oneself to adopt a more optimistic view of life. Spurring the discussion has been the synchronicity between optimism and the very human condition to desire pleasurable emotional experiences and perhaps equally strongly shun painful ones. This chapter examines the optimism discourse occurring in the spheres of both empirical research and popular culture. The authorsintroduce a different perspective on the matter that is influenced by a parallel discourse which has not yet become a part of the lexicon of optimism although the evidence already exists, that of balance achieved through mindfulness.

Chapter 8 – Previous studies have detected different variables influencing the attitude towards individuals with schizophrenia. It has been considered that individual's knowledge about schizophrenia has an important role in shaping attitudes about people diagnosed with the disorder, and that a lack of knowledge may increase prejudice and discrimination of these individuals. However, additional factors related to particular characteristics of the perceiver, such as personality traits, may have a direct influence in the recognition of schizophrenia as a mental disease and the subsequent attitudes related to the disorder.

Chapter 9 – Initially, the "Reconstructive Therapy" of Dr. Jerome Schulte, focused on the treatment of the homicidal psychotic patient. After decades of treatment applying this model with a variety of offenses, Dr. Schulte believed that it could be applied to understand and treat the "Criminal Personality", various offenses as well as treating non-clinical populations of children, adolescents and adults. The goal of therapy became one of promoting personal growth and humanness through the positive resolution of Ericksonian stages. The question remains if the successful resolution of Erickson's Psychosocial stages is relevant to the functioning of a Person with an Intellectual Disability, and Criminal Offenses? A theoretical and initial exploratory analysis suggests that the Reconstructive Therapy model can be relevant to the treatment for Persons with Intellectual Disabilities (ID) and various offenses.

Chapter 10 – New research suggests that the structure of human brain predicts core qualities of the individual's personality. One specific model of personality, developed by Cloninger, was based upon an association of specific personality traits to an underlying neurobiology. This seven-factor model consists of four dimensions of temperament (harm avoidance, novelty seeking, reward dependence, persistence) and three dimensions of character (self-directedness, cooperativeness, self-transcendence). Each dimension represents a specific stimulus-response sensitivity, the particular modes of behavior that resulted, and the specific neurotransmitters involved. Four dimensions of temperament are thought to be genetically independent traits and are moderately inheritable and stable throughout life. Novelty seeking is thought to be derived by the behavioral activation system. Harm avoidance is related to the behavioral inhibition system. It reflects the tendency of an individual to inhibit or interrupt behaviors. Reward dependence refers to the individual's tendency to respond intensely to signals of reward, and it involves maintaining or continuing behaviors that have been previously associated with reinforcement. Persistence is the individual's ability to generate and maintain arousal and motivation internally, in the absence of immediate external reward. It reflects perseverance in behavior despite frustration, fatigue, and lack of reward. In this model, neurotransmitters were hypothesized to be associated with behavioral manifestations: dopamine for novelty seeking (behavioral activation), serotonin for harm avoidance (behavioral inhibition), and noradrenaline for reward dependence (behavioral maintenance). Character reflects individual differences in self-concepts about goals and values in relation to experience. It is predominantly determined by socialization. Temperament provokes perception and emotion, character regulates the cognitive processes. Thus, character leads to the development of a mature self-concept. The three dimensions of character develop over the course of time, and influence personal and social effectiveness into adulthood. Self-directedness expresses individual's competence toward autonomy, reliability, and maturity. Cooperativeness is related to social skills, such as support, collaboration, and partnership. Self-transcendence refers to identification with a unity of all things in the world and it reflects a tendency toward spirituality and idealism. Findings suggest that an association exists between personality dimensions, neurotransmitters' function and regional brain metabolism. As morphometric studies have stated, regional variance in the neuronal volume of specific brain structures seem to underpin the observed range of individual differences in personality traits. In this chapter, I will particularly focus on recent work at the molecular genetic and functional imaging level with respect to specific personality traits.

Chapter 11 - Alzheimer's disease (AD) is a degenerative pathology of the brain, causing dementia. Caregivers of persons with AD (ADcg) have to cope with cognitive impairment, behavioral symptoms and incompetence in daily living and they experience heavy burden. Besides, ADcg are the most important referent for physicians in reporting information about patients with AD (ADp), because ADp show lack of awareness of their changes. The aims of our research were to examine the relationship between specific personality traits of ADcg and perceived stress; moreover, to highlight the caregivers' capacity to be "objective" in evaluating functional abilities of ADp. In the first study, 118 ADcg were assessed using Caregiver Burden Inventory (CBI) and 16 Personality Factors- C form questionnaires (16PF-C). In the second study, 40 ADp and their caregivers were assessed in order to measure awarness using the Deficit Identification Questionnaire (DIQ); ADcg were also administered 16PF-C. Data from the first sample show that Reasoning (B), Emotional Stability (C) and Rule-Consciousness (G) were more strongly associated with caregiver burden; each indicator seems to be significant, to a different extent, for objective, developmental, physical, social and emotional burden. Caregivers characterized by emotional unstability, unable to stand frustration, high self-demanding and with difficulty in self abstracting from concrete problem solving are going to perceive higher distress in caregiving ADp. In the second research, 26 of 40 ADp showed unawareness of their deficits, while 11 ADp were enough aware of their difficulties and only 3 ADp overvalued their impairment: the majority of ADp were unaware of their cognitive impairment and functional deficits in activities of daily living and overestimated their abilities compared to ADcg perception. ADcg DIQ correlated with four 16PF-C factors: Dominance (E), Liveliness (F), Social Boldness (H) and Privateness (N). This indicate an influence of personality on ADcg judgment: in fact, traits of personality such as being deeply involved in evaluating cognitive impairment and functional deficits, ability to perceive problems in daily living, especially for those aspects that could make them feel inadequate in social situations and that engage them emotionally, could influence ADcg judgment about their relatives. In conclusion, focusing on specific personality traits, which are predictive of caregivers' burden, might be helpful in planning psychological approach aimed to improve caregivers' quality of life. In order to evaluate functional abilities of ADp, even detailed scales of awareness provided by ADcg seem not to be objective means to assess ADp functional state, because they are influenced by ADcg personality.

Short commentary - According to the Merriam-Webster dictionary, "Identity" is defined as "the sameness of essential or generic character in different instances". Essentially, how a person views oneself, is different from his personality, namely the totality of the characteristics that make up that person. The importance of identity change in treatment has been identified for well over 40 years, however it continues to be limited in its application to clinical disorders or populations. The nature and importance of identity change will be highlighted, and the recommendation made that it be expanded to treat different offending patterns, and even dysfunctional patterns of "normal" individuals.

In: Personality Traits: Theory, Testing and Influences
Editor: Melissa E. Jordan

ISBN: 978-1-61728-934-7
© 2011 Nova Science Publishers, Inc.

Chapter 1

ADDICTION: FRONTAL PERSONALITY CHANGE BUT NOT PERSONALITY DISORDER COMORBIDITY IMPLICATIONS FOR TREATMENT OF ADDICTIVE DISORDERS

Eduardo J. Pedrero-Pérez[1], Ana López-Durán[2], and Alvaro Olivar-Arroyo[3]

(1) Instituto de Adicciones, Ayuntamiento de Madrid, Madrid, Spain
(2) Universidad de Santiago de Compostela, Spain
(3) Consejería de Educación. Comunidad de Madrid, Spain

ABSTRACT

A high prevalence of co-occurrence among addictive disorders and personality disorders has been documented. Studies have usually found between a 50 and 75 percent of addicted individuals with Axis II concurrent diagnosis. However, such diagnoses often do not take account of several changes related to the course of addiction that affect functioning of the frontal lobe and, consequently, the overall programming of behaviour. Simple diagnosis based on the ICD or DSM classifications, without regard to etiological factors, is just a still photograph reflecting a fractal of a long development process altered by addiction. Impairment of frontal cortical function due to direct effects of the substance or to mediators as stress factors, are the basis of most of the symptoms justifying the diagnosis of personality disorders. Miller's proposals on stable and induced-by-stress disorders, as well as new findings on executive dysfunction linked to addiction must be taken into consideration. Personality disorders, so understood, should be treated differently from the present, including cognitive stimulation techniques and attending to stress and coping, preventing symptomatic prescribing of drugs with dubious benefits and multiple side effects. New neurological and neuropsychological perspectives of addiction do not support concepts such as comorbidity as a priority intervention guide.

INTRODUCTION

Many studies associate addiction to alcohol and other drugs with the presence of symptoms that fulfil the criteria for concurrent diagnosis of other DSM disorders (American Psychiatric Association, 2000). This co-occurrence is observed in relationship with categories classified on Axis I and II and has been studied with the designation of dual diagnosis (First and Gladis, 1996; Krantzler and Tinsley, 2004; Stowell, 1991). Of all the categories diagnosed, personality disorders are among the most frequently associated with substance abuse and dependency (i.e., Pettinati, Pierce, Belden and Meyers, 1999; Weaver, Madden, Charles, Stimson, Renton, Tyrer, et al., 2003). However, there are important differences in the prevalences found regarding the association between drug use and personality disorders in the studies published. Different variables exist that may explain these discrepancies: the selection of samples (drug users, psychiatric population or general population), assessment instruments (diagnostic interviews vs. self-reports), reference classification (DSM or ICD) and when the assessment is performed (at the beginning or during the course of treatment, hospitalised addicts or those in residential treatment).

Regarding the studies with extensive samples carried out in the USA, it is appropriate to highlight the classic Epidemiological Catchment Area of the National Institute of Mental Health (ECA; Regier et al., 1990) which finds a 14.3% prevalence of antisocial personality disorder in subjects dependent on alcohol and 17.8% in those dependent on other substances. Conversely, subjects with antisocial personality disorder present disorders owing to the use of substances in 83.6% of cases. Another important study is the National Epidemiological Survey on Alcohol and Related Conditions (NESARC; Grant, Stinson, Dawson, Chou, Ruan, and Pickering, 2004) in which it was found that 28.6% of persons with alcohol abuse or dependency and 47.7% of persons with drug abuse or dependency have a personality disorder. In the National Comorbidity Survey Replication, the co-occurrence of personality disorders with some disorder owing to the use of substances is situated at 28.5% (Lenzenweger, Lane, Loranger, and Kessler, 2007).

Verheul (2001) carried out a review of the studies on the co-occurrence of personality disorders that use structured interviews as the assessment instrument. In the case of addicts undergoing treatment the prevalence varied between 34.8 and 73.0% (median 56.5%), in psychiatric patients the range was between 45.2 and 80.0% (median 60.4%) and in the general population between 10.0 and 14.8% (median 13.5%). Regarding the assessment instrument used, it is necessary to point out that the figures for prevalence increased substantially when self-report instruments were used such as the Millon Clinical Multiaxial Inventory (MCMI) in its subsequent versions (i.e., Craig, 2000; Echeburúa, Bravo de Medina and Aizpiri, 2007; Nadeau, Landry and Racine, 1999; Pedrero, Puerta, Lagares and Sáez, 2003).

Different models have been proposed to explain the frequent co-occurrence of mental disorders and addictive disorders, but none of these has managed to accumulate sufficient empirical evidence to prove its superiority with regard to the alternative models. These models have focused mainly on determining which diagnosis precedes the other and to what extent its appearance favours the establishment of the other (Mueser, Drake, & Wallach, 1998; Verheul & van den Brink, 2005). Models have also been proposed which emphasise the existence of vulnerabilities that favour the progression from initial consumption to addictive consumption patterns. Verheul (2001) has proposed the existence of three channels for the acquisition of addictive patterns on the basis of specific personality characteristics, so that each one of these would lead with preference to the choice of one or another drug according to the neurotransmitters involved in each one of the patterns. The model has been criticized, not so much owing to the neurological channels involved in the development of the addiction, but due to its incapacity to predict the substance consumed and the impossibility of accounting for polysubstance use (Conway, Kane, Ball, Poling and Rounsaville, 2003). However, it is currently the diathesis-stress models that enjoy the most empirical support. Within these the common factor model may be considered, which proposes that disorders owing to the use of substances and some personality disorders (specifically, antisocial and borderline) share certain components (genetic and behavioural) the joint development of which would be favoured in the presence of a third factor of an environmental nature (Siever & Davis, 1991; Verheul & van den Brink, 2005).

Despite the proliferation of epidemiological studies in recent decades, there is great controversy with regard to the validity of the diagnoses. Some authors have stated that "*official diagnoses are substantially arbitrary, often unreliable, overlapping, and incomplete and have only a limited utility for treatment planning*" (Widiger, Trull, Clarkin, Sanderson, & Costa, 2002; p. 435) and that "*the assessment of personality disorder is currently inaccurate, largely unreliable, frequently wrong, and in need of improvement*" (Tyrer, Coombs, Ibrahimi, Mathilakath, Bajaj Ranger, et al., 2007; p. 51). Underlying these and other criticisms is a generalised disagreement with the categorial methodology for characterizing and diagnosing dysfunctional behaviour patterns. The APA (American Psychiatric Association) itself has for many years been promoting a research agenda for the classification of personality disorders in the DSM-V. This need is based on the awareness that, after more than 30 years, it has not been possible to validate these syndromes, nor to discover common etiologies, no laboratory marker has yet been detected to identify any of the syndromes defined by the DSM, the diagnoses present a high degree of short-term diagnostic instability and the lack of specificity in response to the treatments is almost the rule rather than the exception (Kupfer, First and Regier, 2002). The alternative, accepted by the majority, is the dimensional conceptualisation of personality disorders on the basis of different combinations of underlying traits (Clark, 2007; Saulsman & Page, 2004).

Stability vs. Personality Change

All the criteria included by the DSM-IV-TR (American Psychiatric Association, 2000) to consider the existence of a personality disorder include the need for the dysfunctional pattern to be enduring: (A) An enduring pattern of inner experience and behaviour deviating markedly from the expectations of the individual's culture; (B) The enduring pattern is inflexible and pervasive across a broad range of personal and social situations; (C) The enduring pattern leads to clinically significant distress or impairment in social, occupational or other important areas of functioning; (D) The pattern is stable and of long duration and its onset can be traced back at least to adolescence or early adulthood; (E) The enduring pattern is not better accounted for as a manifestation or consequence of another mental disorder; (F) The enduring pattern is not due to the direct physiological effects of a substance (e.g., a drug of abuse, a medication) or a general medical condition. Similarly, the ICD-10 (World Health

Organization, 1992-1994) considers that evidence is necessary that the individuals present "characteristic and enduring patterns of inner experience and behaviour". This particularity is clearly distinctive from Axis I disorders, the temporal persistence of which is variable and, in any case, limited in time.

Consequently, one of the main topics of controversy and investigation is the stability of personality disorders. Longitudinal methodology has allowed this question to be explored, although the results are contradictory. Many studies find that patients diagnosed with some personality disorder did not fulfil the criteria to reaffirm the diagnosis after one (Shea, Stout, Gunderson, Morey, Grilo, McGlashan, et al., 2002), two (Ferro, Klein, Schwartz, Kasch, & Leader, 1998; Grilo, Sanislow, Gunderson, Pagano, Yen, Zanarini, et al., 2004) or 10 years (Durbin & Klein, 2006). The Collaborative Longitudinal Personality Disorders Study (CLPS; Gunderson, Shea, Skodol, McGlashan, Morey, Stout, et al., 2000) observed a certain stability of the disorders, although a considerable number of patients did not reach the diagnostic thresholds at 12 months (Shea & Yen, 2003). This study found that the Axis II disorders presented a significantly higher stability than those of Axis I, although the intensity tended to decrease over time, so that the criteria for maintaining the diagnosis were gradually unfulfilled (Shea & Yen, 2003). An extensive population study found that the stability of personality disorders, based on various measurements taken over 12 years, was 28% (Baca-Garcia, Perez-Rodriguez, Basurte-Villamor, Fernandez del Moral, Jimenez-Arriero, Gonzalez de Rivera, et al., 2007). In adolescents, the majority of the personality disorders diagnosed do not persist two years after having been diagnosed (Bernstein, Cohen, Velez, Schwab-Stone, Siever, & Shinsato, 1993). Other authors (Fountoulakis & Kaprinis, 2006; McDavid, & Pilkonis, 1996) also reach the conclusion, after reviewing a series of studies, that the categorization of personality disorders is an inadequate procedure and that the stability that should differentiate them from Axis I disorders is not observed. Moreover, the studies that have shown greater stability of personality disorders (Lenzenweger, 1999) have been criticized for the poor variability of the samples that they use, fundamentally of the general population, and, specifically, of university students.

When the sample assessed is following a treatment, personality disorders are reduced by between 72% (Monsen, Odland, Faugli, Daae, & Eilertsen, 1995) and 88% with recurrences of only 6% (Zanarini & Frankenburg, 2001; Zanarini, Frankenburg, Hennen, Reich & Silk, 2006). Other heuristic models estimate that the level of remission reaches 25.8% per year (Perry, Banon, & Ianni, 1999).

In general, there is widespread agreement in that the dimensional models amply exceed the categorial diagnoses, very especially with regard to temporal stability (Grilo & McGlasham, 2009; Skodol, Gunderson, Shea, McGlashan, Morey, Sanislow, et al., 2005). The nuclear traits or latent personality factors in adolescents show considerable stability over time, but categorial diagnoses do not (Grilo, Becker, Edell, & McGlashan, 2001; Krueger, Silva, Caspi, & Moffitt, 1998). The criteria that remain more stable over time are those that refer to traits and attitudes, whilst those that appear more unstable or intermittent are of a behavioural or reactive nature (McGlashan, Grilo, Sanislow, Ralevski, Morey, Gunderson, et al., 2005). It has been proposed that the diagnosis of personality disorders should consider simultaneously two components: (a) diagnosing disorder, that is, assessing the level of psychological and social/interpersonal dysfunction (e.g., integrated sense of self; family and occupational stability) and its acute manifestations (e.g., ideas of reference, aggression, hyperperfectionism, suicidality); and (b) describing individuals' personality traits (Clark,

2009). In the same line, Clark (2007) points out that the studies which analyse the stability of personality disorders conclude that the said disorders include both acute, dysfunctional behaviours that resolve in relatively short periods, and maladaptative temperamental traits that are relatively more stable, similar to normal-range personality traits. Other studies that have applied growth curve analysis find that personality disorders show large variations over time and that they cannot be considered stable entities, even when their link with the underlying traits is considered (Lenzenweger, Johnson, & Willett, 2004).

There is evidence of the stability of the personality traits which are demonstrated in the first years of life and which to a certain extent predict personality styles several decades later (Asendorpf & Denissen, 2006; Caspi, Harrington, Milne, Amell, Theodore, & Moffitt, 2003; Dennissen, Asendorpf, & van Aken, 2008; Roberts & DelVecchio, 2000). The Children in the Community Study, for example, reflects as a general conclusion that the highest point of the symptomatology associated with personality disorders is found in early adolescence, and that it descends lineally until the age of 27 (Cohen, Crawford, Johnson & Kasen, 2005). In the same way, evidence exists that changes occur, especially in early youth, but, in general, across the whole life-span (Caspi, Roberts, & Shiner, 2005), and the adult personality is the product of the permanent interactions between genetic predispositions and environmental conditions (Caspi, McClay, Moffitt, Mill, Martin, Craig, et al., 2002; Caspi & Shiner, 2006).

As a consequence, the available evidence seriously questions the diagnostic entity of the categories of personality disorder. One of the main problems should probably be situated in the erroneous belief that people show a transituational consistency in their behaviour, independently of the environmental conditions in which this takes place (Mischel, 2004). Another problem, linked to the previous belief, is that personality disorders have been studied more frequently from a model of medical disease which is shown to be profoundly inadequate (Potter, 2004). Since personality disorders are not diseases, they can be assessed but not diagnosed definitively: the concept of personality in itself implies the existence of mechanisms for adaptation to certain environmental circumstances that may imply severe changes in the pattern assessed (Millon and Davis, 1996).

Stability of Personality Disorders in Samples of Addicts

Few studies explore the stability of diagnoses in populations of addicts, with the particularity that these samples are usually formed by subjects who are undergoing a treatment of which the objective is precisely to modify the dysfunctional aspects of behaviour. A generalized remission has been found of all the diagnoses associated with abstinence during treatment (Wagner, Krampe, Stawicki, Reinhold, Jahn, Mahlke, et al., 2004). The studies that use the MCMI as an assessment instrument have found certain stability in successive measurements (Craig & Olson, 1998; Lenzenweger, 1999). However, studies also exist that have found significant reductions in the scales of the MCMI after prolonged periods of abstinence and in subjects with adherence to the treatments (Calsyn, Wells, Fleming, & Saxon, 2000). As a general rule, stability is higher in the basic traits than in the symptoms of distress (Calsyn, et al., 2000; de Groot, Franken, van der Meer, & Hendriks, 2003; Schinka, Hughes, Coletti, Hamilton, Renard, Urmann, et al., 1999), although other studies do not find these differences (McMahon & Richards, 1996). In another study the stability of the traits measured by the NEO-FFI was compared with that presented by the DSM criteria with the Structured Clinical Interview for DSM-III-R, in a sample of addicts in residential treatment; the authors did not find differences that justified the claimed superior stability of the traits over the disorders (Ball, Rounsaville, Tennen, & Kranzler, 2001). The reduction of the symptoms is associated with persistence in time of the abstinence (Hesse, Nielsen, & Røjskjær, 2007) and may be related to the reduction of key components of the personality disorders, such as impulsivity, which has also been observed in addicts treated as outpatients (Forcada-Chapa, Pardo-Pavía, & Bondía-Soler, 2006) and those in residential treatment (Bankston, Carroll, Cron, Granmayeh, Marcus, Moeller, et al., 2009).

Factors Affecting the Stability of the Diagnosis: Stress

Empirical evidence exists that individuals frequently present Axis II diagnoses that co-exist with diagnoses of depression. But these personality disorders do not persist in time when the treatment is efficient in reducing the depressive symptomatology (Fava, Farabaugh, Sickinger, Wrigh, Alpert, Sonawalla, et al., 2002). Likewise, personality disorders are also diagnosed more frequently when a concurrent Axis I disorder is present than when the said disorder has remitted (Iketani, Kiriike, Stein, Nagao, Nagata, Minamikawa, et al., 2002). According to Reich (1999a), *"in predisposed individuals, the stress of an Axis I disorder, sometimes even in subclinical form, exaggerates normal personality traits to level of a disorder"*, and he proposed the existence of stress-induced personality disorders (p.711). This author observed that, under strong conditions of stress, which result in Axis I symptomatology, the measurement of personality traits may present elevations, which will return to the baseline once the Axis I disorder has been solved (Reich, 1999b). These changes would not be artefacts of measuring, but should be conceptualised as a personality change (Bronisch & Klerman, 1991). State (stress-induced) personality disorders would present different characteristics from true stable and dysfunctional behavioural patterns, or stable (trait) personality disorders (Reich, 1999b). The individual history or trajectory would be perceptibly different in both cases and the clinical presentation of both modalities would offer significant differences (i.e., greater presence of anxious and depressive symptomatology linked to more sources of stress on Axis IV in the case of the state personality disorders). Some studies have explored the differences between both groups, finding traits, such as sensitivity to criticism or feeling of guilt, which may favour the appearance of states that mimic the existence of a personality disorder (Reich, 2002; Reich & Hofmann, 2004). The clinical importance of distinguishing between stable patterns and transitory states of maladapted behaviour is obvious: the existence of a stress-induced personality disorder may alter the response to habitually efficient treatments (pharmacological and psychotherapeutic); furthermore, to diagnose a stable personality disorder based on acute demonstrations of decompensation of habitually adapted traits is erroneous and may lead to unnecessary, inadequate or useless therapeutic approaches (Reich, 2005).

Although the empirical support for this proposal is limited, Reich has proposed a topic of enormous interest that would oblige reconsideration of the available epidemiological studies that do not control the effect of stress at the time of assessment and diagnosis. Some authors have emphasised this question, warning that a considerable proportion of the variability in the figures for the prevalence of personality disorders diagnosed in addicts may be due to the different moments at which the assessment is performed. The stress of disintoxication and early abstinence may be the cause of an overdiagnosis of personality disorders when the assessment is carried out at that time (Thomas, Melchert, & Banken, 1999). Consequently, and as Ball et al. (2001) warn, "*substance intoxication, dependence, and withdrawal are characterized by marked changes in cognitive, emotional, and social functioning that may mimic many of the symptoms of personality disorders and intensify personality traits*".

But these are not the only sources of stress that may interfere in the assessment of personality disorders at the onset of treatment. Patients who request and commence treatment do so at their worst moment, when the malaise is at a maximum, and it is precisely the malaise that motivates the demand for treatment. The accumulation of negative consequences of consumption (neurobiological, psychological and social) causes a spiral of losses that people experience as a situation of stress (Pedrero-Pérez, Puerta-García, Segura-López, & Martínez-Osorio, 2004). In terms of the Behavioural Choice Theory, the individual experiences a strong increase in opportunity costs, which is revealed via a self-perception of stress and gives rise to the change of behaviour (Vuchinich and Heather, 2003). This situation would justify to a large extent the claimed comorbidity between depression and addiction, which some authors rejected a long time ago: depression only exists in precisely those drug addicts who requested treatment and not in those who persisted with consumption (Rounsaville & Kleber, 1985). Moreover, the depressive symptomatology associated with psychosocial stress or the withdrawal of the substances of abuse tends to remit rapidly (Pedrero-Pérez et al., 2004) and this remission is precisely the factor that best explains the changes in the diagnosis of personality disorder in repeated measurements (Ball et al., 2001).

Moreover, it is important to explain how stress influences brain development and, with it, that of personality, from the first stages of life, as well as the greater possibility of establishing an addictive relationship with substances. Three elements appear as determining, as proposed by Andersen and Teicher (2009). In the first place, compulsive drug use increases due to a highly reactive hypothalamic–pituitary–adrenal axis (HPA). Moreover, exposure to stress is associated with sensitive periods of vulnerability that will contribute to drug abuse vulnerability. And, in the third place, brain regions and circuits need to mature to a certain degree in order for the effects of early stress exposure to manifest. This implies that, probably, people with problems of addiction who attend treatment centres, not only find themselves in a circumstantial situation of stress, but moreover, carry a personal history associated with a high vulnerability to stress.

Factors Affecting the Stability of the Diagnosis: Impulsivity

Impulsivity is a personality trait that precedes addiction and favours its development (Verdejo-García, Lawrence, & Clark, 2008). Furthermore, impulsivity is a nuclear trait of personality disorders most frequently linked to addiction, those of the cluster B (Verheul, 2001). These disorders and addiction as a process would share common genetic substrates that would operate as factors of vulnerability (Jacob, Müller, Schmidt, Hohenberger, Gutknecht, Reif, et al., 2005) in certain environmental conditions (Caspi et al., 2002). Neither is impulsivity as a trait unrelated to the processes of evolutionary development, there is evidence of the importance of parental educational styles for the development of effortful control that reduces problems of externalisation (Eisenberg, Zhou, Spinrad, Valiente, Fabes, & Liew, 2005). Likewise, the characteristics of the home at three years of age appear to be associated with a greater impulsivity in some ethnic groups (Dillworth-Barth, Khurshid & Lowe Vandell, 2007), so that cultural questions possibly influence in this differentiation. Both elements, genetic predisposition and early interactions (especially those associated with attachment mechanisms), have been proposed as shared substrates for the development of impulsive styles of behaviour, understood as the tendency for the preference for risk-taking behaviours (Lende & Smith, 2002).

However, impulsivity is also a consequence of the addictive process (de Wit, 2009; Perry & Carroll, 2008), which includes not only the pharmacological effects of the substances, but also the effect of psychological or emotional events, such as the acute stress associated with consumption (de Wit, 2009; Sinha 2001; Tice, Bratslavsky, & Baumeister, 2001). As a consequence, it must be supposed that a considerable proportion of the impulsive behaviours that suggest the presence of a personality disorder are due to direct and transitory effects of the substance abuse, both owing to its pharmacological effects and to the psychosocial consequences of consumption. This is suggested by the fact that impulsivity is drastically reduced during the first months of treatment (Aklin, 2007; Bankston et al., 2009; Forcada-Chapa et al., 2006), and that the differences in impulsivity between those who developed an addiction in the past and those who did not hardly reach statistical significance (Allen, Moeller, Rhoades, & Cherek, 1998).

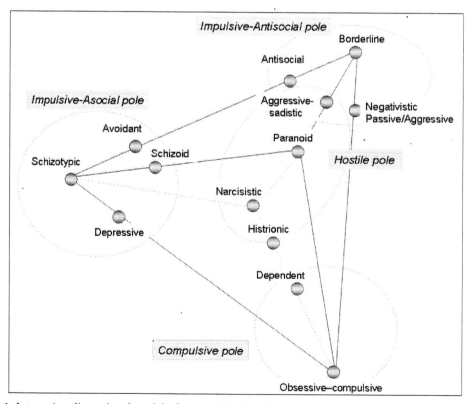

Figure 1. Interactive-dimensional model of personality disorders

Therefore, impulsivity is a less stable characteristic than would correspond to a personality trait, as this concept is understood. If impulsivity is a substrate common to addiction and to certain personality disorders, specifically borderline personality disorder (Bornovalova, Lejuez, Daughters, Rosenthal, & Lynch, 2005) and antisocial personality disorder (Krueger, Markon, Patrick, Benning, & Kramer, 2007), then these disorders may not be stable over time. Millon, in his biosocial model of personality and its disorders, has proposed that in certain circumstances (i.e., acute stress) stable personality patterns decompensate to more severe forms of destructuration, acquiring the external manifestations of a paranoid, schizoid or borderline disorder (Choca, 1999). For example, negativist-passive/aggressive personality disorder may appear in the form of a borderline personality disorder in conditions of decompensation: both share impulsivity as one of the common components, but the exacerbation of emotional components may destructure the behaviour pattern even more until it mimics the extreme disorganisation of behaviour (Pedrero-Pérez, López-Durán, & Olivar-Arroyo, 2006). When categorial diagnoses are made in the initial phases of abandonment of the addictive behaviour or in critical phases of the remission process, without taking into account that there are elements that may exacerbate certain symptoms, the consequence may be an artefactual increase of personality disorders which present a higher degree of severity.

Based on the dimensional analysis of the core-items of the MCMI-II, a model has been proposed that allows personality disorders to be grouped differently from the DSM clusters (Pedrero-Pérez et al., 2006). The model (Figure 1) responds to the hierarchical structuring of the disorders based on their severity, those that Millon considers more serious (schizotypic, borderline and paranoid) occupying the vertices and, at the opposite extreme, the obsessive-compulsive disorders. Disorders with a lesser degree of severity (narcissistic, histrionic and dependent) are situated at the base. The graph allows us, moreover, to know which other disorders each one of them may decompensate towards, taking into account their proximity. Thus, a person with narcissistic disorder may decompensate, in situations of high stress, and if interpersonal sensitivity prevails, towards a paranoid pattern (if distrust predominates), towards an antisocial pattern (if the indiscriminate attack of rules and persons predominates), towards an aggressive-sadistic pattern (if focussing on the people close to them predominates) or towards a negativistic pattern (if passive-aggressive strategies are chosen); but the person may also decompensate, if the tendency for isolation, self-depreciation or the rejection of others prevails, towards a schizoid, avoidant or depressive pattern. In the impulsive-antisocial pole, impulsive personalities, in moments of exacerbation, may decompensate towards a borderline pattern, which would not be stable. The model allows hypothesisation of the stable pattern if the situational effect of the stress is discounted.

Factors Affecting the Stability of the Diagnosis: Personality Change

In a study performed with 749 patients who were beginning treatment for substance abuse/dependency, the factorial structure of the MCMI-II was explored (Pedrero-Pérez, 2009). Surprisingly, in a first orthogonal rotation a principal factor emerged, which explained 14.2% of the total variance of the test, in a group of 7 items that begin with "in the last two years", "since one or two years ago", "in recent years", "a few years ago", as well as other items that suggest obsessive ideation and emotional instability. In a second rotation a principal superfactor appears which integrates, around the previous one, more than 40% of the items of the complete questionnaire (specifically, 74), which refer to Axis I symptomatology: disorders of anxiety, state of mind, of a psychotic nature, etc. Moreover, a considerable proportion of its items limit the appearance of these symptoms to "recent years" or "recent weeks". Therefore, they do not assess stable personality traits or characteristics, but symptomatology of recent appearance or recently experienced by the subject. This superfactor explained 25.5% of the total variance of the test. The rest of the secondary superfactors referred strictly speaking to personality traits, such as opposition/antagonism, neuroticism, compulsion-impulsivity, restriction or aggressivity. These data were substantially different from those obtained in a previous study that performed the same analyses on a sample of patients diagnosed with at least one personality disorder without concurrent addictive behaviour (Besteiro, Lemos, Muñiz, García, & Álvarez, 2007), which suggests that this test does not present a similar functioning in addicts and in other clinical populations.

These data suggest that a change has occurred, abrupt or gradual, in the behaviour or the emotional pattern of the addicted subject: The subjects do not situate the central nucleus of the change in a stable disposition to behave in a certain way, but in something that irrupts into the previous personality of the patient, modifying it. It is not, therefore, a statistical deviation from normality but a qualitative transformation. Consequently, it appears that the MCMI-II does not assess a stable personality pattern in addicts but something closer to that which the ICD-10 defines as 'organic personality disorder' ("*alteration of personality and behaviour can be a residual or concomitant disorder of brain disease, damage or dysfunction*") within the group of "personality and behavioural disorders due to brain disease, damage and dysfunction". It would also be closer to what the DSM-IV-TR designates 'personality change due to a general medical condition' ("*a persistent personality disturbance that represents a change from the individual's previous characteristic personality pattern*"). But we could wonder: What '*brain disease, damage or dysfunction*' can justify that personality change? What '*medical condition*' can explain the change in the habitual behaviour pattern of the subject?

Categorial conceptions do not help us to understand the process via which this personality change takes place. In reality, the simple classification of events based on their observable manifestation at the time of assessment is an inadequate procedure for favouring understanding of the phenomena intended to be studied. The consequence of applying this classificatory methodology is the accumulation of diagnostic labels, which does not inform us at all regarding which relationships exist between the different manifestations that justify the various diagnoses. The question then is: "*Is psychiatry ready to move beyond its descriptive approach to classification and embrace a diagnostic model linked to underlying pathophysiology that is more akin to most of medicine?*" (McGough & McCracken, 2006). Are the rest of the disciplines implicated ready to assume the recent findings regarding the brain processes on which addiction is based?

Neuroscientific Perspective of Addiction

If in previous decades addiction has been considered as a chronic, relapsing mental disease, we currently know that addiction is a process of which the natural course tends towards remission, that it is the shortest-lasting psychiatric disorder, that it is the disorder most influenced by socially mediated consequences, and that addicts can curtail drug use when it is immediately beneficial to do so (Heymann, 2001). As a consequence, a change has occurred from the consideration of "mental disease" towards a more ample concept of "cerebral illness". On the one hand, the distinction between disease (a biological concept) and illness (a broader concept that includes a person's experience and interpretation of his or her condition) (Potter, 2004) is important because the use of an imprecise language may lead to an imprecise form of thought (Lilienfeld, Waldman, & Israel, 1994; Maj, 2005). On the other hand, in the last decade we have obtained more knowledge regarding the brain processes to which addiction is linked, which were unknown in the past. This knowledge, deriving from the study of addictive processes from neurological, neuropsychological, psychophysiological, developmental and epigenetic perspectives, has favoured the proposal of new models of addiction. Unlike previous ones, these models are interested in the pathophysiological and neurobehavioral processes that precede the addiction, sustain it and make its abandonment possible.

Although the initial proposals date from 30 years ago, in the last decade various theories and models have been formulated which set out to explain the mechanisms that underlie addiction, linking the observable behavioural manifestations with the neurobiological substrates on which they are sustained. The classical models of addiction, which had emphasised the role of the so-called "reward circuit" or "pleasure circuit" (the dopaminergic mesolimbic circuit) in drug consumption and its merely pleasurable nature, were superseded by conceptions that showed that the compulsive consumption of drugs was linked to a motivational, but not hedonic mechanism. These models have formulated tentative explanations that try to explain topics such as the loss of control over behaviour, compulsive consumption, the decision to consume above and beyond its consequences, craving, relapse and other known phenomena which had been linked to addiction. On the other hand, the research deriving from each of these models has allowed us better knowledge of the brain structures involved in each one of the processes, and they have allowed us to overcome mind/body, genetic/environmental or biological/psychosocial dualisms, so that the new formulations of addiction allow us to consider the human organism as a whole in action. We will briefly mention below the main theories and models regarding addiction, applicable in current research.

The central thesis of the Incentive Sensitzation Theory (Robinson & Berridge, 2003, 2008) is that repeated exposure to different drugs of abuse may produce (in certain individuals and under certain exposure patterns) persistent neuroadaptations in neurons and brain circuits that are normally responsible for attributing motivational relevance to environmental stimuli. The result of these neuroadaptations is that the circuit becomes hypersensitive to the stimuli related to drug consumption. In accordance with the model, the principal neuroanatomical substrate of the motivational sensitization processes pivots around the nucleus accumbens, which receives phasic dopaminergic projections (mediated by D2 receptors) from the ventral tegmental area and the hippocampus and is projected towards the prefrontal cortex, especially towards the anterior cingulate cortex.

The Allostasis-Stress Model (Koob & Le Moal, 1997, 2008), proposes that addiction is the result of a change in the control of behaviour motivated from positive reinforcement mechanisms, aimed at obtaining rewards, at negative reinforcement mechanisms, aimed at reducing stress and malaise and trying to re-establish a false homeostatic balance (designated "allostasis"). This transition is the product of the progressive deregulation of two mechanisms: (i) the loss of function of the reward system, which is revealed by an increase of the stimulation thresholds necessary to reach an allostatic state – of non-malaise – and (ii) the hyperactivation of anti-reward systems and stress, originally responsible for countering the rewarding effects of drugs and which now go on to dominate the motivational balance of the organism. The neuroanatomic substrates of the model pivot around the axis of the extent amygdala towards the hypothalamic–pituitary–adrenal axis, involving feedback systems of neurotransmitters such as corticotropin, norepinephrine or the opioid system. Subsequent revisions have emphasised the regulatory role of the prefrontal cortex and the cingulate gyrus over the stress systems, proposing that the dysfunction of the prefrontal cortex would diminish the capacity of the individual to regulate motivational states of stress and malaise (Li & Sinha, 2008).

The Impulsive-to-Compulsive Habits Transition Model (Everitt & Robbins, 2005; Everitt, Belin, Economidou, Pelloux, Dalley, & Robbins, 2008) proposes that addiction represents a transition from an initial phase in which drugs are consumed for their reinforcement effects (to which individuals with high levels of premorbid impulsivity would be most vulnerable) towards a phase of dependency in which consumption behaviours are transformed into compulsive rituals which are maintained in spite of their negative consequences (Belin, Mar, Dalley, Robbins, & Everitt, 2008; Dalley, Fryer, Brichard, Robinson, Theobald, Lääne, et al., 2007). This transition would occur as a consequence of the effects of the drugs on the dopaminergic systems involved in motivated learning and the programming of motor conducts. The over-stimulation of these systems produces a progressive automatisation of the motor sequences associated with consumption and a reduction of the activation threshold necessary to trigger these sequences. As a result objective-oriented behaviour is replaced, the individual pursues drugs for the reinforcement he obtains, through an automatic and inflexible behaviour in which the motivated control of consumption disappears. At an anatomic level, this transition would emerge as the displacement of behaviour control from the prefrontal cortex towards the basal ganglia and, within these, from the anterior regions (nucleus accumbens, with rich connections towards the prefrontal cortex and the amygdala) to the posterior regions specialised in the programming and maintenance of motor sequences (dorsal striatum).

The Impaired-Salience Attribution and Response Inhibition Model (Goldstein & Volkow, 2002) explains addiction as the result of the alteration of two complementary systems. On the one hand, the system responsible for detecting and valuing the motivational relevance of the reinforcers performs an exaggerated valuation of the reinforcement properties of the drugs and in turn depreciates the motivational relevance of other natural reinforcers (e.g., food, money, sex, social relationships). On the other hand, there is damage to the inhibition system responsible for halting behaviours which are inappropriate for the demands of the organism and the context, owing to which difficulties exist for the inhibition of motivationally relevant behaviours; in this case, drug consumption. The damage in these two systems would have a transversal repercussion on various phases of the addiction. Likewise, the model specifies that the damage to these systems would affect the functioning of various neuropsychological mechanisms, including (1) memory and conditioning (hippocampus and amygdala), (2) motivation and programming of motor responses (basal ganglia), (3) response inhibition (cingulate cortex) and (4) decision making (orbitofrontal cortex).

The Somatic Marker Theory applied to addictions (Bechara, 2005; Verdejo-García, Bechara, Recknor, & Pérez-García, 2006; Verdejo-García & Bechara, 2009) defines addiction as a dysfunction of the neuropsychological systems involved in decision making, including motivational, emotional, mnesic and response selection mechanisms. Decision making is a process guided by emotional signals ("somatic markers") which anticipate the potential results of different decision options. In normal conditions these emotional markers, understood experimentally as vegetative, muscular, neuroendocrine or neurophysiologic changes, provide an affective context and guide decision making towards adaptive response options for the individual following a homeostatic logic. In addictions, the model proposes that certain substances consumed repeatedly may "hijack" the motivational and emotional systems responsible for the generation of these somatic markers, prioritising the emotional signals associated with consumption and blocking the possibility for the negative experience associated with its adverse consequences to be transformed into productive learning. As a result, the emotional markers associated with consumption may influence at least two neuropsychological systems: (i) the consolidation of specific affective states, such as the feeling of urgency to consume or craving (in the processing of which the insula intervenes, a region specialised in interoceptive processing and injury to which produces the drastic interruption of the feeling of "desire" and the behaviour of smoking) and (ii) the capacity to bias response selection processes towards options of immediate reinforcement (e.g., consumption) even ignoring the inadequacy of these responses according to the context or their potential negative consequences. Therefore, the model bases addictive behaviour on the difficulty in assigning relevant affective states to cognitive scenarios of decision, promoting decisions based on immediate reinforcement that disregard their future consequences (phenomenon defined as "myopia for the future") and the tendency to persist in the error, owing to the difficulty of incorporating affective learning in subsequent decisions. The model specifies a set of brain systems that intervene in (1) the generation of these emotional markers (orbitofrontal cortex and amygdala), (2) the "reading" that the brain gives to these markers in areas specialised in corporal mapping (insular and somatosensory cortices), and (3) the final selection of the response (striatum and anterior cingulate cortex).

Recently, Redish, Jensen, & Johnson (2008) have formulated a conceptual framework integrating these and other theories, which understands addiction as a dysfunction of the decision making processes. This dysfunction derives from the occurrence of neuroadaptations in a set of interactive systems: the planning system, equivalent to the executive system or system for control of object oriented behaviour; the habits system, a trigger of behavioural sequences pre-established according to the presence of contextual keys; and the situational recognition system, which modulates the preponderance of the planning systems versus habits for behaviour control according to the context. In accordance with the model, these systems may promote maladaptive decisions according to the incidence of multiple sources of vulnerability, many of them included in previous models, which include: (i) deviations of the homeostasis and the allostasis involved in motivational destabilisation, (ii) exhilarating reward signals, (iii) overvaluing of the planning or habituation systems or maladjustment between the two, (iv) failures of the system of search and identification of relevant contexts (i.e., illusions of control or distortions of overgeneralisation or overcategorisation), (v) disproportionate increases of the system for the discounting of delayed rewards and (vi) alterations of learning ratios, which may lead to rejection of consistent associations or identification of false or illusory associations between stimuli. The model contemplates various courses of action for these vulnerabilities, from biological predisposition to maladaptive cognitive and affective learning, as well as the possibility of multiple interactions between the different sources of vulnerability. This integrational model has generated various criticisms (see discussion following the cited article), but the agreements are beginning to outnumber the disagreements on the neurocognitive formulation of addictive processes.

There is widespread agreement, transversal to all the models, in the implication of the frontal lobe, and, especially, of the prefrontal cortex, in the genesis, maintenance and abandonment of addictive habits (Verdejo-García, Perez-Garcia, & Bechara, 2006; Verdejo-Garcia, Lopez-Torrecillas, Aguilar de Arcos, & Perez-Garcia, 2005). Specifically, the failures in the executive functioning of the prefrontal cortex (executive dysfunction) have been linked to addiction as cause and consequence (Hester & Garavan, 2004). Another general agreement is related to the fact that the intimate mechanisms of addiction are common to addictive behaviours that involve the use of substances and to those others that do not require the pharmacological action of drugs, such as pathologic gambling (Goudriaan, Oosterlaan, de Beurs, & van den Brink, 2006; Ko, Liu, Hsiao, Yen, Yang, Lin, et al., 2009) or the excessive use of Internet (Sun, Chen, Ma, Zhang, Fu, X. M. & Zhang, 2009). Very recent studies allow the suggestion of a mapping of the zones involved in decision making in variable conditions of risk and in persons who have developed addictive behaviours without substances (Miedl, Fehr, Meyer, & Herrmann, 2010).

The studies mentioned, and others along a similar line, study "the effects of the severity of the addiction on frontal functioning" and "the common etiology of the disorders owing to the use of substances and addictive conducts without drugs". In forthcoming years, research topics will probably turn in another direction: the effects of frontal functioning on the severity of the addiction and the existence of a single neurophysiological-neurobehavioral process with diverse manifestations.

Neuroscientific Perspective of Personality

One of the most important questions in relation to the personality traits proposed by the different models is the search for the neurological substrates and neurobehavioral correlates on which they are sustained. Associations have been found between personality dimensions and a wide variety of neurobiological measures, such as MAO activity (Schalling, Asberg, Edman, & Oreland, 1987), neurotransmitter metabolites in cerebrospinal fluid (Limson, Goldman, Roy, Lamparski, Ravitz, Adinoff, et al., 1991) and various markers associated with in-vivo neuroimaging (Canli, Zhao, Kang, & Gross, 2001; Farde, Gustavsson, & Jonsson, 1997; Fischer, Wik, & Fredrikson, 1997; Gray, Pickering, & Gray, 1994; Haier, Sokolski, Katz, & Buchsbaum, 1987; Kumari, Ffytche, Williams, & Gray, 2004; Sugiura, Kawashima, Nakagawa, Okada, Sato, Goto, et al., 2000). Right frontal and thalamic areas are known to have a strong role in cognitive processing and have been demonstrated to activate during a range of cognitive tasks (Cabeza & Nyberg, 2000), and the right inferior frontal gyrus has been specifically implicated in response inhibition (Aron & Poldrack, 2005).

We will review the findings in relationship with the two principal personality models at the current time: Lexicographic Five Factor Model and Cloninger's Biosocial Model.

Extraversion has been associated with increased glucose metabolic rate in the caudate, putamen and various frontal and temporal areas (Haier et al., 1987), and with perfusion in the basal ganglia, thalamus and inferior frontal gyrus (O'Gorman, Kumari, Williams, Zelaya, Connor, Alsop, et al., 2006). Extraversion has also been shown to predict the brain response to cognitive stimuli (Kumari et al., 2004). Neuroticism is associated with the activity of the frontal lobes and the left temporal lobe (Canli et al., 2001), as well as with a specific activity of the amygdala (Canli, Sivers, Whitfield, Gotlib and Gabrieli, 2002). Neuroticism and extraversion have both been shown to moderate the brain response to emotional stimuli (Canli et al., 2001, 2002). Psychoticism has been associated with decreased glucose metabolic rate in the basal ganglia and thalamus (Haier et al., 1987) as well as with low dopamine activity in the basal ganglia (Gray et al., 1994).

Novelty seeking is specifically associated with dopaminergic activity, and there is strong empirical support for such a relationship (Hansenne, Pinto, Pitchot, Reggers, Scantanburlo, Moor et al., 2002; Suhara, Yasuno, Sudo, Yamamoto, Inoue, Okubo et al., 2001; Wiesbieck, Mauerer, Thome, Jacob and Boening, 1995). Furthermore, other studies associate this dimension with increased cerebral blood flow in the insula and anterior cingulate (Sugiura et al., 2000), cerebellum, cuneus and thalamus (O'Gorman et al., 2006). This personality trait has been consistently linked with the anticipation of the expected rewards, and it is related to grey matter density in several brain regions, including the ventral striatum, insula, and prefrontal cortex (Schweinhardt, Seminowicz, Jaeger, Duncan, & Bushnell, 2009).

Harm avoidance should be associated, according to the theory formulated by Cloninger, with serotonergic activity, but there is no evidence of such a relationship (Ebstein, Gritsenko, Nemanov, Frisch, Osher and Belmaker, 1997) whereas there is evidence of its link to gabaergic activity in the anterior cingulate cortex (Kim, Kim, Cho, Song, Bae, Hong, et al., 2009). This area of the brain receives inputs from and issues outputs to the amygdala, which is a crucial structure regarding anxiety and fear, so that the volume of this area showed positive correlation with the amygdala volume (Pezawas, Meyer-Lindenberg, Drabant, Verchinski, Munoz, Kolachana, et al., 2005). Both structures, anterior cingulate cortex and amygdale, showed correlated activity in functional neuroimaging studies (Pillay, Gruber, Rogowska, Simpson, & Yurgelun-Todd, 2006) and evidence exists of the channels of connection between both structures (Kim & Whalen, 2009). What these findings imply is that harm avoidance reflects, ultimately, the activation and cortical modulation of structures of the limbic system and the taking of secure decisions, via its connection with the insula, as a critical neural substrate to instantiate aversive somatic markers that guide risk-taking decision-making behaviour (Paulus, Rogalsky, Simmons, Feinstein, & Stein, 2003).

Reward dependence is hypothetically associated with noradrenergic activity, although the empirical evidence is contradictory (Curtin, Walker, Peyrin, Soulier, Badan and Schulz, 1997; Garvey, Noyes, Cook, and Blum, 1996). More recently it has been found that opiate receptor availability in the ventral striatum, a core area of the brain reward system, is directly correlated with reward dependence (Schreckenberger, Klega, Gründer, Buchholz, Scheurich, Schirrmacher, et al., 2008). If the anticipation of the reward is associated with dopaminergic activity, and, in consequence, with novelty seeking, the reward dependence would be associated with the gratification obtained by the behaviour in course, which manifests as individual differences in social attachment, dependence on the approval of others, and sentimentality (Cloninger, Svrakic, & Przybeck, 1993) and opioid activity would mediate reward dependence in social contact behaviour via longer-lasting individual differences that can be clinically defined as human personality trait. Harm avoidance and reward dependence are found to correlate with decreased cerebral blood flow in various paralimbic and frontal and temporal regions (Sugiura et al., 2000).

Persistence is a trait associated with the maintenance of behaviour despite receiving intermittent reinforcements, and it is especially linked to the neuronal interconnections between the prefrontal, orbitolateral and medial cortex and the ventral striatum (Gusnard, Ollinger, Shulman, Cloninger, Price, Van Essen et al., 2003).

A very recent study (Gardinia, Cloninger, & Venneri, 2009), using Magnetic Resonance Imaging, has found that novelty seeking correlated positively with grey matter volume in frontal and posterior cingulate regions; harm avoidance showed a negative correlation with grey matter volume in orbito-frontal, occipital and parietal structures; reward dependence was negatively correlated with grey matter volume in the caudate nucleus and in the rectal frontal gyrus; persistence showed a positive correlation with grey matter volume in the precuneus, paracentral lobule and parahippocampal gyrus. Consequently, the authors consider that these results indicate that individual differences in the main personality dimensions may reflect structural variance in specific brain areas. However, it is not clear whether these differences are due, as Cloninger's theoretic model suggests, to genetically determined conditions, stable over time, or whether it might be that any observed morphological brain variability, rather than a predisposing factor which determines individual differences in personality traits, might be a byproduct of differences in personality traits, resulting from repeated behaviours and environmental exposures in the course of life. Although the authors opt for the original explanation, coherent with the model, we have evidence that, at least in addicts to substances, and via structural equations, some supposedly innate and stable dimensions, such as novelty seeking, are explained to a large extent on the basis of early environmental conditions (Lukasiewicz, Neveu, Blecha, Falissard, Reynaud, & Gasquet, 2008).

Regarding character dimensions, it has been proposed that self-directedness would be associated with the prefrontal cortex and the superior functions (Cloninger, 2004, 2006), to the point that the definition of this dimension is superimposed over that of executive functions of the frontal lobe (Lezak, 1982), strictly representing a meta-variable of prefrontal functioning, which is presented at systematically low levels in addicts, regardless of whether or not they fulfil the criteria for a diagnosis on Axis II (Pedrero-Pérez, Ruiz-Sanchez-de-León, Rojo-Mota, Olivar-Arroyo, Llanero-Luque, & Puerta-García, C., in press-a; Ruiz-Sanchez-de-León, Pedrero-Pérez, Olivar-Arroyo, Llanero-Luque, Rojo-Mota, Puerta-García, in press; see Figure 2).

Despite the proliferation of studies, we currently lack a neural map that allows us to interpret the traits in terms of brain functioning. On the basis of this lack, psychometric limitations are found for both the self-report questionnaires and the biochemical and neuroimaging tests, which provide indicators of poor validity. However, the studies already cited offer an encouraging starting point for future studies. This is one of the channels open for research in forthcoming years.

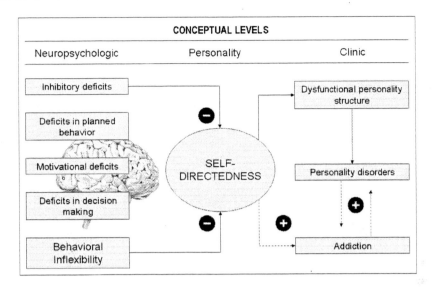

Figure 2. Relationship between variables of different conceptual areas

Neuroscientific Perspective of Personality Disorders

On the other hand, an attempt has also been made to find the neurophysiological basis of categorially formulated personality disorders, as well as their neuropsychological correlates. We will first review the most relevant findings in relationship with the two disorders most frequently linked with addiction: antisocial and borderline personality disorders.

· Subjects diagnosed with borderline personality disorder show deficits in cognitive processing, specifically in tasks that require sustained attention, spatial working memory, and executive functioning, decision-making and planning, as well as other difficulties of control of the affective response (Bazanis, Rogers, Dowson, Taylor, Meux, Staley, et al., 2002; Fertuck, Lenzenweger, Clarkin, Hoermann, & Stanley; 2006; Lenzenweger, Clarkin, Fertuck, Kernberg, 2004). Another study found that this diagnosis was associated with deficits on measures of nonverbal executive function and nonverbal memory but not with alternation learning, response inhibition, divergent thinking, verbal fluency, and verbal working memory, which suggests dysfunction of right hemisphere frontotemporal regions (Dinn, Harris, Aycicegi, Greene, Kirkley, & Reilly, 2004). These deficits and others, such as diminished regulation of impulsive behaviour in persons with this diagnosis may be associated with decreased glucose uptake in medial orbital frontal cortex (Soloff, Meltzer, Becker, Greer, Kelly, & Constantine, 2003). Deficits in attention and executive functions have been proposed as promising endophenotypic markers for this disorder, although it is necessary to consider it from an evolutionary perspective (Fertuck, Lenzenweger, & Clarkin, 2005). These findings allow us to affirm that the current diagnostic category is not adequately formulated, that a large number of the co-occurring disorders would be explained based on a neurocognitive formulation that takes the common substrates into account, and that the perspective of experimental psychopathology is that the features and symptoms of devastating clinical phenomena can be assessed and related to basic biological and psychological mechanisms and systems (Fertuck et al., 2006). Specifically, it has been proposed that there are common neurobiological substrates to borderline personality disorder and addictive disorders, which seriously questions the utility of a dual diagnosis (Bornovalova et al., 2005).

Subjects diagnosed with antisocial personality disorder perform significantly worse in tasks that assess executive functions (Morgan& Lilienfeld, 2000). In general terms, antisocial personality and psychopathy are associated with executive cognitive control deficits, similar to some of the findings we have reviewed in borderline personality disorder (Dolan & Park, 2002). In a study of neuropsychological performance (Dinn & Harris, 2000) the subjects diagnosed with antisocial personality disorder showed greater neuropsychological deficits on measures sensitive to orbitofrontal dysfunction, deficits on the object alternation test may reflect an inability to effectively process feedback information regarding reward and punishment (i.e., the inability to successfully employ punishment cues to guide behaviour), subjects were electrodermally hyporesponsive to aversive stimuli, but they did not demonstrate performance deficits on classical tests of frontal executive function. Amygdala reactivity to emotional stimuli may discriminate borderline from antisocial individuals, who fail to show physiological activation to sad faces and lack empathy for the distress of others (Blair, Jones, Clark, & Smith, 1997).

At the current time, sufficient evidence supports a neurobehavioral basis for borderline (Arza, Díaz-Marsá, López-Micó, Fernández de Pablo, López-Ibor, & Carrasco, 2009; Ruocco, 2005) and antisocial personality pathology (Morgan& Lilienfeld, 2000; Raine, Lencz, Bihrle, LaCasse, & Colletti, 2000), but also for other personality disorders (Voglmaier, Seidman, Niznikiewicz, Dickey, Shenton, & McCarley, 2005). In general terms, the involvement of the prefrontal cortex in the development of the different dysfunctional patterns of personality appears clear (Ruocco & Trobst, 2003).

We know that brain injuries cause deep personality changes and that such changes acquire clinical manifestations that resemble the personality disorders described in the absence of brain damage (Castaño-Monsalve, González-Echeverri, Andrés-Cano, García, & Arizmendi, 2005). A study examined the relationship between personality disorders, measured with the MCMI-III and neuropsychological performance in classical tests, in patients who had suffered closed brain injury (Ruocco & Swirsky-Sacchetti, 2007), characterising the cognitive performance associated with each trait and with each pathological personality pattern. In addition, the authors found a unique set of relations between neuropsychological functioning and passive-aggressive (or negativistic personality disorder, a disorder listed in DSM-IV for further study) symptomatology: when depressive symptomatology was accounted for in the regression model, executive function remained the sole neuropsychological domain significantly associated with passive-aggressive traits. These findings suggest that passive-aggressive traits may be a more severe form of personality pathology with substantial deficits in higher-order regulatory and supervisory functions subserved primarily by the frontal lobes. Moreover,negativistic/passive-aggressive personality disorder usually appears with very high prevalences when samples of addicts are studied with self-report instruments, such as the different versions of the MCMI (Marlowe, Festinger, Kirby, Rubenstein, & Platt, 1998; Nadeau et al., 1999; Pedrero-Pérez et al., 2003). Some authors have suggested that this disorder is superimposed over the symptomatology inherent to substance abuse (Nadeau et al., 1999). Other studies find that it is a disorder with sufficient construct validity in order to be considered a clinical entity (Hopwood, Morey, Markowitz, Pinto, Skodol, Gunderson, et al., 2009). In a study performed on a sample of addicts in treatment (Pedrero-Pérez et al., 2006) a high prevalence of this disorder was found (punctuation criterion in the MCMI-II of 33.3%, being the most punctuated scale at 15.9%) and was associated with the results in two questionnaires: the BFQ (Five Factor Model) and TCI-R (Cloninger's biosocial model). In the first, negativistic/passive-aggressive personality disorder was associated with high levels of extraversion and low levels of emotional stability (high neuroticism): in reality, it appeared as an attenuated form of borderline personality disorder. In relation to the second model, the disorder was associated with high levels of novelty seeking and harm avoidance, as well as the low levels in self-directedness characteristic of all the disorders. In the dimensional study of the MCMI-II, based on the nuclear items of each disorder, negativistic/passive-aggressive personality disorder was situated close to the aggressive/sadistic, borderline and antisocial disorders, and mid-way between these and paranoid, histrionic and narcisistic disorders (see Figure 1). This work concluded that the decision taken in the last edition of the DSM to relegate it to the entity of "category proposed for study" may paradoxically be hindering such study, so that the subjects who could be catalogued as negativist, are being diagnosed as antisocial – if aggressive, impulsive behaviours predominate – dominant and disruptive, as borderline – if problems of the emotional sphere predominate or are added – or as both – supporting a possible spurious comorbidity – or are included in the category, accessed with difficulty by research, of non-specified personality disorder.

Subsequent studies have found a strong correlation between this disorder and frontal symptomatology in daily life (Pedrero-Pérez, Ruiz-Sanchez-de-León, Rojo-Mota, Olivar-Arroyo, Llanero-Luque, & Puerta-García, in press-b), which is congruent with the findings of the study of Ruocco & Swirsky-Sacchetti (2007). Taken as a whole, what these data suggest is that negativistic/passive-aggressive personality disorder in addicts to substances may represent the consequence of a personality change occurring as a consequence of the addiction itself and the executive dysfunction that accompanies it (and perhaps also explains and sustains it): the effects of the substances and of other conditions associated with addiction (e.g., stress) would alter corticofrontal functioning, favour the loss of control over behaviour, increase dysexecutive symptomatology in everyday life and result in ambivalent behaviour, which would be the result of the decompensation of previous stable patterns. This would also justify the proposal of Nadeau et al. (1999), who considered the superposition of these symptoms with those inherent to addiction, as well as the decrease in the severity of this disorder after a few weeks of treatment (Landry, Nadeau, & Racine, 1996; Zimmerman, 1994).

Ernst and Fudge (2009) have proposed a developmental neurobiological model of motivated behaviour. According to their Fractal Triadic Model, motivated behaviour is governed by a carefully orchestrated articulation among three systems, approach, avoidance and regulatory. These three systems map to distinct, but overlapping, neural circuits, whose representatives are the striatum, the amygdala and the medial prefrontal cortex. Ultimately, motivated behaviour would be the consequence of the modulation exercised by the prefrontal cortex on the inputs received from the other two structures. Approach or flight before certain stimuli would be a decision modulated by cortical structures, the function of which would be to inhibit one or another of the subcortical structures. Should the functioning of the prefrontal cortex not be appropriate, it is most probable that the deregulated behaviour would opt alternatively and chaotically for approach or avoidance. This ambivalence suggests an explanation to the finding, already confirmed, of the simultaneous elevation of traits such as novelty seeking and harm avoidance in the negativistic/passive-aggressive profile. When this pattern is stable over time, it is possibly associated with an inadequate learning of frontal control mechanisms, possibly deriving from a family history characterised by unstable attachment, inconsistent educational guidelines, non-contingent reinforcement or other factors (Millon & Davis, 1996). However, it is also possible that executive dysfunction is a product of addiction (Hester & Garavan, 2004; Verdejo-García, A., Bechara, A., et al., 2006) and, to this extent, the deregulation of the subcortical structures represents an ensuing condition that explains both the increase in traits that habitually present a negative correlation (novelty seeking and harm avoidance), and their expression in an ambivalent behaviour pattern chaotically oscillating between approach and avoidance, between aggression and flight, as is the case of the negativistic/passive-aggressive and borderline personality disorders (Pedrero et al., 2006).

Therefore, it is appropriate to think that certain personality patterns may be the consequence of an evolutionary history marked by early stressful experiences, which interact with genetic predispositions, which result in stable physiological changes (e.g., cortisol rhythms), in maladaptive brain functioning (e.g., executive dysfunction) and which modulate stable personality patterns that favour addiction (Caspi et al., 2002; Flory, Yehuda, Grossman, New, Mitropoulou, & Siever, 2009; Gabbard, 2005). But we also know that acute stress is a crucial element in the development and maintenance of addiction (Koob, 2008) and that the consequence of acute-maintained or chronic stress on brain functioning is an alteration in the structure and functioning of the cerebral cortex (Corominas, Roncero, & Casas, 2010; Dias-Ferreira, Sousa, Melo, Morgado, Mesquita, Cerqueira, et al., 2009; Liston, McEwen, & Casey, 2009). We also know that maintained stress may be due not only to the pharmacological effects of the substances, but also to the stimulatory restriction that accompanies addiction (Stairs & Bardo, 2009). We also know of some studies that find a reduction in the thickness of the prefrontal cortex the magnitude of which correlates with the time of consumption of the substance, but not with the age of commencement of the consumption, which allows us to attribute it with higher probability to effects related to consumption and not to previous conditions that may favour it (Makris, Gasic, Kennedy, Hodge, Kaiser, Lee, et al., 2008).

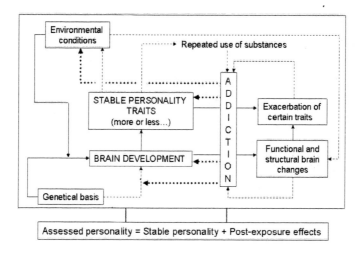

Figure 3. Interactive model of personality and addiction

From this perspective, part of the symptomatology detected in the assessment of addicted subjects must be considered in terms of organic damage or more or less stable neurological alteration, but not in terms of personality. For example, the damage in the frontal lobe favours decision making based on utilitarian moral judgements (Koenigs, Young, Adolphs, Tranel, Cushman, Hauser, et al., 2007), the appearance of uninhibited, aggressive and explosive behaviours, affective instability, apathy, paranoia and perseverance (Max, Levin, Schachar, Landis, Saunders, Ewing-Cobbs, et al., 2006; Max, Robertson, & Lansing, 2001) and the loss of conscience regarding the inherent difficulties (Rankin, Baldwin, Pace-Savitsky, Kramer, & Miller, 2005). All of these are signs habitually known in the addiction clinic.

A Key Difference: Recovery

This neuroscientific perspective of addiction and its relationship with personality disorders necessarily requires consideration that both share, to a considerable extent, common substrates: certain personality traits favour the approach to substances, the repetition of consumptions and the establishment of maladaptive habits; but also that the addiction itself (understood as a pattern of repeated behaviour and its consequences, not only neuropharmacological) generates post-exposure effects that result in neurological changes which modify the behaviour, altering the previous personality, in the same terms that can be observed in brain damage of different etiology (Yücel, Lubman, Solowij, & Brewer, 2007). This conception of addiction as neurobehavioral self-powered complex differs perceptibly from previous conceptions that were limited to a mere symptomatological observance of the concurrence of manifestations of various types, configuring a simplistic vision of mere comorbidity or self-medication.

However, a crucial difference is that the changes generated as a consequence of the addictive process are to a great extent reversible, unlike those produced by other causes (traumatic, degenerative, tumoural, etc.). Despite the fact that the alterations may persist during long periods of time (Tanabe, Tregellas, Dalwani, Thompson, Owens, Crowley, & Banich, 2009), and therefore deficits may be seen in the neuropsychological performance (Prosser, Eisenberg, Davey, Steinfeld, Cohen, London, et al., 2008; Rapeli, Fabritius, Kalska, & Alho, 2009), we also have solid evidence that the structural recovery of the affected brain areas begins very early in the abstinence (Bartsch, Homola, Biller, Smith, Weijers, Wiesbeck, et al., 2007) and that the neuropsychological performance may become similar to that of controls in the absence of treatment (Selby & Azrin, 1998). We know that this recovery may be favoured by certain pharmacological interventions (Vocci, 2008) but also by means of cognitive training (Draganski, Gaser, Busch, Schuierer, Bogdahn, & May, 2004) which allows recovery even of the cortical substrate most closely linked to addiction (McNab, Varrone, Farde, Jucaite, Bystritsky, Forssberg, et al., 2009). And this without considering that the majority of addicts abandon the habit and return to their daily activity without even requiring professional attention (Carballo, Fernández-Hermida, Secades-Villa, Sobell, Dum, & García Rodríguez, 2007). Moreover, mention has already been made in another section of the considerable remission rates of personality disorders diagnosed at the onset of a treatment.

CONCLUSIONS

In accordance with that expressed above we can summarise that:

1. Personality disorders do not constitute, as they are formulated at present, a category with sufficient construct validity: the stability over time of the diagnoses is low, which is not coherent with the supposed stability of personality.
2. The stability of the diagnoses of personality disorders in addicts is even lower: the symptoms disappear after extremely short periods of time.
3. Even though many researchers advocate a reformulation of Axis II disorders, which takes into account the more stable traits, instead of the symptoms and behaviours present at the time of assessment, this would not solve the problem of diagnosis in addicts: the addiction itself (understood as a process) modifies traits that are considered stable (e.g., impulsivity).
4. A neurological and neuropsychological perspective is required for the understanding of personality, its disorders and complex phenomena such as addiction. The phenomenological classifications are insufficient and induce error, considering as 'comorbidity' what are, in neurological terms, unitary phenomena, product of a common etiopathogeny. As Goldberg (2009) points out: "*Our personality is determined to a large extent by our neurobiology, and personality disorders, unlike skin disease, are caused by changes in the brain. The frontal lobes have more to do with our 'personalities' than any other part of the brain, and frontal lobe damage produces profound personality change*" (p. 156).
5. Addiction should be considered as a process that alters brain functioning, especially that of the prefrontal cortex. Consequently, addiction alters the previous personality of the patient and the product cannot be considered a 'personality disorder', but a change of personality of neurological origin. Experience in the clinic allows as to remember how, very frequently, we hear patients declare that "I was never like that", or members of their families stating that "this is not my son, he has never behaved like this before".
6. This change is less severe than that observed in other neuropsychiatric disorders, such as schizophrenia ("*We conclude that relative to other psychopathological disorders – such as schizophrenia – the severity of neuropsychological impairment in cocaine addiction is modest, albeit not indicative of the absence of neurocognitive dysfunction. The impact of such small differences in performance on quality of life, and possibly of craving and relapse, may be substantial*"; Goldstein, Leskovjan, Hoff, Hitzemann, Bashan, Khalsa, et al., 2004) and may be reversed, to a greater or lesser extent, if reversal is achieved of the neurological and neuropsychological changes produced by the addictive process.
7. From this neuroscientific perspective, the available bibliographic data must be reviewed in a new direction. Far from two morbid entities co-existing (in Spanish speaking countries the unacceptable concept of 'dual pathology' is becoming popular), what the data suggest is that addicts request treatment when the conditions (environmental, psychological and metabolic) are critical, and access the treatments in a situation that makes the learning of new behaviours impossible, which may

justify the high rates of relapse habitually observed on the treatment programmes ("... *the greatest impairment occurs initially during early treatment when therapy is the most intense. Thus there may be a temporal mismatch between the learning that is expected of the patient and his or her ability to process and retain new material that constitutes the therapeutic approach*"; Vocci, 2008). The introduction, in these initial phases of the treatments, of cognitive training programmes, supported by drugs that modulate the altered functions (without blocking the learning capacities) and a psychotherapeutic intervention of a motivational nature, may improve the conditions of adherence of the patients and favour their subsequent inclusion, once they have recovered the necessary cognitive conditions, in more demanding programmes, such as the relapse prevention.

Consequently, there is sufficient empirical evidence to affirm that when an addict is assessed it is not his personality, as this construct is defined in the various disciplines and classifications, that is really explored, but the additive product of the stable traits that characterise his habitual pattern of behaviour plus those other traits, or exacerbation of traits, which are the product of his consumption behaviour. The studies that explore the 'comorbidity' between addiction and personality disorders must be reviewed in the light of new neuroscientific knowledge. Methods of assessment are required that take these aspects into account, in the line of certain methods already proposed (Rounsaville, Kranzler, Ball, Tennen, Poling, & Triffleman, 1998), able to measure personality beyond the circumstantial changes with criteria based on scientific evidence (Widiger & Samuel, 2005).

REFERENCES

Aklin, W. M. (2007). *Impact of residential substance abuse treatment on affect and personality-related variables across inner-city substance abusers*.Doctoral Dissertation.Retrieved from http://www.lib.umd.edu/drum/bitstream/1903/7215/1/umi-umd-4611.pdf.University of Maryland.

Allen, T. J., Moeller, F. G., Rhoades, H. M. & Cherek, D. R. (1998).Impulsivity and history of drug dependence.*Drug and Alcohol Dependence, 50*, 137-145.

American Psychiatric Association (2000).*Diagnostic and statistical manual of mental disorders (4th ed revised)*. Washington DC: American Psychiatric Press.

Andersen, S. L. & Teicher, M. H. (2009). Desperately driven and no brakes: Developmental stress exposure and subsequent risk for substance abuse. *Neuroscience and Biobehavioral Reviews, 33*, 516-524.

Aron, A. R. & Poldrack, P. A. (2005). The cognitive neuroscience of response inhibition: relevance for genetic research in attention-deficit/hyperactivity disorder. *Biological Psychiatry, 57*, 1285-1292.

Arza, R., Díaz-Marsá, M., López-Micó, C., Fernández de Pablo, N., López-Ibor, J. J. & Carrasco, J. L. (2009). Alteraciones neuropsicológicas en el trastorno límite de la personalidad: estrategias de detección. *Actas Españolas de Psiquiatría, 37*, 185-190.

Asendorpf, J. B. & Denissen, J. J. A. (2006).Predictive validity of personality types versus personality dimensions from early childhood to adulthood: implications for the distinction betweer core and surface traits. *Merrill-Palmer Quarterly, 52*, 486-513.

Baca-Garcia, E., Perez-Rodriguez, M. M., Basurte-Villamor, I., Fernandez del Moral, A. L., Jimenez-Arriero, M. A. & Gonzalez de Rivera, J. L., et al. (2007). Diagnostic stability of psychiatric disorders in clinical practice.*British Journal of Psychiatry, 190*, 210-216.

Ball, S. A., Rounsaville, B. J., Tennen, H. & Kranzler, H. R. (2001). Reliability of personality disorder symptoms and personality traits in substance-dependent inpatients.*Journal of Abnormal Psychology, 2*, 341-352.

Bankston, S. M., Carroll, D. D., Cron, S. G., Granmayeh, L. K., Marcus, M. T., Moeller, F. G. et al. (2009). Substance Abuser Impulsivity Decreases with a Nine-Month Stay in a Therapeutic Community. *American Journal of Drug and Alcohol Abuse, 35*, 417-420.

Bartsch, A. J., Homola,G., Biller, A., Smith, S. M., Weijers, H. G., Wiesbeck, G. A., et al. (2007). Manifestations of early brain recovery associated with abstinence from alcoholism. *Brain, 130*, 36-47.

Bazanis, E., Rogers, R. D., Dowson, J. H., Taylor, P., Meux, C., Staley, C., et al. (2002). Neurocognitive deficits in decision-making and planning of patients with DSM-III-R borderline personality disorder.*Psychological Medicine, 32*, 1395-1405.

Bechara, A. (2005). Decision making, impulse control and loss of willpower to resist drugs: a neurocognitive perspective. *Nature Neuroscience, 8*, 1458-1463.

Belin, D., Mar, A. C., Dalley, J. W., Robbins, T. W. & Everitt, B. J. (2008). High impulsivity predicts the switch to compulsive cocaine-taking. *Science, 320*, 1352-1355.

Bernstein, D. P., Cohen, P., Velez, C. N., Schwab-Stone, M., Siever, L. J. & Shinsato, L. (1993). Prevalence and stability of the DSM-III-R personality disorders in a community-based survey of adolescents. *American Journal of Psychiatry, 150*, 1237-1243.

Besteiro, J., Lemos, S., Muñiz, J., García, E. & Álvarez, M. (2007). Dimensiones de los trastornos de personalidad en el MCMI-II. *International Journal of Clinical and Health Psychology, 7*, 295-306.

Blair, R. J., Jones, L., Clark, F. & Smith, M. (1997). The psychopathic individual: A lack of responsiveness to distress cues? *Psychophysiology, 34*, 192-198.

Bornovalova, M. A., Lejuez, C. W., Daughters, S. B., Rosenthal, M. Z. & Lynch, T. R. (2005). Impulsivity as a common process across borderline personality and substance use disorders.*Clinical Psychology Review, 25*, 790-812.

Bronisch, T. & Klerman, G. L. (1991) Personality functioning: change and stability in relationship to symptoms and psychopathology. *Journal of Personality Disorders, 5*, 307-317.

Cabeza, R. & Nyberg, L. (2000).Imaging cognition II: an empirical review of 275 PET and fMRI studies.*Journal of Cognitive Neuroscience, 12*, 1-47.

Calsyn, D. A., Wells, E. A., Fleming, C. & Saxon, A. J. (2000).Changes in Millon Clinical Multiaxial Inventory among opiate addicts as a function of retention in methadone maintenance treatment and recent drug use.*American Journal of Drug and Alcohol Abuse, 26*, 297-309.

Canli, T., Sivers, H., Whitfield, S. L., Gotlib, I. H., Gabrieli, J. D. (2002). Amygdala response to happy faces as a function of extraversion.*Science, 296*, 2191.

Canli, T., Zhao, Z., Kang, E., Gross, J. (2001). An fMRI study of personality influences on brain reactivity to emotional stimuli. *Behavioral Neuroscience, 115*, 33-42.

Carballo, J. L., Fernández Hermida, J. R., Secades Villa, R., Sobell, L., Dum, M. & García Rodríguez, O. (2007). Natural recovery from alcohol and drug problems: A methological review of the literature from 1999 through 2005. In H. Klingemann & L. Sobell (Eds.), *Promoting self-change from problem substance use: Practical implications for policy, prevention, and treatment.* London: Springer Verlag.

Caspi, A. & Shiner, R. G. (2006).Personality development across the life course. In: Eisenberg, N.; Damon, W. & Lerner, R. M., editors. *Handbook of child psychology: Vol. 3, Social, emotional, and personality development. 6th ed*(p. 300-365). Hoboken, NJ: John Wiley & Sons Inc.

Caspi, A., Harrington, H., Milne, B., Amell, J. W., Theodore, R. F. & Moffitt, T. E. (2003). Children's behavioral styles at age 3 are linked to their adult personality traits at age 26. *Journal of Personality, 71*, 494-513.

Caspi, A., McClay, J., Moffitt, T. E., Mill, J., Martin, J., Craig, I. W., et al. (2002). Role of genotype in the cycle of violence in maltreated children.*Science, 297*, 851-854.

Caspi, A., Roberts, B. W. & Shiner, R. L. (2005). Personality development: stability and change. *Annual Review of Psychology, 56*, 453-484.

Castaño-Monsalve, B., González-Echeverri, G., Andrés-Cano, P., García, J. & Arizmendi, I. (2005). Comparative study of psychiatric disorders in general traumatism and brain injured patients. *Actas Españolas de Psiquiatría, 33*, 96-101.

Choca, J. P. (1999). Evolution of Millon's personality prototypes.*Journal of Personality Assessment, 72*, 353-364.

Clark, L. A. (2007). Assessment and diagnosis of personality disorder: Perennial issues and an emerging reconceptualization. *Annual Review of Psychology, 58*, 227-257.

Clark, L. A. (2009). Stability and change in personality disorder. *Current Directions in Psychological Science, 18*, 27-31.

Cloninger, C. R. (2004). *Feeling Good: The Science of Well-Being.* New York: Oxford University Press.

Cloninger, C. R. (2006). Commentary on Paris: personality as a dynamic psychobiological system. In T. A. Widiger, E. Simonsen, P. Sirovatka, & D. A. Regier (eds.), *Dimensional models of personality disorders: refining the Research Agenda for DSM-V* (pp. 73-76). Washington DC: American Psychiatric Publishing.

Cloninger, C. R., Svrakic, D. M. & Przybeck, T. R. (1993).A psychobiological model of temperament and character.*Archives of General Psychiatry, 50*, 975-990.

Cohen, P., Crawford, T. N., Johnson, J. G. & Kasen, S. (2005). The Children in the Community Study of developmental course of personality disorder.*Journal of Personality Disorders*, 19, 466–486.

Conway, K. P., Kane, R. J., Ball, S. A., Poling, J. C. & Rounsaville, B. J. (2003).Personality, substance of choice, and polysubstance involvement among substance dependent patients.*Drug and Alcohol Dependence, 71*, 65-75.

Corominas, M., Roncero, C. & Casas, M. (2010). Corticotropin releasing factor and neuroplasticity in cocaine addiction.*Life Sciences, 86*, 1-9.

Craig, R. J. & Olson, R. (1998).Stability of the MCMI-III in a substance-abusing inpatient sample.*Psychological Reports, 83*, 1273-1274.

Craig, R. J. (2000). Prevalence of personality disorders among cocaine and heroin addicts.*Substance Abuse, 21*, 87-94.

Curtin, F., Walker, J. P., Peyrin, L., Soulier, V., Badan, M. & Schulz, P. (1997). Reward dependence is positively related to urinary monoamines in normal men. *Biological Psychiatry, 42*, 275-281.

Dalley, J. W., Fryer, T. D., Brichard, L., Robinson, E. S. J., Theobald, D. E. H., Lääne, K., et al. (2007). Nucleus accumbens D2/3 receptors predict trait impulsivity and cocaine reinforcement. *Science, 315*, 1267-1270.

de Groot, M. H., Franken, I. H.A., van der Meer, C. W. & Hendriks, V. M. (2003). Stability and change in dimensional ratings of personality disorders in drug abuse patients during treatment. *Journal of Substance Abuse Treatment, 24*, 115-120.

de Wit, H. (2009). Impulsivity as a determinant and consequence of drug use: A review of underlying processes. *Addiction Biology, 14*, 22-31.

Dennissen, J. J. A., Asendorpf, J. B. & van Aken, M. A. G. (2008). Childhood personality predicts long-term trajectories of shyness and aggressiveness in the context of demographic transitions in emerging adulthood. *Journal of Personality, 76*, 67-99.

Dias-Ferreira, E., Sousa, J. C., Melo, I., Morgado, P., Mesquita, A. R., Cerqueira, J. J., et al. (2009). Chronic stress causes frontostriatal reorganization and affects decision-making. *Science, 325*, 621- 625.

Dilworth-Bart, J. E., Khurshid, A. & Vandell, D. L. (2007). Do maternal stress and home environment mediate the relation between early income to need and 54-months attentional abilities? *Infant and Child Development, 16*, 525-552.

Dinn, W. M. & Harris, C. L. (2000). Neurocognitive function in antisocial personality disorder. *Psychiatry Research, 97*, 173-190.

Dinn, W. M., Harris, C. L., Aycicegi, A., Greene, P. B., Kirkley, S. M. & Reilly, C. (2004).Neurocognitive function in borderline personality disorder.*Progress in Neuro-Psychopharmacology and Biological Psychiatry, 28*, 329-341.

Dolan, M. & Park, I. (2002).The neuropsychology of antisocial personality disorder.*Psychological Medicine, 32*, 417–427.

Draganski, B., Gaser, C., Busch, V., Schuierer, G., Bogdahn, U. & May, A. (2004). Changes in grey matter induced by training. Newly honed juggling skills show up as a transient feature on a brain-imaging scan. *Nature, 427*, 311-312.

Durbin, C. E. & Klein, D. N. (2006). Ten-year stability of personality disorders among outpatients with mood disorders. *Journal of Abnormal Psychology, 115*, 75-84.

Ebstein, R. P., Gritsenko, I., Nemanov, L., Frisch, A., Osher, Y. & Belmaker, R. H. (1997). No association between the serotonin transporter gene regulatory region polymorphism and the Tridimensional Personality Questionnaire (TPQ) temperament of harm avoidance. *Molecular Psychiatry, 2*, 224-226.

Echeburùa, E., Bravo de Medina, R. & Aizpiri, J. (2007). Comorbidity of alcohol dependence and personality disorders: a comparative study. *Alcohol & Alcoholism, 42*, 618-622.

Eisenberg, N., Zhou, Q., Spinrad, T. L, Valiente, C., Fabes, R. A.,& Liew, J. (2005).Relations among positive parenting, children's effortful control, and externalizing problems: A three-wave longitudinal study. *Child Development, 76*, 1055–1071.

Ernst, M. & Fudge, J. L. (2009). A developmental neurobiological model of motivated behavior: Anatomy, connectivity and ontogeny of the triadic nodes. *Neuroscience and Biobehavioral Reviews, 33*, 367-382.

Everitt, B. J. & Robbins, T. W. (2005). Neural systems of reinforcement for drug addiction: from actions to habits to compulsion. *Nature Neuroscience, 8*, 1481-1489.

Everitt, B. J., Belin, D., Economidou, D., Pelloux, Y., Dalley, J. W. & Robbins, T. W. (2008).Neural mechanisms underlying the vulnerability to develop compulsive drugseeking habits and addiction.*Philosophical Transactions of the Royal Society B (Biological Sciences), 363*, 3125-3135.

Farde, L., Gustavsson, J. P. & Jonsson, E. (1997).D2 dopamine receptors and personality traits.*Nature, 385*, 590.

Fava, M., Farabaugh, A. H., Sickinger, A. H., Wrigh, E., Alpert, J. E., Sonawalla, S., et al. (2002).Personality disorders and depression.*Psychological Medicine, 32*, 1049-1105.

Ferro, T., Klein, D. N., Schwartz, J. E., Kasch, K. L. & Leader, J. B. (1998). 30-Month stability of personality disorder diagnoses in depressed outpatients. *American Journal of Psychiatry, 155*, 653-659.

Fertuck, E. A., Lenzenweger, M. F. & Clarkin, J. F. (2005). The association between attentional and executive controls in the expression of borderline personality disorder features: a preliminary study. *Psychopathology, 38*, 75-81.

Fertuck, E. A., Lenzenweger, M. F., Clarkin, J. F., Hoermann, S. & Stanley, B. (2006).Executive neurocognition, memory systems, and borderline personality disorder.*Clinical Psychology Review, 26*, 346-375.

First, M. B. & Gladis, M. M. (1993).Diagnosis and differential diagnosis of psychiatric and substance use disorders. In J. Solomon, S. Zimberg, & E. Shollar (eds.), *Dual diagnosis: evaluation, treatment, training, and program development* (pp.23-37). New York: Kluwer Academic/Plenum Publishers.

Fischer, H., Wik, G. & Fredrikson, M. (1997). Extraversion, neuroticism, and brain function: a PET study of personality. *Personality and Individual Differences, 23*, 345-352.

Flory, J. D., Yehuda, R., Grossman, R., New, A. S., Mitropoulou, V. & Siever, L. J. (2009). Childhood trauma and basal cortisol in people with personality disorders. *Comprehensive Psychiatry, 50*, 34-37.

Forcada-Chapa, R., Pardo-Pavía, N. & Bondía-Soler, B. (2006). Impulsividad en dependientes de cocaína que abandonan el consumo. *Adicciones, 18*, 111-118.

Fountoulakis, K. N. & Kaprinis, G. S. (2006). Personality disorders: new data versus old concepts. *Current Opinion in Psychiatry, 19*, 90-94.

Gabbard, G. O. (2005). Mind, brain, and personality disorders. *American Journal of Psychiatry, 162*, 648-655.

Gardinia, S., Cloninger, C. R. & Venneri, A. (2009). Individual differences in personality traits reflect structural variance in specific brain regions. *Brain Research Bulletin, 79*, 265-270.

Garvey, M. J., Noyes, R., Cook, B. & Blum, N. (1996).Preliminary confirmation of the proposed link between reward-dependence traits and norepinephrine.*Psychiatry Research, 65*, 61-64.

Goldberg, E. (2009). *The new executive brain: frontal lobes in a complex world.* New York: Oxford University Press.

Goldstein, R. Z. & Volkow, N. D. (2002). Drug addiction and its underlying neurobiological basis: Neuroimaging evidence for the involvement of the frontal cortex. *American Journal of Psychiatry, 159*, 1642-1652.

Goldstein, R. Z., Leskovjan, A. C., Hoff, A. L., Hitzemann, R., Bashan, F., Khalsa, S. S., et al. (2004). Severity of neuropsychological impairment in cocaine and alcohol addiction: association with metabolism in the prefrontal cortex. *Neuropsychologia, 42*, 1447-1458.

Goudriaan, A. E., Oosterlaan, J., de Beurs, E. & van den Brink, W. (2006). Neurocognitive functions in pathological gambling: a comparison with alcohol dependence, Tourette syndrome and normal controls. *Addiction, 101*, 534-547.

Grant, B. F., Stinson, F. S., Dawson, D. A., Chou, S. P., Ruan, W. J. & Pickering, R. P. (2004). Co-occurrence of 12-month alcohol and drug use disorders and personality disorders in the United States.*Archives of General Psychiatry, 61*, 361-368.

Gray, N. S., Pickering, A. D. & Gray, J. A. (1994). Psychoticism and dopamine D2 binding in the basal ganglia using single photon emission computed tomography. *Personality and Individual Differences, 17*, 431-434.

Grilo, C. M. & McGlasham, T. H. (2009).Course and outcome. In: J. M. Oldham, A. E. Skodol, & D. S. Bender (eds.), *Essentials of Personality Disorders* (pp.63-79). Arlington VA: American Psychiatric Publishing.

Grilo, C. M., Becker, D. F., Edell, W. S. & McGlashan, T. H. (2001). Stability and change of DSM-III-R personality disorder dimensions in adolescents followed up 2 years after psychiatric hospitalization. *Comprehensive Psychiatry, 42*, 364-368.

Grilo, C. M., Sanislow, C. A., Gunderson, J. G., Pagano, M. E., Yen, S., Zanarini, M. C., et al. (2004). Two-year stability and change of schizotypal, borderline, avoidant, and obsessive-compulsive personality disorders. *Journal of Consulting and Clinical Psychology, 72*, 767-775.

Gunderson, J. G., Shea, M. T., Skodol, A. E., McGlashan, T. H., Morey, L. C., Stout, R. L., et al. (2000). The Collaborative Longitudinal Personality Disorders Study: development, aims, design, and sample characteristics. *Journal of Personality Disorders, 14*, 300-315.

Gusnard, D. A., Ollinger, J. M., Shulman, G. L., Cloninger, C. R., Price, J. L., Van Essen, D. C., et al. (2003). Persistence and brain circuitry.*PNAS, 100*, 3479-3484.

Haier, R. J., Sokolski, K., Katz, M., &Buchsbaum, M. S. (1987).The study of personality with positron emission tomography. In: Strelau, J., Eysenck, H.J. (eds.), *Personality Dimensions and Arousal* (pp. 251-267). New York: Plenum Press.

Hansenne, M., Pinto, E., Pitchot, W., Reggers, J., Scantanburlo, G., Moor, M. & Ansseau, M. (2002). Further evidence on the relationship between dopamine and novelty seeking: a neuroendocrine study. *Personality and Individual Differences, 33*, 967-977.

Hesse, M., Nielsen, P. & Røjskjær, S. (2007). Stability and change in Millon Clinical Multiaxial Inventory II personality disorder scores in treated alcohol dependent subjects: relationship to post-treatment abstinence. *International Journal of Mental Health and Addiction, 5*, 254-262.

Hester, R. & Garavan, H. (2004). Executive dysfunction in cocaine addiction: evidence for discordant frontal, cingulate, and cerebellar activity. *Journal of Neuroscience, 24*, 11017-11022.

Heyman, G. M. (2001). Is addiction a chronic, relapsing disease? In: P. B Heymann & W. N. Brownsberger (eds.), *Drug addiction and drug policy: the struggle to control dependence* (pp. 81-117). Cambridge (MA): Harvard University Press.

Hopwood, C. J., Morey, L. C., Markowitz, J. C., Pinto, A., Skodol, A. E., Gunderson, J. G., et al. (2009). The construct validity of passive-aggressive personality disorder.*Psychiatry: Interpersonal & Biological Processes, 72*, 256-267.

Iketani, T., Kiriike, N., Stein, M.B., Nagao, K. Nagata, T., Minamikawa, N. et al. (2002).Personality disorder comorbidity in panic disorder patients with or without current major depression.*Depression and Anxiety, 15*, 176-182.

Jacob, C. P., Müller, J., Schmidt, M., Hohenberger, K., Gutknecht, L., Reif, A., et al. (2005).Cluster B personality disorders are associated with allelic variation of Monoamine Oxidase A activity. *Neuropsychopharmacology, 30*, 1711-1718.

Kim, H. J., Kim, J. E., Cho, G., Song, I. C., Bae, S., Hong, S. J., et al. (2009). Associations between anterior cingulate cortex glutamate and gamma-aminobutyric acid concentrations and the harm avoidance temperament.*Neuroscience Letters, 464*, 103-107.

Kim, M. J. & Whalen, P. J. (2009). The structural integrity of an amygdala–prefrontal pathway predicts trait anxiety. *Journal of Neuroscience, 29*, 11614-11618.

Ko, C. H., Liu, G. C., Hsiao, S., Yen, J. Y., Yang, M. J., Lin, W. C., et al. (2009). Brain activities associated with gaming urge of online gaming addiction.*Journal of Psychiatric Research, 43*, 739-747.

Koenigs, M., Young, L., Adolphs, R., Tranel, D., Cushman, F., Hauser, M., et al. (2007). Damage to the prefrontal cortex increases utilitarian moral judgements. *Nature, 446*, 908-911.

Koob, G. F. & Le Moal, M. (1997). Drug abuse: hedonic homeostatic dysregulation. *Science, 278*, 52-58.

Koob, G. F. & Le Moal, M. (2008). Neurobiological mechanisms for opponent motivational processes in addiction.*Philosophical Transactions of the Royal Society B (Biological Sciences), 363*, 3113-3123.

Koob, G. F. (2008). A role for brain stress systems in addiction. *Neuron, 59*, 11-34.

Krantzler, H. R. & Tinsley, J. A. (2004). *Dual diagnosis and psychiatric treatment.* New York: Marcel Dekker.

Krueger, R. F., Markon, K. E., Patrick, C. J., Benning, A. D. & Kramer, M. D. (2007). Linking antisocial behavior, substance use, and personality: an integrative quantitative model of the adult externalizing spectrum.*Journal of Abnormal Psychology, 116*, 645-666.

Krueger, R. F., Silva, P. A., Caspi, A. & Moffitt, T. E. (1998). The structure and stability of common mental disorders. *Journal of Abnormal Psychology, 107*, 216-227.

Kumari, V., Ffytche, D. H., Williams, S. C. R. & Gray, J. A. (2004). Personality predicts brain responses to cognitive demands. *Journal of Neuroscience, 24*, 10636-10641.

Kupfer, D. J., First, M. B. & Regier, D. E. (2002).Introduction.In D. J. Kupfer, M. B. First, & D. A. Regier (eds.), *A research agenda for DSM-V (pp. XV-XXIII)*. Washington DC: American Psychiatric Association.

Landry, M., Nadeau, L. & Racine, S. (1996). *La prévalence des troubles de la personnalité dans huit centres de réadaptation du Québec*. Cahier de recherche. Montréal: Recherche et Intervention sur les substances psychoactives.

Lende, D. H. & Smith, E. O. (2002). Evolution meets biopsychosociality: an analysis of addictive behaviour. *Addiction, 97*, 447-458.

Lenzenweger, M. F. (1999). Stability and Change in Personality Disorder Features. The Longitudinal Study of Personality Disorders.*Archives of General Psychiatry, 56*, 1009-1015.

Lenzenweger, M. F., Clarkin, J. F., Fertuck, E. A., &Kernberg, O. F. (2004). Executive neurocognitive functioning and neurobehavioral systems indicators in borderline personality disorder: a preliminary study. *Journal of Personality Disorders, 18*, 421-438.

Lenzenweger, M. F., Johnson, M. D. & Willett, J. B. (2004). Individual growth curve analysis illuminates stability and change in personality disorder features. The Longitudinal Study of Personality Disorders.*Archives of General Psychiatry, 61*, 1015-1024.

Lenzenweger, M. F., Lane, M. C., Loranger, A. W., & Kessler, R. C. (2007).DSM-IV personality disorders in the National Comorbidity Survey Replication.*Biological Psychiatry, 62*, 553-564.

Lezak, M. D. (1982). The problem of assesing executive functions.*International Journal of Psychology, 17*, 281-297.

Li, C. S. & Sinha, R. (2008). Inhibitory control and emotional stress regulation: neuroimaging evidence for frontal-limbic dysfunction in psycho-stimulant addiction. *Neuroscience & Biobehavioral Reviews, 32*, 581-597.

Lilienfeld, S. O., Waldman, I. D. & Israel, A. C. (1994).A critical examination of the use of the term and concept of comorbidity in psychopathology research.*Clinical Psychology: Science and Practice, 1*, 71-83.

Limson, R., Goldman, D., Roy, A., Lamparski, D., Ravitz, B., Adinoff, B., &Linnoila, M. (1991).Personality and cerebrospinal fluid monoamine metabolites in alcoholics and controls.*Archives of General Psychiatry, 48*, 437-441.

Liston, C., McEwen, B. S. & Casey, B. J. (2009). Psychosocial stress reversibly disrupts prefrontal processing and attentional control. *PNAS, 106*, 912-917.

Lukasiewicz, M., Neveu, X., Blecha, L., Falissard, B., Reynaud, M. & Gasquet, I. (2008). Pathways to substance-related disorder: a structural model approach exploring the influence of temperament, character, and childhood adversity in a national cohort of prisoners. *Alcohol & Alcoholism, 43*, 287-295.

Maj, M. (2005). 'Psychiatric comorbidity': an artefact of current diagnostic systems? *British Journal of Psychiatry, 186*, 182-184.

Makris, N., Gasic, G. P., Kennedy, D. N., Hodge, S. M., Kaiser, J. R., Lee, M. J., et al. (2008). Cortical thickness abnormalities in cocaine addiction.A reflection of both drug use and a pre-existing disposition to drug abuse?*Neuron, 60*, 174-188.

Marlowe, D. B., Festinger, D. S., Kirby, K. C., Rubenstein, D. F., &Platt, J. J. (1998).Congruence of the MCMI-II and MCMI-III in cocaine dependence.*Journal of Personality Assessment, 71*, 15-28.

Max, J. E., Levin, H. S., Schachar, R. J., Landis, J., Saunders, A. E., Ewing-Cobbs, L., et al. (2006). Predictors of personality change due to traumatic brain injury in children and adolescents six to twenty-four months after injury. *Journal of Neuropsychiatry and Clinical Neurosciences, 18*, 21-32.

Max, J. E., Robertson, B. A. M. & Lansing, A. E. (2001).The phenomenology of personality change due to traumatic brain injury in children and adolescents.*Journal of Neuropsychiatry and Clinical Neurosciences, 13*, 161-170.

McDavid, J. D. & Pilkonis, P. A. (1996). The stability of personality disorder diagnoses. *Journal of Personality Disorders, 10*, 1-15.

McGlashan, T. H., Grilo, C. M., Sanislow, C. A., Ralevski, E., Morey, L. C., Gunderson, J. G., et al. (2005). Two-year prevalence and stability of individual DSM-IV criteria for schizotypal, borderline, avoidant, and obsessive-compulsive personality disorders: toward a hybrid model of Axis II disorders. *American Journal of Psychiatry, 162*, 883-889.

McGough, J. J. & McCracken, J. T. (2006). Adult attention deficit hyperactivity disorder: moving beyond DSM-IV. *American Journal of Psychiatry, 163*, 1673-1675.

McMahon, R. C. & Richards, S. K. (1996). Profile patterns, consistency, and change in the Millon Clinical Multiaxial Inventory-II in cocaine abusers. *Journal of Clinical Psychology, 52,* 75-79.

McNab, F., Varrone, A., Farde, L., Jucaite, A., Bystritsky, P., Forssberg, H., et al. (2009). Changes in cortical dopamine D1 receptor binding associated with cognitive training. *Science, 323,* 800-802.

Miedl, S. F., Fehr, T., Meyer, G. & Herrmann, M. (2010).Neurobiological correlates of problem gambling in a quasi-realistic blackjack scenario as revealed by fMRI.*Psychiatry Research, 181,* 165-173.

Millon, T. & Davis, R. D. (1996). Conceptual and clinical foundations. In T. Millon & R. D. Davis, *Disorders of Personality: DSM-IV and Beyond* (pp. 3-215). New York: John Wiley & Sons.

Millon, T. & Davis, R. D. (1996). Negativistic personality disorders: the vacillating pattern. In Millon, T. & Davis, R. D., *Disorders of Personality: DSM-IV and Beyond* (pp.,541- 574). New York: John Wiley & Sons.

Mischel, W. (2004).Toward an integrative science of the person.*Annual Review of Psychology, 55,* 1-22.

Monsen, J. T., Odland, T., Faugli, A., Daae, E. & Eilertsen, D. (1995). Personality disorders: Changes and stability after intensive psychotherapy focusing on affect consciousness. *Psychotherapy Research, 5,* 33-48.

Morgan, A. B. & Lilienfeld, S. O. (2000).A meta-analytic review of the relation between antisocial behavior and neuropsychological measures of executive function.*Clinical Psychology Review, 20,* 113-136.

Mueser, K. T., Drake, R. E. & Wallach, M. A. (1998). Dual diagnosis: a review of etiological theories. *Addictive Behaviors, 23,* 717-734.

Nadeau, L., Landry, M. & Racine, S. (1999). Prevalence of personality disorders among clients in treatment for addiction.*Canadian Journal of Psychiatry, 44,* 592-596.

O'Gorman, R. L. Kumari, V., Williams, S. C. R., Zelaya, F. O., Connor, S. E. J., Alsop, D. C., et al. (2006). Personality factors correlate with regional cerebral perfusion. *NeuroImage, 31,* 489-495.

Paulus, M. P., Rogalsky, C., Simmons, A., Feinstein, J. S. & Stein, M. B. (2003). Increased activation in the right insula during risk-taking decision making is related to harm avoidance and neuroticism. *Neuroimage, 19,* 1439-1448.

Pedrero-Pérez, E. J. (2009). Personality disorder dimensions of MCMI-II in treated substance addicts. *Adicciones, 21,* 29-38.

Pedrero-Pérez, E. J., López-Durán, A. & Olivar-Arroyo, Á. (2006). Negativistic personality disorder related with substance abuse. *Trastornos Adictivos, 8,* 22-41.

Pedrero-Pérez, E. J., Puerta-García, C., Lagares-Roibas, A. & Sáez-Maldonado, A. (2003). Prevalencia e intensidad de trastornos de personalidad en adictos a sustancias en tratamiento en un centro de atención a las drogodependencias. *Trastornos Adictivos, 5,* 241-255.

Pedrero-Pérez, E. J., Puerta-García, C., Segura-López, I. & Martínez-Osorio, S. M. (2004). Evolution of psicopathologic symptoms of drug dependents throughout the treatment.*Trastornos Adictivos, 6,* 176-191.

Pedrero-Pérez, E. J., Ruiz-Sanchez-de-León, J. M., Rojo-Mota, G., Olivar-Arroyo, Á., Llanero-Luque, M. & Puerta-García, C. *Personality differences between alcohol abusers* *and matched controls: relation to frontal symptoms and subtypes of addicts.*Psicothema, in press (a).

Pedrero-Pérez, E. J., Ruiz-Sanchez-de-León, J. M., Rojo-Mota, G., Olivar-Arroyo, Á., Llanero-Luque, M. & Puerta-García, C. *Personality disorders and symptoms of executive dysfunction in addicts: the influence of the frontal lobe in stable personality and their changes.*In press (b).

Perry, J. C., Banon, E. & Ianni, F. (1999). Effectiveness of psychotherapy for personality disorders. *American Journal of Psychiatry, 156*, 1312-1321.

Perry, J. L. & Carroll, M. E. (2008).The role of impulsive behavior in drug abuse.*Psychopharmacology, 200*, 1-26.

Pettinati, H, Pierce, J., Belden, P. & Meyers, K. (1999).The relationship of axis II personality disorders to other known predictors of addiction treatment outcome.*American Journal of Addictions, 8*, 136-147.

Pezawas, L., Meyer-Lindenberg, A., Drabant, E. M., Verchinski, B. A., Munoz, K. E., Kolachana, B. S., et al. (2005). 5-HTTLPR polymorphism impacts human cingulate-amygdala interactions: a genetic susceptibility mechanism for depression. *Nature Neuroscience, 8*, 828-834.

Pillay, S. S., Gruber, S.A., Rogowska, J., Simpson, N. & Yurgelun-Todd, D.A. (2006).fMRI of fearful facial affect recognition in panic disorder: the cingulate gyrus-amygdala connection, *Journal of Affective Disorders, 94*, 173-181.

Potter, N. N. (2004). Perplexing issues in personality disorders. *Current Opinion in Psychiatry, 17*, 487-492.

Prosser, J. M., Eisenberg, D., Davey, E. E., Steinfeld, M., Cohen, L. J., London, E. D., et al. (2008).Character pathology and neuropsychological test performance in remitted opiate dependence.*Substance Abuse Treatment, Prevention, and Policy, 3*, 23.

Raine, A., Lencz, T., Bihrle, S., LaCasse, L. & Colletti, P. (2000).reduced prefrontal gray matter volume and reduced autonomic activity in antisocial personality disorder. *Archives of General Psychiatry, 57*, 119-127.

Rankin, K. P., Baldwin, E., Pace-Savitsky, C., Kramer, J. H. & Miller, B. L. (2005). Self awareness and personality change in dementia. *Journal of Neurology, Neurosurgery & Psychiatry, 76*, 632-639.

Rapeli, P., Fabritius, C., Kalska, H. & Alho, H. (2009). Memory function in opioid-dependent patients treated with methadone or buprenorphine along with benzodiazepine: longitudinal change in comparison to healthy individuals. *Substance Abuse Treatment, Prevention, and Policy, 4*, 6.

Redish, A. D., Jensen, S. & Johnson, A. (2008). A unified framework for addiction: vulnerabilities in the decision process. *Behavioral and Brain Sciences, 31*, 415-437; discussion 437-487.

Regier, D. A., Farmer, M.E., Rae, D. S., Locke, B. Z., Keith, S. J., Judd, L.L. et al. (1990). Comorbidity of mental disorders with alcohol and other drug abuse.*JAMA, 264*, 2511-2518.

Reich, J. & Hofmann, S. (2004). State personality disorder in social phobia. *Annals of Clinical Psychiatry, 16*, 139-144.

Reich, J. (1999a). Comorbid anxiety and depression and personality disorder: A possible stress-induced personality disorder syndrome. *Psychiatric Annals, 29*, 707-712.

Reich, J. (1999b). An empirical examination of the concept of "stress-induced" personality disorder.*Psychiatric Annals, 29*, 701-706.

Reich, J. (2002). Clinical correlates of stress-induced personality disorder. *Psychiatric Annals, 32*, 581-588.

Reich, J. (2005). State and trait in personality disorders. In J. H. Reich (ed.), *Personality disorders: current research and treatments* (pp. 3-20). New York: Taylor & Francis.

Roberts, B. W. & DelVecchio, W. (2000). Consistency of personality traits from childhood to old age: A quantitative review of longitudinal studies. *Psychological Bulletin, 126*, 3-25.

Robinson, T. E. & Berridge, K. C. (2003).Addiction.*Annual Review of Psychology, 54*, 25-53.

Robinson, T. E. & Berridge, K. C. (2008). The incentive sensitization theory of addiction: some current issues. *Philosophical Transactions of the Royal Society B (Biological Sciences), 363*, 3137-3146.

Rounsaville, B. J. & Kleber, H. (1985).Untreated opiate addicts. How do they iffer from those seeking treatment? *Archives of General Psychiatry, 42*, 1072-1077.

Rounsaville, B. J., Kranzler, H. R., Ball, S., Tennen, H., Poling, J. & Triffleman, E. (1998). Personality disorders in substance abusers: relation to substance use. *Journal of Nervous and Mental Disease, 186*, 87-95.

Ruiz-Sanchez-de-León, J. M., Pedrero-Pérez, E. J., Olivar-Arroyo, Á., Llanero-Luque, M., Rojo-Mota, G. & Puerta-García, C. *Personality and frontal symptomatology in addicts and non-clinical population: toward a neuropsychology of personality.*In press.

Ruocco, A. C. & Swirsky-Sacchetti, T. (2007).Personality disorder symptomatology and neuropsychological functioning in closed head injury.*Journal of Neuropsychiatry and Clinical Neurosciences, 19*, 27-35.

Ruocco, A. C. & Trobst, K.K. (2003).Frontal lobe functioning and personality disorder symptomatology.*Archives of Clinical Neuropsychology, 18*, 737.

Ruocco, A. C. (2005). The neuropsychology of borderline personality disorder: a meta-analysis and review. *Psychiatry Research, 137*, 191-202.

Saulsman, L. M. & Page, A. C. (2004). The five-factor model and personality disorder empirical literature: A meta-analytic review. *Clinical Psychology Review, 23*, 1055-1085.

Schalling, D., Asberg, M., Edman, G. & Oreland, L. (1987). Markers for vulnerability to psychopathology: temperament and traits associated with platelet MAO activity. *Acta Psychiatrica Scandinavica, 76*, 172-182.

Schinka, J. A., Hughes, P. H., Coletti, S. D., Hamilton, N. L., Renard, C. G., Urmann, C. F., et al. (1999). Changes in personality characteristics in women treated in a therapeutic community. *Journal of Substance Abuse Treatment, 16*, 137– 142.

Schreckenberger, M., Klega, A., Gründer, G., Buchholz, H. G., Scheurich, A., Schirrmacher, R., et al. (2008). Opioid receptor PET reveals the psychobiologic correlates of reward processing. *Journal of Nuclear Medicine, 49*, 1257-1261.

Schweinhardt, P., Seminowicz, D. A., Jaeger, E., Duncan, G. H. & Bushnell, M. C. (2009). The anatomy of the mesolimbic reward system: a link between personality and the placebo analgesic response. *Journal of Neuroscience, 29*, 4882-4887.

Selby, M. J. & Azrin, R. L. (1998).Neuropsychological functioning in drug abusers.*Drug and Alcohol Dependence, 50*, 39-45.

Shea, M. T. & Yen, S. (2003). Stability as a distinction between Axis I and Axis II disorders.*Journal of Personality Disorders, 17*, 373-386.

Shea, M. T., Stout, R., Gunderson, J., Morey, L. C., Grilo, C. M., McGlashan, T., et al. (2002). Short-Term diagnostic stability of schizotypal, borderline, avoidant, and obsessive-compulsive personality disorders. *American Journal of Psychiatry, 159*, 2036-2041.

Siever, L. J. & Davis, K. L. (1991). A psychological perspective on the personality disorders. *American Journal of Psychiatry, 148*, 1647-1658.

Sinha, R. (2001). How does stress increase risk of drug abuse and relapse? *Psychopharmacology (Berl), 158*, 343-359.

Skodol, A. E., Gunderson, J. G., Shea, M. T., McGlashan, T. H., Morey, L. H., Sanislow, C. A., et al. (2005).The Collaborative Longitudinal Personality Disorders Study (CLPS): Overview and Implications. *Journal of Personality Disorders, 19*, 487-504.

Soloff, P. H., Meltzer, C. C., Becker, C., Greer, P. J., Kelly, T. M. & Constantine, D. (2003).Impulsivity and prefrontal hypometabolism in borderline personality disorder.*Psychiatry Research: Neuroimaging, 123*, 153-163.

Stairs, D. J. & Bardo, M. T. (2009). Neurobehavioral effects of environmental enrichment and drug abuse vulnerability. *Pharmacology, Biochemistry and Behavior, 92*, 377-382.

Stowell, R. J. (1991). Dual diagnosis issues.*Psychiatric Annals, 21*, 98-104.

Sugiura, M., Kawashima, R., Nakagawa, M., Okada, K., Sato, T., Goto, R., et al. (2000).Correlation between human personality and neural activity in cerebral cortex.*NeuroImage, 11*, 541– 546.

Suhara, T., Yasuno, F., Sudo, Y., Yamamoto, M., Inoue, M., Okubo, et al. (2001). Dopamine D2 receptors in the insular cortex and personality trait of novelty seeking.*Neuroimage, 13*, 891-895.

Sun, D. L., Chen, Z. J., Ma, N., Zhang, X. C., Fu, X. M. & Zhang, D. R. (2009). Decision-Making and Prepotent Response Inhibition Functions in Excessive Internet Users.*CNS Spectrum, 14*, 75-81.

Tanabe, J., Tregellas, J. R., Dalwani, M., Thompson, L., Owens, E., Crowley, T. & Banich, M. (2009). Medial orbitofrontal cortex gray matter is reduced in abstinent substance-dependent individuals. *Biological Psychiatry, 65*, 160-164.

Thomas, V. H., Melchert, T. P. & Banken, J. A. (1999). Substance dependence and personality disorders: comorbidity and treatment outcome in an inpatient treatment population. *Journal of Studies on Alcohol, 60*, 271-277.

Tice, D. M., Bratslavsky, E. & Baumeister, R. F. (2001). Emotional distress regulation takes precedence over impulse control: if you feel bad, do it! *Journal of Personality and Social Psychology, 80*, 53-67.

Tyrer, P., Coombs, N., Ibrahimi, F., Mathilakath, A., Bajaj P, Ranger, M. et al. (2007). Critical developments in the assessment of personality disorder.*British Journal of Psychiatry, 190* (Supl. 49), S51-S59.

Verdejo-Garcia, A. & Bechara, A. (2009).A somatic marker theory of addiction.*Neuropharmacology, 56 Suppl 1*, S48-S62.

Verdejo-Garcia, A. J., Lopez-Torrecillas, F., Aguilar de Arcos, F. & Perez-Garcia, M. (2005). Differential effects of MDMA, cocaine, and cannabis use severity on distinctive components of the executive functions in polysubstance users: a multiple regression analysis. *Addictive Behaviors, 30*, 89-.101.

Verdejo-García, A., Bechara, A., Recknor, E. C. & Pérez-García, M. (2006). Executive dysfunction in substance dependent individuals during drug use and abstinence: An examination of the behavioral, cognitive and emotional correlates of addiction. *Journal of the International Neuropsychological Society, 12*, 405-415.

Verdejo-García, A., Lawrence, A. J. & Clark, L. (2008). Impulsivity as a vulnerability marker for substance-use disorders: Review of findings from high-risk research, problem gamblers and genetic association Studies. *Neuroscience and Biobehavioral Reviews, 32*, 777-810.

Verdejo-García, A., Perez-Garcia, M. & Bechara, A. (2006) Emotion, decision-making and substance dependence: A somatic-marker model of addiction. *Current Neuropharmacology, 4*, 17-31.

Verheul, R. & van den Brink, W. (2005). Causal pathways between substance use disorders and personality pathology. *Australian Psychologist, 40*, 127-136.

Verheul, R. (2001). Co-morbidity of personality disorders in individuals with substance use disorders. *European Psychiatry, 16*, 274-282.

Vocci, F. J. (2008).Cognitive remediation in the treatment of stimulant abuse disorders: a research agenda. *Experimental and Clinical Psychopharmacology, 16*, 484-497.

Voglmaier, M. M., Seidman, L. J., Niznikiewicz, M. A., Dickey, C. C., Shenton, M. E. & McCarley, R. W. (2005).A comparative profile analysis of neuropsychological function in men and women with schizotypal personality disorder.*Schizophrenia Research, 74*, 43-49.

Vuchinich, R. & Heather, N. (2003).*Choice, behavioural economics and addiction*. London: Pergamon.

Wagner, T., Krampe, H., Stawicki, S., Reinhold, J., Jahn, H., Mahlke, K., et al. (2004). Substantial decrease of psychiatric comorbidity in chronic alcoholics upon integrated outpatient treatment – results of a prospective study. *Journal of Psychiatric Research, 38*, 619-635.

Weaver, T., Madden, P., Charles, V., Stimson, G., Renton, A., Tyrer, P. et al. (2003). Comorbidity of substance misuse and mental illness in community mental health and substance misuse services.*British Journal of Psychiatry, 183*, 304-313.

Widiger, T. A. & Samuel, D. B. (2005). Evidence-based assessment of personality disorders. *Psychological Assessment, 17*, 278-287.

Widiger, T. A., Costa, P. T. J. & McCrae, R. R. (2002).A proposal for Axis II: Diagnosing personality disorders using the Five-Factor Model. In P.T. Costa Jr, T.A. Widiger (eds.), *Personality Disorders and the Five-Factor Model of Personality* (2nd ed.; pp. 431-456). Washington, DC: American Psychological Association.

Wiesbieck, G. A., Mauerer, C., Thome, J., Jacob, F. & Boening, J. (1995). Neuroendocrine support for a relationship between «novelty seeking» and dopaminergic function in alcohol-dependent men. *Psychoneuroendocrinology, 20*, 755-761.

World Health Organization (1992-1994). *International Statistical Classification of Diseases and Related Health Problems; Tenth Revision*. Geneva: World Health Organization.

Yücel, M., Lubman, D. I., Solowij, N. & Brewer, W. J. (2007). Understanding drug addiction: a neuropsychological perspective. *Australian and New Zealand Journal of Psychiatry, 41*, 957-968.

Zanarini, M. C. & Frankenburg, F. R. (2001).Attainment and maintenance of reliability of axis I and II disorders over the course of a longitudinal study.*Comprehensive Psychiatry, 42*, 369-374.

Zanarini, M. C., Frankenburg, F. R., Hennen, J., Reich, B. & Silk, K. R. (2006).Prediction of the 10-year course of borderline personality disorder.*American Journal of Psychiatry, 163*, 827-832.

Zimmerman, M. (1994).Diagnosing personality disorders: a review of issues and research methods.*Archives of General Psychiatry, 51*, 225-245.

In: Personality Traits: Theory, Testing and Influences
Editor: Melissa E. Jordan

ISBN: 978-1-61728-934-7
© 2011 Nova Science Publishers, Inc.

Chapter 2

CIRCADIAN PREFERENCE AND PERSONALITY: A MINIREVIEW

Lorenzo Tonetti[*]

Department of Psychology, University of Bologna, Bologna, Italy

ABSTRACT

The aim of this chapter is to update the status of the art of the relationship between morningness-eveningness preference and personality. To this end, keeping in mind the wide number of personality models available in literature, this chapter discusses three of them: 1) Eysenck's model; 2) Big Five model; 3) Cloninger's model. On the basis of main data reported in papers, it is suggested that future studies should focus on the Cloninger's psychobiological model of personality because it takes into account both biological (temperament dimensions) and socio-cultural (character dimensions) aspects, being thus useful to address their respective importance linking circadian rhythms with personality characteristics. To this aim, cross-cultural comparisons are specifically needed. Implications of this chapter in several applied areas are also discussed.

INTRODUCTION

Chronobiology has clearly shown that living creatures have one or more "endogenous clocks" or "endogenous biological clocks" (Gillette &Sejnowski, 2005). From the chronobiological perspective, biological functions' rhythms are driven by those endogenous oscillators. The term "circadian" was used for the first time by Franz Halberg in 1959 describing the approximation to the 24 hours of an endogenous rhythm. However the timing of rhythms generated by biological clocks shows interindividual differences between humans.

One of the most robust individual differences in circadian rhythms is circadian preference, which is described by a continuum between two extremes (Natale & Cicogna,

---

[*] Corresponding author: Department of Psychology, Viale Berti Pichat 5, 40127 Bologna – Italy, Phone: +39-051-2091877, Fax: +39-051-243086, Email: lorenzo.tonetti2@unibo.it

2002): morning types (occasionally labelled "larks") go to bed and awake early; evening types (at times labelled "owls") have later bedtime and wake up time and are tired when waking up. Intermediate types or neither types represent the larger part of the population (around 60%-70%) and demonstrate patterns of behaviour being a part of an intermediate area between the two extreme types of this continuum. Chronotypes mainly differ in their circadian phase which is delayed in evening than morning types (Mongrain et al., 2004).Even if phase differences could be explained by individual's life style, this kind of relationship between circadian period and circadian preference has been detected from a physiological (Duffy et al., 2001) and molecular point of view (Brown et al., 2008), and also when extreme circadian types were examined under constant routine conditions (Kerkhof & Van Dongen, 1996).

Circadian preference changes over the individual's life. Morning preference is more frequent up to 10 years and after 50 years (Roenneberg et al., 2004). Adolescence is characterized by a shift from a prevalent morning preference to an evening preference (Carskadon et al., 1993; Diaz-Morales et al., 2007; Ishihara et al., 1990; Laberge et al., 2001; Tonetti et al., 2008; Yang et al., 2005). This shift started from the age of 12–13 years in different cultures (Caci et al., 2005c; Carskadon et al., 1993; Gau & Soong, 2003; Ishihara et al., 1990; Laberge et al., 2001; Park et al., 1999; Russo et al., 2007; Shinkoda et al., 2000; Tonetti et al., 2008), pointing out a crucial role of biological aspects. This shift ended at around 18–20 years, and it has been assumed that the conclusion of this process could be considered as a possible marker of the end of adolescence (Roenneberg et al., 2004; Tonetti et al., 2008).

Gender is another variable thought to be able to affect circadian typology. Some papers have highlighted no significant gender differences in morningness-eveningness preference (Greenwood, 1994; Neubauer, 1992). However some studies involving large samples have shown that women are significantly more morning types than men (Adan & Natale, 2002; Chelminski et al., 1997; Lehnkering & Siegmund, 2007; Tonetti et al., 2008). Confirming these results, Natale and Danesi (2002) reported that sleep phase difference between males and females is statistically significant but quantitatively small. Thus gender differences in circadian typology have been highlighted in large samples only. Due to the relatively low prevalence of extreme circadian types in the general population, the sample size may have an effect on the power of statistical tests used to detect the association between gender and circadian preference.

Moreover the age variance in the sample might determine the inconsistency in results (Caci et al., 2005a). Randler (2007) has shown that a large variance in age within a study covered gender differences. Apparently this is due to the systematic changes in sleep timing over the life span which tend to obscure individual differences. Randler (2007) suggested that studies detecting the relationship between gender and sleep timing should preferably provide the same mean age for both genders.

Most of the results quoted above has been highlighted in studies using self-reporting tools of circadian preference, many of which have been validated with external criterion (Caci et al., 2008). In spite of the high number of available circadian questionnaires, the currently most used tool in chronopsychology is the Morningness-Eveningness Questionnaire (Horne & Östberg, 1976).

The Morningness-Eveningness Questionnaire has been also adapted to assess morningness-eveningness preference in children and adolescents: the Morningness-Eveningness Questionnaire for Children and Adolescents (Ishihara et al., 1990).

In the last years circadian preference has been related with several behavioural aspects, such as school and academic performance, alcohol and tobacco use, involvement in risky behaviours. More specifically, Randler and Frech (2009) have shown that circadian typology can affect school performance of adolescents, with morning types performing better in school achievement. Fernandez-Mendoza et al. (2010) confirmed these data in a sample of university students, showing that evening types reported more often than morning types poorer memory and the need to get more sleep as necessary to improve their academic performance. As regards tobacco and alcohol use, Randler (2008a) highlighted that German university students smokers tended towards evening preference and consumed more alcohol. Similar results have been detected in a Spanish population of university students (Fernandez-Mendoza et al., 2010), with evening types reporting more frequent use of tobacco and alcohol on daily basis than morning types. Referring to the involvement in risky behaviours, Tonetti et al. (2010) reported that both Italian and Spanish evening types are more sensation seekers than morning types. Thus evening types show higher tendency to engage in risky behaviour than morning types, also as shown above referring to tobacco and alcohol consumption.

Several research papers have investigated the relationship between circadian typology and personality and are reported in three reviews. Those reviews did not focus only on personality differences between circadian types, but also examined the relationship between circadian preference on one hand and other aspects as gender and age on the other. The first one was carried out by Kerkhof in 1985, where the studies on the association between circadian preference and the Eysenck's personality factor of introversion-extraversion were analysed. Even if non significant in most cases, those studies showed a negative correlation between morningness and extraversion. However Kerkhof concluded that those results did not support the idea of a direct relationship between circadian typology and introversion-extraversion. A second review was put forward by Tankova, Adan and Buela-Casal in 1994. Also those authorsanalyzed the Eysenck's personality model, showing that eveningness and extraversion were probably indirectly linked. The last review on this issue was published in 2008 by Cavallera and Giudici. Those authors also discussed one study referred to the Cloninger's personality model (Caci et al., 2004), which showed that morningness was positively related with persistence and negatively with novelty seeking.

Because human behaviour mainly reflects personality features, this chapter aims to update the status of the art of the relationship between morningness-eveningness preference and personality, with reference to the following three models: 1) Eysenck's model; 2) Big Five model; 3) Cloninger's model. This minireview focuses on these models because they are the most frequently used in the chronopsychological research and because it is extremely hard to analyse all those available in literature, since their wide number. For example two models excluded from this chapter are the Zuckerman's Alternative Five Factor (Zuckerman et al., 1993) and Millon's (Millon, 1994) models.

CIRCADIAN PREFERENCE AND EYSENCK'S PERSONALITY MODEL

The three-factors Eysenck model derives from a psychobiological approach to personality and is based on three personality dimensions: extraversion, neuroticism and psychoticism (Eysenck, 1967; Eysenck et al., 1985). The extraversion components are sociability and impulsivity. Neuroticism describes the emotional stability and psychoticism dimension allows us to detect conduct disorders and their level. The Eysenck Personality Questionnaire (Eysenck & Eysenck, 1975) identifies the three Eysenck personality factors. A revised version of this tool has been proposed (Eysenck Personality Questionnaire-revised) (Eysenck et al., 1985) and has been translated in several languages.

As stated above, the association between circadian typology and three Eysenck's personality factors was firstly analysed in the reviews by Kerkhof (1985) and Tankova et al. (1994). More specifically, some studies have shown a positive relationship between extraversion and eveningness (Adan, 1992; Mecacci et al., 1986; Neubauer, 1992), while others, with regard to the neuroticism dimension (Mura & Levy, 1986; Neubauer, 1992), have highlighted that evening types are more neurotic than morning types. On the contrary Mecacci et al. (1986) found a higher neuroticism degree in morning versus evening types, while, with regard to psychoticism, evening types scored higher than morning types.

Only three studies have been published since the last review referred to this personality model and are shown in Table 1. The research report by Mitchell and Redman (1993) confirmed a positive association between extraversion and eveningness (Adan, 1992; Mecacci et al., 1986; Neubauer, 1992), showing no differences between extreme circadian types in neuroticism dimension and a higher psychoticism level in evening than morning types (Mecacci et al., 1986). These results have been confirmed only referring to the psychoticism dimension in the study by Mecacci and Rochetti (1998). Moreover Langford and Glendon (2002) showed a higher degree of extraversion in evening types and higher neuroticism scores in morning types (Mecacci et al., 1986).

The higher extraversion degree in evening types has not always been detected, also as shown in Table 1. The reviews put forward by Kerkhof (1985) and Tankova et al. (1994) highlighted that the relationship between morningness-eveningness and introversion-extraversion may reflect an indirect, rather than a direct association. It has been suggested that this association could be detected separately considering sociability and impulsivity components of extraversion (Eysenck & Eysenck, 1963) and that arousal may modulate this relationship. More specifically, Blake (1967) showed a phase advance of body temperature rhythm in introverts and assumed a time of day effect with introverts executing better in the morning (high arousal) on one hand and on the other extraverts executing better in the evening (high arousal). Revelle et al. (1980) supposed that interactive effects of time of day, arousal and impulsivity may be due to an association between impulsivity and circadian arousal rhythm phase, with individuals high in impulsiveness characterized by a delayed peak arousal than those low in impulsiveness. Following this hypothesis, high impulsivity but not high sociability should be linked to eveningness (Caci, et al., 2004; Caci et al., 2005b; Neubauer, 1992).However Larsen (1985) found that MEQ scores were negatively associated with sociability, but not impulsivity. Moreover other papers linked the observed time of day effects to sociability component (Matthews, 1988; Wilson, 1990). Thus the results about the suggested modulating role of impulsivity on the relationship between eveningness and extraversion are not conclusive.

As regards neuroticism dimension, the higher prevalence of this personality factors in evening types (Table 1) may be related to the association between eveningness and anxiety symptoms (Gaspar-Barba et al., 2009). However Langford and Glendon (2002) showed a positive association between morningness and neuroticism, confirming previous data reported by Mecacci et al. (1986). The discrepancy between results shown in Mecacci and Rochetti (1998) and Langford and Glendon (2002) papers could be probably due to the different age of their samples. In fact Mecacci and Rochetti (1998) studied a sample of university students, while Langford and Glendon (2002) have taken into account adult participants.

Finally the positive association between eveningness and psychoticism (Table 1) may be due to the relationship between eveningness and different types of psychopathology: bipolar disorder (Hakkarainen et al., 2003; Wood et al., 2009), depression (Chelminski et al., 1999; Drennan et al., 1991; Gaspar-Barba et al., 2009; Hidalgo et al., 2009), drug addiction (Adan, 1994) and seasonal depression (Johansson et al., 2003; Natale et al., 2005).

CIRCADIAN PREFERENCE AND BIG FIVE PERSONALITY MODEL

The Big Five model provides valuable insights into the domain of personality and is one of the most used models for personality classification (Costa & McCrae, 1992). It derives from a psycholexical approach. The five factors are: extraversion, agreeableness, conscientiousness, neuroticism and openness. Extraversion is represented by facets such as activity, assertiveness, and self-confidence. Agreeableness refers to concern and sensitiveness toward others and their needs. Conscientiousness refers to self-regulation in both proactive and inhibitory mode. Neuroticism refers to the inability to cope adequately with one's own anxiety and emotionality and to control irritation and anger. Openness refers to propensity to novelty, tolerance of different values, interest toward different habits and lifestyles. The Big Five Questionnaire-2 (Caprara et al., 2007) is frequently used to assess the big five personality factors and includes 134 items on a 5-point Likert scale: 24 items for each of the 5 factors and 14 items belonging to a Lie scale.

All studies published on this personality model are relatively recent and are shown in Table 2. These papers (DeYoung et al., 2007; Gray & Watson, 2002; Hogben et al., 2007; Jackson & Gerard, 1996; Randler, 2008b; Tonetti et al., 2009) showed similar results referring to two personality domains, in spite of the different instruments used to assess circadian typology (Morningness-Eveningness Questionnaire and Composite Scale of Morningness): no difference between extreme circadian types in extraversion and a higher conscientiousness level in morning than evening types. The fact that these research papers employed different circadian preference self-reporting tools is not a limitation mainly for two reasons. Firstly, Morningness-Eveningness Questionnaire and Composite Scale of Morningness have shown to have good convergent validity (Caci et al., 2009b), so they measure the same construct. Secondly DeYoung et al. (2007), who used the Morningness-Eveningness Questionnaire, obtained the same results as Randler (2008b) who used the Composite Scale of Morningness.

Table 1. Review of the studies that have explored the relationship between the three Eysenck personality factors and circadian preference

Authors	Year	Participants	Participants' nationality	Extreme circadian types	Tools	Extraversion	Neuroticism	Psychoticism
Mitchell and Redman	1993	116 (44 M; 72 F)	Australian	47 MT (11 M; 36 F) 69 ET (33 M; 36 F)	MEQ; EPQ	ET>MT	N.S.	ET>MT
Mecacci and Rochetti	1998	232 (111 M; 121 F)	Italian	Not specified	MEQ; EPQ	N.S.	ET>MT	ET>MT
Langford and Glendon	2002	101 (28 M; 73 F)	Australian	35 MT; 33 ET	MEQ; EPQ-R	ET>MT	MT>ET	Not specified

Abbreviations: M = male; F = female; MT = morning type; ET = evening type; MEQ = Morningness-Eveningness Questionnaire; EPQ = Eysenck Personality Questionnaire; EPQ-R = Eysenck Personality Questionnaire-Revised.

Participants of these studies were university students, except for Langford and Glendon work which examined a university administrative staff.

Table 2. Review of the studies that have analysed the association between the Big Five personality model and circadian typology

Authors	Year	Participants	Participants' nationality	Extreme circadian types	Tools	Extraversion	Agreeableness	Conscientiousness	Neuroticism	Openness
Jackson and Gerard	1996	360 (132 M; 228 F)	United States	113 MT 122 ET	CSM; JACLM	N.S.	N.S.	MT>ET	N.S.	N.S.
Gray and Watson	2002	334 (121 M; 213 F)	United States	Not available*	Sleep Log; adapted form of NEO-PI	N.S.	N.S.	MT>ET	N.S.	N.S.
DeYoung et al.	2007	279 (87 M; 192 F)	Canadian	Not specified	MEQ; BFI	N.S.	MT>ET	MT>ET	ET>MT	N.S.
Hogben et al.	2007	617 (205 M; 412 F)	British	Not specified	MEQ; NEO-FFI	N.S.	MT>ET	MT>ET	N.S.	ET>MT
Randler	2008 b	1231 (579 M; 625 F)	German	Not specified	CSM; BFI-10	N.S.	MT>ET	MT>ET	ET>MT	N.S.
Tonetti et al.	2009	503 (223 M; 280 F)	Italian	104 MT (45 M; 59 F) 105 ET (45 M; 60 F)	MEQ; BFO	N.S.	N.S.	MT>ET	ET>MT	N.S.

Abbreviations: M = male; F = female; MT = morning type; ET = evening type; CSM = Composite Scale of Morningness; MEQ = Morningness-Eveningness Questionnaire; JACLM = John's Adjective Check List Markers; NEO-PI = NEO-Personality Inventory; BFI = Big Five Inventory; NEO-FFI = NEO-Five Factor Inventory; BFI-10 = short version of the Big Five Inventory with 10 items; BFO = Big Five Observer.

Most participants of these studies were university students. * Authors did not directly determine circadian preference, but used a sleep log.

Table 3. Review of the studies that have examined the link between Cloninger's personality dimensions and circadian preference

Authors	Year	Participants	Participants' nationality	Extreme circadian types	Tools	HA	NS	RD	PS	SD	C	ST
Caci et al.	2004	129 M	French	Not specified	CSM; TCI	N.S.	ET>MT	N.S.	MT>ET	N.S.	N.S.	N.S.
Adan et al.	2010	862 (362 M; 500 F)	Spanish	155 MT (60 M; 95 F) 184 ET (86 M; 98 F)	MEQr; TCI-56	MT>ET	ET>MT	N.S.	MT>ET	MT>ET	N.S.	N.S.

Abbreviations: M = male; F = female; MT = morning type; ET = evening type; CSM = Composite Scale of Morningness; MEQr = reduced version of the Morningness-Eveningness Questionnaire; TCI = Temperament and Character Inventory; TCI-56 = reduced Temperament and Character Inventory; HA= harm avoidance; NS = novelty seeking; RD = reward dependence; PS = persistence; SD = self-directedness; C = cooperativeness; ST = self-transcendence. Participants of these studies were university students.

Since the works shown in Table 2 were led in different countries, it is possible that biological factors play a primary role in determining the association between personality and circadian preference, not directly confirming the plausibleness of the neurobiological model of personality put forward by DeYoung (2006) and DeYoung et al. (2002, 2007). This model, based on the Big Five, connects the metatrait stability (combination of neuroticism reversed, agreeableness, conscientiousness) with variability in serotonergic function, and the metatrait plasticity (combination of extraversion and openness) with variability in dopaminergic function. High serotonergic function was linked with lower levels of neuroticism in healthy females (Brummett et al., 2008) and in healthy males neuroticism and conscientiousness were related, negatively and positively, with high serotonergic function (Manuck et al., 1998). Bearing in mind that metatrait stability is linked to morningness (DeYoung et al., 2007) and serotonin is implicated in stabilization of circadian rhythms in Drosophila (Yuan et al., 2005), mammalians (Edgar et al., 1993) and maybe humans too, it is possible to hypothesize that higher degrees of serotonin correspond to higher levels of stability and morningness. This model could be further corroborated by the association between decreased levels of serotonin and depression on one hand (Owens & Nemeroff, 1994) and depression and evening preference on the other (Chelminski et al., 1999; Drennan et al., 1991; Gaspar-Barba et al., 2009). Hence low serotonergic degrees might be linked to eveningness.

Two studies shown in Table 2 completely agree with this model (DeYoung et al., 2007; Randler, 2008b), other two (Gray & Watson, 2002; Jackson & Gerard, 1996) have shown that one component of the supposed metatrait stability was linked to morningness and the remaining have highlighted the expected relationship for two personality factors on three (Hogben et al., 2007; Tonetti et al., 2009). The lack of a complete agreement between the model of DeYoung and empirical data is not surprising since it rarely occurs and it could be judged satisfactory that four studies on six have shown the supposed relationship at least for two personality dimensions on three.

However the Big Five Questionnaire-2 as well other instruments that assess the Big Five personality domains grow out from a psycholexical approach and thus do not seem adequate to explore the plausibility of the neurobiological model put forward by DeYoung. On the contrary to this aim it might be more valuable employing a self-reporting tool as the Temperament and Character Inventory (Cloninger et al., 1994), which derives from a psychobiological model of personality (Cloninger et al., 1993). To this end, the next paragraph reviews the studies that have dealt with the relationship between circadian preference and the Cloninger's personality dimensions.

CIRCADIAN PREFERENCE AND CLONINGER'S PERSONALITY MODEL

The psychobiological model of personality put forward by Cloninger et al. (1993) considers personality as the result of the interaction between temperament and character. Temperament is considered as inherited manifesting itself early in development, while character is thought to be less inheritable than temperament and to develop during life, getting structured through learnt socio-cultural mechanisms. There are four dimensions of temperament (novelty seeking, harm avoidance, reward dependence, and persistence) and three dimensions of character (self-directedness, cooperativeness, and self-transcendence).

Novelty seeking is related with the system of behavioural activation or reward. Harm avoidance reflects the activity of the system of behavioural inhibition or punishment. Reward dependence is related to social reinforcement and sensitivity to social stimuli. Persistence implies the tendency to maintain behaviour in extinction conditions. Self-directedness represents the capacity to regulate behaviour in order to adjust it to one's principles, goals and personal beliefs. Cooperativeness involves the subject's prosocial behaviour as a measure of social adaptation. Self-transcendence is related to the identification with what is conceived as essential and consequential parts of a unified whole. The Temperament and Character Inventory (Cloninger et al., 1994) is an useful self-reporting tool of the Cloninger's psychobiological model, as well as other formats of this inventory: the Temperament and Character Inventory-Revised (Fossati et al., 2007) and the reduced Temperament and Character Inventory (Adan et al., 2009).

The relationship between morningness-eveningness preference and Cloninger's personality dimensions has been rarely investigated. In fact only two studies examined that association (see Table 3). The first one was led by Caci et al. (2004) which showed that morningness in a sample of French university students was positively linked with persistence and negatively with novelty seeking. Adan et al. (2010) confirmed these results in a sample of Spanish university students and expanded the differences between extreme circadian types also to harm avoidance and self-directedness dimensions, where evening types scored lower than morning types.

The relationship between circadian preference and temperament dimensions seems thus quite similar in French (Caci et al., 2004) and Spanish (Adan et al., 2010) university students, in spite of the different self-reporting tools of circadian preference (the reduced version of the Morningness-Eveningness Questionnaire in Adan et al. paper versus the Composite Scale of Morningness in Caci et al. work) and the Cloninger's personality dimensions (the reduced Temperament and Character Inventory in Adan et al. work rather than the full Temperament and Character Inventory in Caci et al. study). Bearing in mind that circadian preference is mainly linked with genetic and biological aspects (Barclay et al., 2010; Hur, 2007; Lee et al., 2007; Roenneberg et al., 2004; Tonetti et al., 2008; Vink et al., 2001), these data could confirm that temperament dimensions are inherited manifesting themselves early in development (Cloninger et al., 1993).

CONCLUSION

On the basis of this chapter, it is possible to suggest that future studies should focus on the Cloninger's psychobiological model of personality, for several reasons. Firstly because this model takes into account both biological (temperament dimensions) and socio-cultural (character dimensions) aspects and thus it could be useful aiming to address their respective importance linking circadian rhythms with personality characteristics. Secondly because circadian preference is associated not only with biological and genetic (Barclay et al., 2010; Hur, 2007; Lee et al., 2007; Roenneberg et al., 2004; Tonetti et al., 2008; Vink et al., 2001) but also with socio-cultural (Adan & Natale, 2002; Diaz-Morales & Randler, 2008; Randler & Diaz-Morales, 2007) factors, and Cloninger's model considers both those aspects, contrary to the Eysenck and Big Five models. Moreover the Eysenck's model seems to be less reliable than the Cloninger's model, since studies detecting circadian preference differences in the three factors model led to contradictory results (Kerkhof, 1985; Tankova et al., 1994), as also shown in this chapter.

In order to detect the role of biological and socio-cultural factors in the association between circadian typology and personality features, further studies should perform some cross-cultural comparisons. Indeed in this way it will be possible to ascertain the effects of biological (such as circadian typology) and socio-cultural (such as nationality) dimensions. On the basis of the fact that temperament dimensions are considered as innate, morningness-eveningness preference is attended to influence more temperament than character personality dimensions. Moreover if biological factors play the main role in regulating the association between circadian preference and temperament dimensions, then future research papers should report similar data to those shown by Caci et al. (2004) and Adan et al. (2010). On the contrary, considering that character dimensions are less inheritable and more affected by socio-cultural factors, it is possible to assume that nationality will have a more marked effect on character than temperament domains.

Moreover future cross-cultural comparisons should examine societies with a different timing of human activities aiming to detect if this change could be related to a different association between circadian preference and personality features. In fact the higher novelty seeking observed in evening types could be in some measure accounted by social jetlag (Wittmann et al., 2006), which is thought as the difference between social and biological time. The social jetlag is higher in evening types because their endogenous sleep-wake rhythm generally does not adjust to social timetables. Thus evening types could attempt to balance the negative effects of social jetlag (as sleepiness) performing risky behaviors, aiming to preserve an adequate arousal level.

Another still open question regards the age changes in circadian preference, with evening preference more frequent than morning preference in young adults (Tonetti et al., 2008) and the opposite during adulthood (Roenneberg et al., 2004). Furthermore also temperament and character dimensions vary with age. In fact a decline in novelty seeking between young adulthood and adulthood was observed (Mikolajczyk et al., 2008; Trouillet & Gana, 2008). It is interesting to note that the developmental pathways of eveningness and novelty seeking seem quite similar and that biological factors are supposed to affect circadian typology (Roenneberg et al., 2004; Tonetti et al., 2008) and also novelty seeking (Tsuchimine et al., 2009). On the basis of these considerations, further longitudinal studies are required to test, from a developmental point of view, the relationship between circadian preference and Cloninger's personality dimensions. This is also necessary since the only two studies carried out on this topic investigated just university student samples.

Further studies could have implications into applied working areas, especially those related to human resources recruitment. If the relationship between circadian types and some personality features will be confirmed, this could lead to including a brief self-reporting tool of circadian typology (for example the reduced version of the Morningness-Eveningness Questionnaire) into the assessment procedure to detect the ideal candidate to perform a job requiring certain personality characteristics. Moreover this could be valuable since temperament dimensions have been related with subjective stress and performance during different tasks (Ravaja et al., 2006), with high novelty seekers performing better during a reaction time task while high persistence in women was related with better performance appraisal in a public speaking task. Furthermore temperament could be related to creativity, which is basically required to adequately perform some kinds of jobs (Caselli, 2009).

Another working implication is related to the career counselling. Eley et al. (2008, 2009), referring to the model of personality put forward by Cloninger et al. (1993), pointed out a psychobiological profile of rural general practitioners. This profile is characterized by low level of harm avoidance and or high level of novelty seeking and self-directedness. Thus it seems useful administering a self-assessment tool of Cloninger's personality dimensions to medical students aiming to orientate them towards a fitting work, carrying out an effective career counselling. Aiming to improve the usefulness of career counselling, it could be possible to use a short self-reporting tool of morningness-eveningness preference in addition and/or substitution of Temperament and Character Inventory, if the relationship between circadian typology and Cloninger's personality dimensions will be confirmed.

An additional implication regards the clinical area. Temperament and character dimensions have been related with some psychiatric disorders (Gurpegui et al., 2009). More specifically novelty seeking is high in patients suffering from attention deficit hyperactivity disorder(Anckarsäter et al., 2006) and substance use disorders (Le Bon et al., 2004). The character dimension of self-directedness (lower scores) is related to depression (Cloninger et al., 2006) and personality disorders (Svrakic et al., 2002). Also circadian preference has been linked to several psychiatric conditions: attention deficit hyperactivity disorder (Caci et al., 2009a), bipolar disorder (Hakkarainen et al., 2003; Wood et al., 2009), depression (Chelminski et al., 1999; Drennan et al., 1991; Gaspar-Barba et al., 2009; Hidalgo et al., 2009) and drug addiction (Adan, 1994). As a consequence of further confirmations of a relationship between morningness-eveningness preference and Cloninger's dimensions of personality, the assessment of circadian typology could help to identify as soon as possible people risking to develop certain psychiatric disorders.

Further implication is related to school performance, which is supposed to be affected from both circadian preference (Randler & Frech, 2009) and temperament traits (Gerra et al., 2005). The poor scholastic achievement in evening types could be partially explained by the school jet lag (Tonetti, 2007), which is due to a transition to an earlier school start time along with adolescents' sleep phase delay, that leads to sleepiness. Furthermore it is possible that eveningness in adolescence represents a risk factor for poor performance because youth are tested at their nonoptimal time of day (Goldstein et al., 2007). This information leadsus to suggest a new intervention based on the delaying of school starting time, that allows adolescents to get more sleep and be more refreshed during school hours.

The last implication regards the prevention of behavioral problems observed in evening types, such as alcohol and tobacco use, involvement in risky behaviours (Fernandez-Mendoza et al., 2010; Randler, 2008a; Tonetti et al., 2010), which are also associated with temperament traits as novelty seeking (Leventhal et al., 2007; Sher et al., 2000). Future interventions of prevention should also assess circadian preference and personality features aiming to precociously detect individuals at higher risk to develop behavioral problems.

ACKNOWLEDGMENTS

I am very grateful to Dr. Marco Fabbri for his insightful and constructive review.

REFERENCES

Adan, A. & Natale, V. (2002). Gender differences in morningness-eveningness preference.*Chronobiology International, 19*, 709-720.

Adan, A. (1992).The influence of age, work schedule and personality on morningness dimension.*International Journal of Psychophysiology, 12*, 95–99.

Adan, A. (1994).Chronotype and personality factors in the daily consumption of alcohol and psychostimulants.*Addiction, 89*, 455–462.

Adan, A., Lachica, J., Caci, H. & Natale, V. (2010). Circadian typology and Temperament and Character personality dimensions.*Chronobiology International, 27*, 181-193.

Adan, A., Serra-Grabulosa, J. M., Caci, H. & Natale, V. (2009). A reduced Temperament and Character Inventory (TCI-56).Psychometric properties in a non-clinical sample.*Personality and Individual Differences, 46*, 687–692.

Anckarsäter, H., Stahlberg, O., Larson, T., Hakansson, C., Jutblad, S. B., Niklasson, L., Nyden, A., Wentz, E., Westergren, S., Cloninger, C. R., Gillberg, C. & Rastam, M. (2006).The impact of ADHD and autism spectrum disorders on temperament, character, and personality development.*American Journal of Psychiatry, 163*, 1239-1244.

Barclay, N. L., Eley, T. C., Buysse, D. J., Archer, S. N. & Gregory, A. M. (2010). Diurnal preference and sleep quality: same genes? A study of young adult twins.*Chronobiology International, 27*, 278-296.

Blake, M. J. (1967). Relationship between circadian rhythm of body temperature and introversion–extraversion.*Nature, 215*, 896-897.

Brown, S. A., Kunz, D., Dumas, A., Westermark, P. O., Vanselow, K., Tilmann-Wahnschaffe, A., Herzel, H. & Kramer, A. (2008). Molecular insights into human daily behavior.*Proceedings of the National Academy of Sciences of the United States of America, 105*, 1602-1607.

Brummett, B. H., Boyle, S. H., Kuhn, C. M., Siegler, I. C. & Williams, R. B. (2008). Associations among central nervous system serotonergic function and neuroticism are moderated by gender. *Biological Psychology, 78*, 200-203.

Caci, H., Adan, A., Bohle, P., Natale, V., Pornpitakpan, C. & Tilley, A. (2005a). Transcultural properties of the Composite Scale of Morningness: The relevance of the "morning affect" factor. Chronobiology *International, 22*, 523-540.

Caci, H., Bouchez, J. & Baylè, F. J. (2009a). Inattentive symptoms of ADHD are related to evening orientation. *Journal of Attention Disorders, 13*, 36-41.

Caci, H., Deschaux, O., Adan, A. & Natale, V. (2009b).Comparing three morningness scales: Age and gender effects, structure and cut-off criteria. *Sleep Medicine, 10*, 240-245.

Caci, H., Mattei, V., Bayle, F. J., Nadalet, L., Dossios, C., Robert, P. & Boyer, P. (2005b). Impulsivity but not venturesomeness is related to morningness. *Psychiatry Research, 134*, 259-265.

Caci, H., Natale, V. & Adan, A. (2008). Do scales for measuring morningness-eveningness exist all over the world? In A.L. Leglise (Ed), *Progress in circadian rhythm research* (209-222). New York: Nova Science Publisher.

Caci, H., Robert, P. & Boyer, P. (2004). Novelty seekers and impulsive subjects are low in morningness. *European Psychiatry, 19*, 79-84.

Caci, H., Robert, P., Dossios, C. & Boyer, P. (2005c). Morningness-eveningness for children scales: psychometric properties and month of birth effect. *Encephale, 31,* 56-64.

Caprara, G. V., Barbaranelli, C., Borgogni, L. & Vecchione, M. (2007). *Bfq–2.Big Five Questionnaire-2.Manuale.*[Bfq–2.Big Five Questionnaire-2.Manual]. Firenze: Organizzazioni Speciali.

Carskadon, M. A., Vieira, C. & Acebo, C. (1993). Association between puberty and delayed phase preference.*Sleep, 16,* 258-262.

Caselli, R. J. (2009). Creativity.An organizational schema.*Cognitive and Behavioral Neurology, 22,* 143-154.

Cavallera, G. M. & Giudici, S. (2008). Morningness and eveningness personality: A survey in literature from 1995 up till 2006. *Personality and Individual Differences, 44,* 3-21.

Chelminski, I., Ferraro, F. R., Petros, T. & Plaud, J. J. (1997). Horne and Östberg questionnaire: a score distribution in a large sample of young adults. *Personality and Individual Differences, 23,* 647-652.

Chelminski, I., Ferraro, F. R., Petros, T. V. & Plaud, J. J. (1999). An analysis of the "eveningness-morningness" dimension in "depressive" college students.*Journal of AffectiveDisorders, 52,* 19-29.

Cloninger, C. R., Przybeck, T. R., Svrakic, D. M. & Wetzel, R. (1994).*The Temperament and Character Inventory (TCI): a guide to its development and use.* St. Louis: Washington University Press.

Cloninger, C. R., Svrakic, D. M. & Przybeck, T. R. (1993).A psychobiological model of temperament and character.*Archives of General Psychiatry, 50,* 975-990.

Cloninger, C. R., Svrakic, D. M. & Przybeck, T. R. (2006). Can personality assessment predict future depression? A twelve month follow-up of 631subjects.*Journal of AffectiveDisorders, 92,* 35-44.

Costa, P. T. & McCrae, R. R. (1992). Revised NEO Personality Inventory (NEO PI-R) and NEO Five-Factor Inventory (NEO-FFI).Odessa: *Psychological Assessment Resources.*

DeYoung, C. G. (2006). Higher-order factors of the Big Five in a multi-informant sample. *Journal of Personality and Social Psychology, 91,* 1138-1151.

DeYoung, C. G., Hasher, L., Djikic, M., Criger, B. & Peterson, J. B. (2007). Morning people are stable people: Circadian rhythm and the higher-order factors of the big five. *Personality and Individual Differences, 43,* 267–276.

DeYoung, C. G., Peterson, J. B. & Higgins, D. M. (2002). Higher-order factors of the Big Five predict conformity: are there neuroses of health? *Personality and Individual Differences,33,* 533-552.

Diaz-Morales, J. F. & Randler, C. (2008).Morningness-eveningness among German and Spanish adolescents 12-18 years.*European Psychologist, 13,* 214-221.

Diaz-Morales, J. F., Davila de Leon, M. C. & Sorroche, M. G. (2007).Validity of the Morningness Eveningness Scale for children among Spanish adolescents.*Chronobiology International, 24,* 435-447.

Drennan, M. D., Klauber, M. R., Kripke, D. F. & Goyette, L. M. (1991). The effects of depression and age on the Horne-Östberg morningness eveningness score. *Journal of Affective Disorders,23,* 93-98.

Duffy, J. F., Rimmer, D. W. & Czeisler, C. A. (2001). Association of intrinsic circadian period with morningness-eveningness, usual wake time, and circadian phase.*Behavioral Neuroscience, 115,* 895-899.

Edgar, D. M., Miller, J. D., Prosser, R. A., Dean, R. R. & Dement, W. C. (1993). Serotonin and the mammalian circadian system: II. Phase-shifting rat behavioral rhythms with serotonergic agonists.*Journal of Biological Rhythms, 8,* 17-31.

Eley, D., Young, L. & Przybeck, T. R. (2009).Exploring the temperament and character traits of rural and urban doctors.*The Journal of Rural Health, 25,* 43-49.

Eley, D., Young, L. & Shrapnel, M. (2008). Rural temperament and character: a new perspective on retention of rural doctors. *Australian Journal of Rural Health, 16,* 12-22.

Eysenck, H. J. & Eysenck, S. B. G. (1963).On the dual nature of extraversion.*British Journal of Social and Clinical Psychology, 2,* 46-55.

Eysenck, H. J. & Eysenck, S. B. G. (1975).Manual of the Eysenck Personality Questionnaire. London: *Hodder and Stoughton.*

Eysenck, H. J.(1967). The biological basis of personality. Springfield: Charles C. Thomas.

Eysenck, S. B. G., Eysenck, H. J. & Barrett, P. (1985).A revised version of the psychoticism scale.*Personality and Individual Differences, 6,* 21-29.

Fernandez-Mendoza, J., Ilioudi, C., Montes, M. I., Olavarrieta-Bernardino, S., Aguirre-Berrocal, A., De La Cruz-Troca, J. J. & Vela-Bueno, A. (2010). Circadian preference, nighttime sleep and daytime functioning in young adulthood.*Sleep and Biological Rhythms, 8,* 52-62.

Fossati, A., Cloninger, C. R., Villa, D., Borroni, S., Grazioli, F., Giarolli, L., Battaglia, M. & Maffei, C. (2007). Reliability and validity of the Italian version of the Temperament and Character Inventory Revised in an outpatient sample. *Comprehensive Psychiatry, 48,* 380-387.

Gaspar-Barba, E., Calati, R., Cruz-Fuentes, C. S., Ontiveros-Uribe, M. P., Natale, V., De Ronchi, D. & Serretti, A. (2009). Depressive symptomatology is influenced· by chronotypes. *Journal of Affective Disorders, 119,* 100-106.

Gau, S. F. & Soong, W. T. (2003). The transition of sleep-wake patterns in early adolescence. *Sleep, 26,* 449-454.

Gerra, G., Garofano, L., Zaimovic, A., Moi, G., Branchi, B., Bussandri, M., Brambilla, F. & Donnini, C. (2005). Association of the serotonin transporter promoter polymorphism with smoking behavior among adolescents.*American Journal of Medical Genetics Part B (Neuropsychiatric Genetics), 135B,* 73-78.

Gillette, M. U. & Sejnowski, T. J. (2005). Biological clocks coordinately keep life on time. *Science, 309,* 1196-1198.

Goldstein, D., Hahn, C. S., Hasher, L., Wiprzycka, U. J. & Zelazo, P. D. (2007). Time of day, intellectual performance, and behavioral problems in morning versus evening type adolescents: is there a synchrony effect? *Personality and Individual Differences, 42,* 431-440.

Gray, E. K. & Watson, D. (2002).General and specific traits of personality and their relation to sleep and academic performance.*Journal of Personality, 70,* 177-206.

Greenwood, K. M. (1994). Long-term stability and psychometric properties of the Composite Scale of Morningness.*Ergonomics, 37,* 377-383.

Gurpegui, M., Jurado, D., Fernández-Molina, C. M., Moreno-Abril, O., Luna, J. D. & Alarcón, R. D.(2009). Personality profiles and minor affective psychopathology in a non-clinical sample: an empirical verification of Cloninger's theoretical model. *Journal of Affective Disorders, 119,* 34-42.

Hakkarainen, R., Johansson, C., Kieseppä, T., Partonen, T., Koskenvuo, M., Kaprio, J. &Lönnqvist, J. (2003).Seasonal changes, sleep length and circadian preference amongtwins with bipolar disorder. *BMC Psychiatry*, *3*, 6.

Halberg, F. (1959).Physiologic 24-hour periodicity in human beings and mice, the lighting regimen and dalily routine.In R. B. Withrow (Ed.), Photoperiodism and related phenomena in plants and animals (pp. 803-807). Washington: American Association for the *Advancement of Science*.

Hidalgo, M. P., Caumo, W., Posser, M., Coccaro, S. B., Camozzato, A. L. & Chaves, M. L. (2009). Relationship between depressive mood and chronotype in healthy subjects.*Psychiatry and Clinical Neurosciences*, *63*, 283-290.

Hogben, A. L., Ellis, J., Archer, S. N. & von Schantz, M. (2007). Conscientiousness is a predictor of diurnal preference. *Chronobiology International*, *24*, 1249-1254.

Horne, J. & Östberg, O. (1976).A self-assessment questionnaire to determine morningness-eveningness in human circadian rhythms.*International Journal of Chronobiology*, *4*, 97-110.

Hur, Y. M. (2007). Stability of genetic influence on morningness– eveningness: A cross-sectional examination of South Korean twins from preadolescence to young adulthood. *Journal of Sleep Research*, *16*, 17-23.

Ishihara, K., Honma, Y. & Miyake, S. (1990). Investigation of the children's version of the morningness-eveningness questionnaire with primary and junior high school pupils in Japan.*Perceptual and Motor Skills*, *71*, 1353-1354.

Jackson, L. A. & Gerard, D. A. (1996).Diurnal types, the "big five" personality factors, and other personal characteristics. *Journal of Social Behavior and Personality*, *11*, 273–284.

Johansson, C., Willeit, M., Smedh, C., Ekholm, J., Paunio, T., Kieseppa, T., Lichtermann, D., Praschak-Rieder, N., Neumeister, A., Nilsson, L. G., Kasper, S., Peltonen, L., Adolfsson, R., Schalling, M. & Partonen, T. (2003). Circadian clock-related polymorphisms in seasonal affective disorder and their relevance to diurnal preference.*Neuropsychopharmacology*, *28*, 734-739.

Kerkhof, G. A. & Van Dongen, H. P. A. (1996). Morning-type and evening-type individuals differ in the phase position of their endogenous circadian oscillator. *NeuroscienceLetters*, *218*, 153-156.

Kerkhof, G. A. (1985). Inter-individual differences in the human circadian system: A review. *BiologicalPsychology*, *20*, 83-112.

Laberge, L., Petit, D., Simard, C., Vitaro, F., Tremblay, R. E. & Montplaisir, J. (2001). Development of sleep patterns in early adolescence. *Journal of SleepResearch*, *10*, 59-67.

Langford, C. & Glendon, I. A. (2002). Effects of neuroticism, extraversion, circadian type and age on reported driver stress. *Work &Stress*, *16*, 316-334.

Larsen, R. J. (1985). Individual differences in circadian activity rhythm and personality.*Personality and Individual Differences*, *6*, 305-311.

Le Bon, O., Basiaux, P., Streel, E., Tecco, J., Hanak, C., Hansenne, M., Ansseau, M., Pelc, I., Verbanck, P. & Dupont, S. (2004). Personality profile and drug of choice; a multivariate analysis using Cloninger's TCI on heroin addicts, alcoholics, and a random population group.*Drug and Alcohol Dependence*, *73*, 175-182.

Lee, H. J., Paik, J. W., Kang, S. G., Lim, S. W. & Kim, L. (2007). Allelic variants interaction of clock gene and g-protein beta 3 subunit gene with diurnal preference.*Chronobiology International*, *24*, 589-597.

Lehnkering, H. & Siegmund, R. (2007). Influence of chronotype, season, and sex of subject on sleep behavior of young adults. *Chronobiology International*, *24*, 875-888.

Leventhal, A. M., Waters, A. J., Boyd, S., Moolchan, E. T., Helshman, S. J., Lerman, C. & Pickworth, W. B. (2007). Associations between Cloninger's temperament dimensions and acute tobacco withdrawal.*Addictive Behaviors*, *32*, 2976-2989.

Manuck, S. B., Flory, J. D., McCaffery, J. M., Matthews, K. A., Mann, J. J. & Muldoon, M. F. (1998). Aggression, impulsivity, and central nervous system serotonergic responsivity in a nonpatient sample.*Neuropsychopharmacology*, *19*, 287–299.

Matthews, G. (1988). Morningness-eveningness as a dimension of personality: trait, state and psychophysiological correlates. *European Journal of Personality*, *2*, 277-293.

Mecacci, L. & Rocchetti, G. (1998). Morning and evening types: Stress related personality aspects. *Personality and Individual Differences*, *25*, 537–542.

Mecacci, L., Zani, A., Rocchetti, G. & Lucioli, R. (1986). The relationship between morningness–eveningness, ageing, and personality.*Personality and Individual Differences*, *7*, 911-913.

Mikolajczyk, E., Zietek, J., Samochowiec, A. & Samochowiec, J. (2008). Personality dimensions measured using the Temperament and Character Inventory (TCI) and NEO-FFI on a Polish sample. *International Journal of Methods in Psychiatric Research*, *17*, 210-219.

Millon, T. (1994). The Millon inventories: clinical and personality assessment. New York: *The Guilford Press*.

Mitchell, P. J. & Redman, J. R. (1993).The relationship between morningness-eveningness, personality and habitual caffeine consumption.*Personality and Individual Differences*, *15*, 105-108.

Mongrain, V., Lavoie, S., Selmaoui, B., Parquet, J. & Dumont, M. (2004). Phase relationship between sleep-wake cycle and underlying circadian rhythms in morningness-eveningness. *Journal of Biological Rhythms*, *19*, 248-257.

Mura, E. L. & Levy, D. A. (1986). Relationship between neuroticism and circadian rhythms. *Psychological Reports*, *58*, 298.

Natale, V. & Cicogna, P. C. (2002). Morningness-eveningness dimension: is it really a continuum? *Personality and Individual Differences*, *32*, 809-816.

Natale, V. & Danesi, E. (2002). Gender and circadian typology. *Biological Rhythm Research*, *33*, 261-269.

Natale, V., Adan, A. & Scapellato, P. (2005). Are seasonality of mood and eveningness closely associated? *Psychiatry Research*, *136*, 51-60.

Neubauer, A. C. (1992). Psychometric comparison of two circadian rhythm questionnaires and their relationship with personality.*Personality and Individual Differences*, *13*, 125–132.

Owens, M. J. & Nemeroff, C. B. (1994). Role of serotonin in the pathophysiology of depression: focus on the serotonin transporter. *Clinical Chemistry*, *40*, 288-295.

Park, Y. M., Matsumoto, K., Seo, Y.J. & Shinkoda, H. (1999).Sleep and chronotype for children in Japan.*Perceptual and Motor Skills*, *88*, 1315-1329.

Randler, C. & Diaz-Morales, J. F. (2007). Morningness in German and Spanish students: a comparative study. *European Journal of Personality*, *21*, 419-427.

Randler, C. & Frech, D. (2009). Young people's time-of-day preferences affect their school performance. *Journal of Youth Studies*, *12*, 653-667.

Randler, C. (2007). Gender differences in morningness-eveningness assessed by self-report questionnaires: a meta-analysis. *Personality and Individual Differences, 43,* 1667-1675.

Randler, C. (2008a). Differences between smokers and nonsmokers in morningness-eveningness.*Social Behavior and Personality, 36,* 673-680.

Randler, C. (2008b). Morningness-eveningness, sleep-wake variables and big five personality factors.*Personality and Individual Differences, 45,* 191-196.

Ravaja, N., Keltikangas-Jarvinen, L. & Kettunen, J. (2006). Cloninger's temperament dimensions and threat, stress, and performance appraisals during different challenges among young adults.*Journal of Personality, 74,* 287-310.

Revelle, W., Humphreys, M. S., Simon, L. & Gilliland, K. (1980). The interactive effect of personality, time of day, and caffeine: a test of the arousal model. *Journal ofExperimental Psychology: General, 109,* 1-31.

Roenneberg, T., Kuehnle, T., Pramstaller. P. P., Ricken, J., Havel, M., Guth, A. & Merrow, M. (2004). A marker for the end of adolescence.*Current Biology, 14,* R1038-R1039.

Russo, P. M., Bruni, O., Lucidi, F., Ferri, R. & Violani, C. (2007). Sleep habits and circadian preference in Italian children and adolescents. *Journal of Sleep Research, 16,* 163-169.

Sher, K. J., Bartholow, B. D. & Wood, M. D. (2000). Personality and substance use disorders: a prospective study. *Journal of Consulting and Clinical Psychology, 68,*818–829.

Shinkoda, H., Matsumoto, K., Park, Y. M. & Nagashima H. (2000). Sleep-wake habits of schoolchildren according to grade. *Psychiatry and Clinical Neurosciences, 54,* 287-289.

Svrakic, D. M., Draganic, S., Hill, K., Bayon, C., Przybeck, T. R. & Cloninger, C. R. (2002). Temperament, character, and personality disorders: etiologic, diagnostic, treatment issues. *Acta Psychiatrica Scandinavica, 106,* 189-195.

Tankova, I., Adan, A. & Buela-Casal, G. (1994). Circadian typology and individual differences.A review.*Personality and Individual Differences, 16,* 671–684.

Tonetti, L. (2007). Validity of the Morningness-Eveningness Questionnaire for adolescents (MEQ-A).*Sleep and Hypnosis, 9,* 47-51.

Tonetti, L., Adan, A., Caci, H., De Pascalis, V., Fabbri, M. & Natale, V. (2010). Morningness-Eveningness preference and sensation seeking.*European Psychiatry, 25,* 111-115.

Tonetti, L., Fabbri, M. & Natale, V. (2008). Sex difference in sleep time preference and sleep need: a cross-sectional survey among Italian pre-adolescents, adolescents, and adults. *Chronobiology International, 25,* 745-759.

Tonetti, L., Fabbri, M. & Natale, V. (2009). Relationship between circadian typology and big five personality domains.*Chronobiology International, 26,* 337-347.

Trouillet, R. & Gana, K. (2008). Age differences in temperament, character and depressive mood: a cross-sectional study. *Clinical Psychology and Psychotherapy, 15,* 266-275.

Tsuchimine, S., Yasui-Furukori, N., Kaneda, A., Saito, M., Sugawara, N. & Kaneko, S. (2009). Minor genetic variants of the dopamine D4 receptor (DRD4) polymorphism are associated with novelty seeking in healthy Japanese subjects. Progress in Neuro-*Psychopharmacology & Biological Psychiatry, 33,* 1232-1235.

Vink, J. M., Groot, A. S., Kerkhof, G. A. & Boomsma, D. I. (2001).Genetic analysis of morningness and eveningness.*Chronobiology International, 18,* 809–822.

Wilson, G. D. (1990). Personality, time of day and arousal.*Personality and Individual Differences, 11,* 153-168.

Wittmann, M., Dinich, J., Merrow, M. & Roenneberg, T. (2006). Social jetlag: misalignment of biological and social time. *Chronobiology International, 23*, 497-509.

Wood, J., Birmaher, B., Axelson, D., Ehmann, M., Kalas, C., Monk, K., Turkin, S., Kupfer, D. J., Brent, D., Monk, T. H. & Nimgainkar, V. L. (2009).Replicable differences in preferred circadian phase between bipolar disorder patients and control individuals.*Psychiatry Research, 166*, 201-209.

Yang, C-K., Kim, J. K., Patel, S. R. & Lee, J-H. (2005). Age-related changes in sleep/wake patterns among Korean teenagers. *Pediatrics, 115*, 250-256.

Yuan, Q., Lin, F., Zheng, X. & Sehgal, A. (2005). Serotonin modulates circadian entrainment in *Drosophilia.Neuron, 47*, 115-127.

Zuckerman, M., Kuhlman, D. M., Joireman, J., Teta, P. & Kraft, M. (1993). A comparison of three structural models for personality: the big three, the big five, and the alternative five. *Journal of Personality and Social Psychology, 65*, 757-768.

In: Personality Traits: Theory, Testing and Influences
Editor: Melissa E. Jordan

ISBN: 978-1-61728-934-7
© 2011 Nova Science Publishers, Inc.

Chapter 3

THE IMAGINARY COMPANION EXPERIENCE IN ADULTS: ASSET, DISORDER OR PERSONALITY FEATURE?

Lino Faccini
Consulting Psychologist, Long Island NY, USA

ABSTRACT

Clinical and Forensic cases are reviewed regarding how an examiner should conceptualize the adult experience of having Imaginary Companions (IC). Some clinical and forensic research indicates that there is an overlap between adult IC and Dissociative experiences/disorders. However, other forensic case studies, a phenomenological perspective and expert opinion also indicate that the adult IC experience can occur in other clinical disorders, with personality disorders, and as the sole feature of one's clinical presentation. Also, research has identified that adult ICs can be linked to acts of violence, sex offending and self-harm. The diagnostic dilemma of how to conceptualize and diagnose these cases is most pertinent when ICs are involved and blamed for the commission of violent and criminal acts. Since the creation and dismissing of Adult ICs is a conscious and voluntary experience, the legal plea of Not Guilty by Reason of (Insanity) Mental Disease or Defect is not appropriate. Several different diagnostic possibilities are presented, consistent with DSM IV-TR. The Fantasy Prone Personality is also presented as another diagnostic classification possibility but with no current counterpart in the DSM IV-TR. The current gap in our knowledge in how to diagnose the presentation of ICs in adults, especially when they are involved in the commission of criminal acts should prompt more dialogue between clinicians, forensic examiners and researchers to develop a new diagnostic nomenclature.

The creation of Imaginary Companions (IC) that persist into adulthood can influence one's adult functioning and lead to clinical disorders and even forensic consequences. Currently, there exists a gap in our diagnostic nomenclature in how to regard, and diagnose the existence of ICs in the forensic evaluation. Cases were reviewed from the clinical and forensic literature regarding how to conceptualize the adult IC experience. A number of studies suggest an over-lap between the adult IC experience and dissociative and other clinical disorders. However, other studies, a phenomenological perspective and expert opinion describes them as different phenomena. Cases involving IC involvement and acts of violence will also be presented, and the difficulties of how to diagnose these cases is highlighted and suggestions are offered, including the Fantasy Prone Personality (Disorder). Although the Fantasy-Prone Personality is not regarded as a valid diagnostic category according to DSM IV-TR, the focus of this article is to highlight the current ambiguity in how to regard the adult IC phenomena, the personality type who continues to possess one into adulthood, and to suggest the Fantasy Prone Personality as one possible diagnostic alternative as well as other diagnostic options.

DEFINITION AND CHARACTERISTICS OF AN IMAGINARY COMPANION

An IC was described by Svendsen [1] as an invisible character named in conversation with other persons, or played with directly for a period of time, having an air of reality for the child, but no apparent objective basis. Although most of the work on the nature and function of ICs have been documented with children then adolescents, there are clinical and forensic case studies of adults with ICs. Ralph Allison MD, a retired Forensic Psychiatrist, has contributed significantly to understanding the nature of adult's ICs. Basically, Dr. Allison [2] states "Imagination is a process used by the (Original) Personality for the purpose of creating mental entities (such as ICs) for a wide variety of purposes. There are no limits to human imagination, so MEs can be created in any size, age, sex or physical form. They may live inside or outside of their creator's body, as well as placed in objects. They are fueled by raw emotions and are not designed for survival purposes. They may have limited and changing characteristics, as they can be constantly redesigned by the imagination of the (original) personality, as needs and desires change. Since all but the demented can imagine, Imaginary Playmates are ubiquitous throughout mankind. Since they are chosen to be made by the (original) personality, the creation of Imaginary Playmates is voluntary. The (original) personality can destroy any and all Imaginary Playmates, once the person makes up their mind to do so. All that is needed is the will to get rid of them and take responsibility for what they have been doing in the person's behalf...In addition, when ICs are internalized, they can act superficially like alter-personalities but are not formed (created) out of dissociation". In essence, Dr. Allison has identified the following about Imaginary Companions:

they are consciously and voluntarily created via one's emotional imagination and can be discarded when the disadvantages of having them outweigh the advantages.
can be internal or external to the body
can be placed in objects
can be given/embody a variety of emotions
they have a limited capacity to think or pick targets
they can occur at any age - can be in conflict with the creator and can intermittently control his/her body and actions - can contain and manage conflicting feelings
may sound or speak differently than the person when they are internalized and in control
several IICs can communicate with others at 1 time - should not be considered grounds for a Not Criminally Responsible plea in court since the IC was created voluntarily

Overlap between ICs and Dissociative Disorders

With adults, the IC condition is limited to case study presentations. For example, Hawksworth and Schwartz [3], in their book *The Five of Me: The Autobiography of a Multiple Personality Disorder,* present the case of a Mr. Hawksworth who had ICs before he dissociated with three alters, and at the age of 43 "returned" to take control of his body and subsequently also destroying the two ICs. In particular, Mr. Hawksworth had created two ICs before he dissociated at the age of four. One IC was "Johnny" who was created to provide companionship and also to take the blame for the "bad" acts; Johnny resided in a Charlie McCarthy doll. The other IC was "Peter" who was created after he read *Peter Pan.* "He is able to express emotions I, too, had always felt, but which I had to hide because they hadn't fit my father's concept of masculinity". At the age of 43, he destroyed both ICs after he returned to take charge of his body. In essence, Mr. Hawksworth's case clearly illustrates that there can be an overlap between Multiple Personality Disorder (MPD) and the adult IC experience, and that the adult IC experience can precede MPD. Another case of ICs following the presence of MPD involves the case of Marie (Allison [4]). She possessed 69 alter personalities and created "evil demon" ICs to persuade Dr. Allison not to move out of town. The ICs took control of her body and tried to choke and hit Dr. Allison with objects. Subsequently, she was hospitalized and then destroyed the ICs, by an act of will, while in the hospital.

In regard to other dissociative disorders and the presence of ICs, Lewis et al. [5] reported that 10 out of 12 adults in her sample of murderers with Dissociative Identity Disorder (DID) all experienced "vivid and longstanding imaginary companions who seemed to be precursors of their alternate personality states"; however only 5 of the 12 adults had ICs that continued into adulthood. In essence in her sample, ICs preceded the DID disorders. Furthermore, Faccini [6] presented a case of a person with Mild Mental Retardation and a total of 10 ICs, three of whom could take control of his body and influence him to commit acts of pedophilia, exhibitionism, obscene phone calling and child abduction. In addition, one of the ICs, the baby, would initially shrink the size of his penis if he didn't comply with her demands which could culminate in "her" changing his gender, changing his genitals from a penis to a vagina, and shrinking the size of his body. In particular, his clinical presentation seemed to be consistent with the diagnoses of Gender Identity Disorder, Atypical Depersonalization Disorder and Schizoid traits. In this case, an atypical Depersonalization Disorder preceded the presence of the ICs. Furthermore, Sawa et al. [7] presented adult cases involving ICs who provided guidance to see a therapist after a self-cutting episode, another case of a female whose IC expressed thoughts that she suppressed, and a third case where the IC contained and expressed her violent anger. Of the three case studies, all three were diagnosed with dissociative and conversion disorders. Finally, Allison [8] presented a case where a businessman in California had an IC who killed his wife. He was found Not Guilty By Reason of Insanity, because of a diagnosis of MPD, and sent to a Forensic Hospital. However, Allison believed that this man's IC killed the wife not an alter personality. After the person was able to express his own anger appropriately, the IC disappeared and couldn't be found even with the assistance of hypnosis. Subsequently, this man was discharged from the Forensic Hospital.

Mediating Variables between ICs and Dissociative Disorders

Of the studies presented thus far, all of the individuals were diagnosed with a dissociative disorder. The issue of whether the adult IC experience has significant overlap with dissociative experience is a pertinent issue. Some research has tried to investigate the direct relationship while others have tried to find other mediating variables/conditions.

Dierker, Davis and Sanders [9] studied college student's retrospective reports of having a childhood IC and the degree of dissociation, and imaginative involvement. They found that "college students who remember a childhood IC would be more dissociative as well as higher in imaginative involvement than those who do not was clearly confirmed for women, and was partially supported for men...not surprisingly, those whose experience was vivid and real were also more involved with their companions...our results suggest that individuals from the normal population who have vivid imaginary companions experiences are similar to DID groups in having elevated dissociative and imaginative capabilities". Dierker (unpublished study cited in Holocomb [10]) "proposed that it was the vividness of an IC experience and not necessarily the existence of a dissociative disorder posed as an indicator of DES scores". Consistent with these findings, Bonne et al. [11] postulated that "individuals who possess ICs in childhood are more likely to express creative aptitudes as adults... this capacity for vivid fantasy has been deemed indicative of vulnerability towards dissociative phenomenon and depersonalization." However, Holcomb [10] summarized that "dissociation experiences carries aspects of hypnotizability, and to a lesser extent the ability for an individual to become 'absorbed' in a specific area or aspect of his/her life". She concludes that the individual having an IC "may possess an imaginative disposition...but also scored higher on two other subscales of the DES namely depersonalization, derealization and amnesia". In essence, heightened imaginative capabilities towards vivid and real images, and increased hypnotic ability are assets but may also predispose one towards possible dissociative experiences.

To better understand the relationship between ICs and alters/MPD/DID, Sanders [12] offers the following perspective regarding ICs and alters. She states "one possible relationship between an IC and an alter is that in the developmental history of the multiple there is a change in the phenomenological experience such that the imaginary companion becomes an alter. An alternative is that there is no real transition. It may be that for the multiple, the childhood imaginary companion experience is subjectively the same as the alter personality experience, once the childhood experience is seen in a new light. That is to say, that "what was once considered to be an 'imaginary companion' is now seen to have been an alter personality"; although informative, Dr. Sanders appears to be discussing the presence of IC within someone with Multiple Personality Disorder. Although there can be some overlap between ICs and alters, Allison [13] described how they are different and then presents a compelling phenomenological perspective in differentiating them. Allison states that ICs are formed voluntarily, not involuntarily by dissociation as with alters, can be discarded and need not be integrated into the creator like alters. Mainly ICs are created via emotional imagination and not through dissociation "which is a post traumatic process of breaking in two that which was originally one" and that "imagination is the creation of something that did not exist before" [13], and that ICs can exist inside or outside of the body whereas alters can only exist inside of the body/mind. Also, ICs can be very changeable as opposed to alters who are more fixed, and the person "allows" the IC control whereas the alter may be called forth at different times depending on the situation and the type of coping needed.

From a phenomenological standpoint, "when an alter reports seeing an IC, they describe it as wispy, ill defined, colorless, with no substance. It may be described as being all emotion…They know it is not one of them, and they imply that it can be removed without harm to the entire organism". Otherwise "an alter inside of the mind, will appear definite, with strong colors, appearing like a person, or a swirl of colors, with firm ideas and strong opinions. They will know it is like themselves, and they will generally know its name". [13]. As stated by Dr. Allison, the phenomenological perspective of someone who has both ICs and alter personalities described them as very different; therefore to consider ICs as misidentified alter personalities doesn't appear to be consistent with the phenomenological perspective or Dr. Allison's clinical experience.

Overlap between ICs and Other Clinical Disorders

Although research suggests that there may be a degree of overlap between the IC experience and dissociation, other forensic case studies have presented individuals who have ICs into adulthood who weren't diagnosed with any dissociative disorders. In essence, cases have been identified where ICs coexisted with Schizoaffective Disorders, Schizophrenia, Paranoid type with depression, and a case of Major Depressive Disorder, Polysubstance Abuse and Borderline Personality Disorder. In particular, the 2002 case of Kyle Hulbert and the murder of the scientist Robert Schwartz is a case where ICs were created for the sake of companionship by an adult. Hulbert was convinced by the daughter of Robert Schwartz that he was abusing and poisoning her regularly. As a result, Hulbert killed him. As per Psychiatrist Dr. Howard Glick, he presented testimony that Hulbert had ICs of vampires and dragons which he considered his family as part of his clinical presentation, which also included symptoms of a Schizoaffective Disorder and paranoia. Despite a history of psychiatric instability, he was still convicted of first degree murder and sentenced to life in prison. Another case involving an adult with an IC is that of the Virginia Tech shooter, Chao Seung-Hui. Reportedly, a room mate of Chao's stated that he had an imaginary super model girlfriend whom he called Jelly. It may have been that Chao created and needed an IC for companionship especially since he was a loner. Reportedly while in Middle School, he was diagnosed with selective mutism and major depression. Subsequently, various diagnoses such as depression, "psychopathy", and paranoid schizophrenia were also proposed, with the latter diagnosis being preferred by mental health professionals.

In regards to a criminal case, the case of James Gallagher also illustrates that someone diagnosed with Schizophrenia, paranoid type and Imaginary Companions can co-exist; he was charges with the murder of an unsuspecting neighbor who was just trimming the hedges between their properties. The plea entered against the charges of first degree murder was initially NGRI but subsequently, Mr. Gallagher plead no contest to second degree murder.

Furthermore, Allison [2] presented three case studies of men who continued to have imaginary companions. As per Allison, Fred the "Cabbie Killer" was initially found Incompetent to Stand Trial for the murder of an innocent cab driver. He was sent to Atascadero Forensic Hospital and found to be malingering Multiple Personality Disorder, with a more accurate diagnosis of Schizoaffective Disorder. However, Fred actually did have a number of IC's including Mr. Mann who was perfect and proper, Chuck the Bully, and

Madam Amrak. In fact, Dr. Allison states that when he was evaluating Fred for a forensic evaluation, he was assaulted by the Chuck IC. Dr. Allison commented that Fred had "created a series of ICs to contain and manage his conflicting feelings…and other antisocial mental entities were made by the identification with his father and fueled by his intense anger at the man". Unfortunately, his anger was misdirected towards an unsuspecting cab driver killing him. The second case study involved Ted "the Transvestite Bomb Maker". He had created three male and two female ICs. In particular, the first male IC threatened to cut his girlfriend's throat with a knife; Tammy a 7, 10, or 12 year old IC was the "little homemaker" who would cook for him, and was in control of his body when he wore female clothing; Tamara, a 17 or 42 year old "crazy older woman" served as Ted's alter ego being sophisticated, angry, and mean similar to his real mother; Rick was "the macho one" who liked manly activities such as fishing, hunting, mountain climbing, dancing and motorcycle racing; in addition it was Rick who also thought that he was a US Navy Seal and that he had been sent to Russia on a Mission. Finally, Eric who was 25 years old harbored thoughts of killing himself, as Ted presents "he is my frustration, anger, makes me cut myself, hurt myself, and burn myself". Allison considered Fred's diagnosis to be Major Depression, Polysubstance Abuse and Borderline Personality Disorder. In summary, in regards to clinical diagnoses associated with persons who also have ICs, these have included Dissociative Identity Disorders (5 cases), Schizophrenia Spectrum Disorders (6 cases), Dissociative Disorders (4 cases), and Multiple Personality Disorders (3 cases).

Cases Only Involving ICs

Thus far, cases have been identified where ICs have coexisted with dissociative and other clinical disorders; however there are also cases where the ICs are the only part of the clinical presentation. For instance, this phenomenon of talking to an imaginary companion may occur more so with persons with Down's Syndrome. Down's Syndrome is a congenital disorder associated with intellectual disabilities. Patti [14] found that 30% of their 177 adults with Down's Syndrome talked to an imaginary companion; these ICs took the form of hand puppets, talking to one's finger, a stuffed animal or an internalized movie character or a staff member. Another case that may only present an adult with an IC is that of the Australian Murder case involving Christopher Maddox. Mr. Maddox attributed the 2007 attack, murder and mutilation of a neighbor to the orders to do so from an IC named "Bert". Subsequently, Mr. Maddox plead guilty to murder. In this case no clinical diagnosis was identified. Also, Allison [13] describes the case of Carrie, who was first diagnosed with MPD by Dr. Allison, but then he reconsidered and believed that she mainly had ICs. In particular, she had 11 ICs of which Wanda was the one who was filled with hatred and anger, and Debra (the only alter), would save Carrie from suicide attempts. Primarily, Carrie was considered to be a case of having ICs. Also, he mentions the case of a death row inmate who had three ICs. One IC "the rescuer" disappeared due to not being needed while in prison; two other ICs that were still present in the prison included the "killer" who dealt drugs and the "snitch" who negotiated with his defense attorney. Despite the presence of the ICs, the prisoner was described a usually friendly to the guards. In addition, Allison [8] reported a case of a Mr. C who ended up in jail due to assault only to end up killing his prison cell mate. Mr. C was described by Allison as "civilized and polite most of the time" however he had an IC that was a "hit man" who lived by the "convict code". Allison continued by saying "he placed all of his forbidden urges and impulses he dared not express himself...put all of his anger into this IC, which lay dormant for years"; no clinical disorder was identified in this case. Although possible, Mr. Christopher Dee [personal communication, November 4, 2009] believes that serial sexual murderer, Arthur Shawcross, "invented a playmate during his formative years...This was a buddy he could relate all his troubles to and even he went fishing with him, and took him along on his animal torture expeditions...I think that his imaginary friend was with him until he died".

Overlap between ICs and Personality Disorders

So far, cases have been presented indicating that MPD can precede the existence of ICs, ICs can exist first followed by a MPD/DID disorders, or that they can coexist at the same time. However, ICs have been identified in individuals with personality disorders also. In particular, ICs have been present in individuals with such personality disorder as Avoidant, Schizoid (as in Faccini's case of the person with Mild MR), and in Borderline or possibly Mixed Personality Disorder with Borderline and Antisocial features (Allison's case of Ted).

The case of Jerry "Scotty" Heidler illustrates the occurrence of a childhood then an adult IC that existed in someone later diagnosed with Borderline Personality Disorder. In particular, Heidler shot to death four members of the Daniel's family then kidnapped and sodomized another daughter. His foster mother, Sylvia Boatright, stated at his trial that he had a mouse IC that he carried around in his hand and talked to frequently. It was suggested that his talking to the mouse was to compensate for his lack of having any real friends. Interestingly, this fact was brought up at his trial as coinciding with his first hospitalization, and as one aspect of a "mental illness" that contributed to his offenses. However, he was still convicted of murder and kidnapping. At least theoretically, the tendency of someone with Schizotypal Personality Disorder could "turn to the make believe world of their imagination that would provide them with a pseudocommunity of fantasized persons and objects to which they can safely relate" seems to provide the necessary conditions for the creation of ICs, according to Theodore Millon [15]. Similarly, Phillip Long MD [16], when discussing the treatment of Schizoid Personality Disorder, states that the patient may "oscillate between fears of clinging to the therapist followed by fleeing through fantasy and withdrawal...the patient may eventually reveal a plethora of fantasies, imaginary friends, and fears of unbearable dependency". For instance, a case of a person with Mild Mental Retardation and Schizoid Personality Traits was presented earlier under Faccini [6]. For a summary of the cases presenter thus far, as well as diagnoses and the functions of the IC, refer to Table 1.

Lack of Guidelines on How to Diagnose the IC's Influence or Effect

To date, there has been neither a discussion nor options for how to diagnose the influence or effect of ICs when they are involved in clinical or personality problems or when no other diagnosis is made. Because DSM IV-TR doesn't provide any guidance on how to diagnose such clinical presentations, usually other comorbid disorders are diagnosed. (see Table 2).

Table 1. Adult IC cases, corresponding diagnoses and the function of their ICs

Case	Diagnoses/Disorder	ICs	ICs Function
1. Hawksworth and Schwartz (1977)	Multiple Personality Disorder	1. Johnny IC 2. Peter IC	+ companionship + contain/express emo.
2. Marie in Allison [1999]	Multiple Personality Disorder	Evil devil IC	- alter ego
3. Lewis et al. [1997]	5-Dissoc. Identity Disorder	Unknown	Unknown
4. Faccini [2009]	Depersonalization Disorder, Gender Identity Dis, Paraphilia NOS, Schizoid Traits	1. Baby 2. Red-Haired Girl 3. Teen with glasses 4. Evil 1 5. Evil 2 6. Barney 7. Elmo 8. Mom and Dad	−comp/−alter ego +guidance/ +companion −cont/exp emo/ - companion -comp/-alter ego -comp/-alter ego - companion -companion + nurturance/love
5. Sawa et al.[2004]	3 Dissociative Disorders 3 Conversion Disorders	1IC 1IC(mouthpiece) 1IC (attacking self/others)	+guidance/+ support + cont/exp/emo - contain/exp emo
6. Allison [2006]	Multiple Personality Disorder	Killer IC	- contain/express emo
7. 2002 Criminal Case of K. Hulbert	Schizoaffective Disorder with paranoia	Vampire ICs Dragon IC	- companionship - companionship
8. 2007 Case of Chao Seung-Hui	Schizophrenia, paranoid (?) Depression (?) Psychopathy (?)	1IC supermodel girl friend Jelly	- companionship
9. Criminal Case of James Gallagher	Schizophrenia, paranoid	1IC	unknown
10. Allison [1997] Fred the Cabbie Killer	Schizoaffective Disorder	Mr. Mann IC Chuck the Bully Madam Amrak	+ alter ego - alter ego - contain/exp emo
11. Allison [1997] Ted the Transvestite Bombmaker	Major Depression Polysubstance Abuse Borderline Personality	1 Male IC Rick IC Eric IC Tamara IC	- contain/exp emo - alter ego - contain/exp emo - alter ego
		Tammy IC	+ alter ego
12. Patti et al.[2009]	Down's Syndrome	53 ICs	Unknown

Table 1. (Continued)

Case	Diagnoses/Disorder	ICs	ICs Function
13. 2007 Criminal Case of Chris Maddox	unknown	1IC Bert	- alter ego or contain/exp emo (?)
14. Allison [1998] Case of Carrie	None	10 ICs 1 Wanda	unknown - contain/exp emo
15. Allison [1998] Death Row Inmate	None	1 IC Rescuer 1 IC Killer 1 IC Snitch	+ guidance - alter ego + guidance
16. Allison [2006] Case of Mr. C	None	1 IC Hitman	- alter ego/- contain/exp emo
17. Criminal Case of Arthur Shawcross	Paraphilia NOS (Serial Sexual Murder)	1 IC	+ companionship
18. Criminal Case of Jerry "Scotty" Heindler	Borderline Personality Disorder	1 IC Mouse	+ companionship
19. 1979 Criminal Case of Harold Ray Redfeairn	Schizophrenia, paranoid	1 IC	Unknown
20. Criminal Case of John Ray Weber	Sexual Sadism	1 IC NATAS	- alter ego

Table 2. Table of Clinical Diagnoses given to Disorders with accompanying ICs and The Frequency of their Adaptive and Maladaptive Functions

Diagnoses/Disorder	Frequency of Cited Cases	Function of the IC Adaptive	Maladaptive
Down Syndrome	53	Primarily adaptive: plan, rehearse, debrief, calm, problem solve- No frequency available	None
Dissociative Disorders	12		
-Dissociative Identity Disorder	5	8	9
-Dissociative Disorder	4		
-Multiple Personality	3		
Schizophrenic Spectrum	6		
-Schizophrenic, paranoid	3	1	5
-Schizoaffective Disorder	3		
Borderline Personality Disorder	2		
Paraphilias NOS	2		
Sexual Sadism	1		
Schizoid Personality Traits	1		
Polysubstance Abuse	1		

Note. Lewis et al. (1997) sample was not included in the Dissociative Disorders tally; Redfeairn and Gallagher cases were not included in the Schzophrenic Spectrum Disorders tally.

Surprisingly, the most frequent disorder where adults have ICs, with a total of 53 cases, was within the disorder of Down's Syndrome. Secondly, Dissociative Disorders, with 12 total cases, were the next most prevalently diagnosed when an adult had an IC. Next, the Schizophrenic Spectrum Disorders were diagnosed in 6 cases. Subsequently, Paraphilia NOS, Sexual Sadism, Schizoid Personality Traits, and Polysubstance abuse were all diagnosed to a lesser extent. The adaptive and maladaptive functions of the ICs for adults and their relationship with each disorder will be examined in section on Functional method.

In particular, the importance of proper diagnosis is most needed in forensic cases where the defendant and his attorney may enter a plea of Not Criminally responsible mistaking a crime committed with an IC's influence for an alter personality and thus suspecting a Dissociative Identity Disorder or some other major mental illness. Since the IC is created voluntarily, the issue of entering a plea of Not Guilty By Reason of Mental Disease or Defect should not be appropriate. In addition, one of the main functions of having an IC as an adult is to attribute antisocial acts to it (i.e. negative alter ego function). In this way, if a Not Criminally Responsible plea is entered then a lack of accountability may be further reinforced. According to Dr. Allison [2] "in forensic psychiatry, a major issue which often needs to be addressed is whether the illegal act was 'voluntary' or 'involuntary'. The law commonly considers a voluntary act which violates a criminal statute to be worthy of punishment, but the same act done involuntarily might not warrant punishment, and the perpetrator might be referred for treatment of a mental entity (IC or alter) which only intermittently controls the defendant's body, then the psychiatric examiner must determine whether or not that ME was created voluntarily or involuntarily". An example of a defense attributing violent actions to the person's IC and then making a claim for Not Guilty by Reason of Mental Disease or Defect can be found in the case of Harold Ray Redfeairn. Redfeairn was charged with holding up a dealership and a motel, in Ohio in 1979, and then for shooting and the attempted murder of a pursuing police officer. First, he was found Not Competent to Stand Trial but then was found competent and tried in 1981. He was diagnosed with Paranoid Schizophrenia with frequent hallucinations, and persistent delusions involving battling the devil. In adulthood, he testified that he continued to have an IC who talked to him. According to his attorney [17], "the IC had a whole lot to do with what happened in that car" referring to the pursuit and shooting of the officer; the goal was to try and have Mr. Redfeairn be committed to a state forensic hospital. However, Mr. Redfeairn was convicted of attempted aggravated murder and three counts of aggravated robbery. As this case exemplifies, the presence of having an adult IC can be misused as a basis for a Not Criminally Responsible plea with the possible goal of obtaining an easier stay in a forensic hospital rather than being held accountable and being sent to prison. Another case where ICs may have contributed to the commission of criminal acts involves the case of the disorganized serial killer, John Ray Weber. As recounted by Psychiatrist Michael Stone [18], "Weber was declared mentally ill by his defense attorneys-partly on the strength of his previous hospitalizations". In his youth, he had an imaginary friend "who he conversed with in his head and whom he called NATAS-'SATAN' that is spelled backwards. That seems to have been his explanation for his evil mind". However, he was considered a "sexual sadist" and he was still convicted of murder and received a life sentence.

Overly Simplistic Alternatives

Since the issue of diagnosis may have direct implications for how these type of cases can be regarded by clinicians and the legal system, there are several possibilities of how the presence of ICs can be accounted for while using the present diagnostic nomenclature coding for clinical and personality disorders and other conditions across three of the five axes of DSM IV-TR; the optimal goal would involve being able to make a proper diagnosis of one's clinical disorders that may underlie one's criminal actions while not providing a misdiagnosis that could lead to a Not Criminally Responsible plea. For instance, when the IC acts in an antisocial manner, then one possibility is to code it as a V code under Axis I namely Adult Antisocial Behavior. Another alternative, when the presence of the IC influences the control of one's impulses, then one could use the Impulse Control Disorder, NOS diagnosis possibly with a parenthetical qualifier "with Imaginary Companion Influence". An additional possibility involves when the presence of the IC causes significant stress for the person, then possibly it can be coded under Axis IV Psychosocial Stressors- Imaginary Companion Influence.

The Fantasy Prone Personality

In regard to associated Personality types, the presence of Imaginary Companions is included in one category of personality types that has been identified in the professional literature but not in DSM IV-TR. The "fantasy prone personality" was first identified by Wilson and Barber in 1983 and was described as "there exists a small group of individuals (possibly 4% of the population) who fantasize a large part of the time, who typically 'see', 'smell', 'touch', and fully experience what they fantasize; and who can be labeled fantasy-prone individuals" as cited in Posters [19]. In addition, Wilson and Barber identified 14 characteristics, or some regard them as personality traits, of "fantasy-proneness" namely: having imaginary playmates as a child, adopting a fantasy identity, being an excellent hypnotic subject, experiencing imagined sensations as real, reliving past experiences, having vivid sensory perceptions, having out-of-body-experiences, being involved in healing, receiving poems, messages, etc from spirits, higher intelligences and the like, experiencing waking dreams, encountering apparitions, fantasizing frequently as a child, seeing classical hypnagogic imagery and claiming psychic powers. Essentially they believed that having six or more of these 14 characteristics could qualify one to be regarded as "fantasy prone".

Although Fantasy Prone Personality is not recognized as a valid DSM IV-TR Personality (Disorder), some studies have examined if other mainstream clinical personality disorders could account for its characteristics. For instance, Merritt [20] reported "fantasizers (fantasy prone personality) were much more likely to produce MMPI codes associated with a vulnerability to Schizophrenia (70%) than were controls (3.33%)...66.7% of the fantasizers produced three or more elevated clinical scales on the MMPI. The modal MMPI profile for the fantasizers was an 8-9 code (the modal diagnosis being Schizophrenia associated with this code type), indicating that fantasizers appear at heightened risk for eccentric thinking and a Cluster A or B personality organization". In addition, fantasy proneness has been associated with being abused as a child whereupon it is believed that the child withdraws more into fantasy, with Schizotypy in adulthood (Sanchez-Bernardos, and Avia [21]). Also, they were "more likely than controls to meet formal diagnostic criteria for a DSM-IV Cluster A personality disorders at the clinical level, to meet significantly more overall diagnostic criteria across personality disorder clusters, and to produce significantly higher scores on the Dissociation Experiences Scale" (Waldo [22]).

Although a sub-population of individuals with a fantasy prone personality may qualify for an already established clinical personality disorders, however the degree of ease and depth of these individuals' fantasizing ability is extraordinary when witnessed in one's clinical practice; this observation is consistent with the fact that these individuals may be "highly trance prone and in the top 4% of hypnotic capacity or a Grade 5 on the hypnotic induction scale" as Spiegel and Spiegel [23] report. In addition, fantasy proneness has been associated with such assets as increased creativity and imagination (Lynn and Rhue [24]), as well as by high hypnotizability and degree of absorption/ability to concentrate (Rhue and Lynn [24]), while not being related to reality monitoring errors (Aleman & deHaan [25]). To illustrate this point, the person with the Mild Mental Retardation and ICs presented in Faccini [6] exhibited an extraordinary ability to imagine his ICs and even various kid TV shows. In particular, this individual was being prepared to undergo the voluntary banishing of his ICs via the bottle routine (refer to Allison [8] for a description of the procedure). In order to make the practice of the procedure more concrete, the suggestion was given to start at his feet, with his hands cupped to represent a "net" as he was to sweep from his feet to his head and collecting all of his ICs. Once they were all collected in the "net", he was to expel them via his exhaling his breathe. As a means to check if he really understood that he was collecting all of his ICs, that were inside of his body, he was asked if he was able to collect all of them. At this point, the individual stopped, and while pointing to each as though he was counting them in his cupped hand, accounted for all 12 of his ICs while seeing them. In essence, this experience happened during a regular therapy session, without the aid of hypnosis etc. In addition, when he was trying to decrease viewing "Barney", the kid's show on TV (as one means of decreasing his participation in child-oriented activities as one means of managing his pedophilia), he described that he was able to imagine whole skits in his head from the TV show. These two examples highlight the incredible ability and asset to vividly imagine his ICs or whole segments of TV shows.

In essence, the same mechanisms that have been identified in the experience of ICs have also been identified in the fantasy prone personality. In essence, the fact that having ICs as a child is one criteria for this personality pattern means that this personality style may be meaningful in how to regard ICs and the adult personalities who continue to have them. In addition, the other characteristics of the Fantasy Prone Personality, (namely being so highly hypnotizable, having difficulty distinguishing fantasy from reality, experiencing imagined sensations as real, and having vivid sensory perceptions) are consistent with the experience of adults with IC, and that they can be perceived as real and vivid. As a result, the Fantasy Prone Personality may offer another avenue in how to better regard the adult experience of ICs, or the "Fantasy Prone Personality Disorder" when there exists an IC in an adult along with the clinical or forensic presentation.

Table 3. Frequencies of the IC's function in Adults

Adaptive	Companionship 3.5 ICs
	Guidance 3 ICs
	Containing/expressing difficult emotions 3 ICs
	Positive Alter Ego 2 ICs
	Nurturance/Love 2 ICs
Maladaptive/	Negative Alter Ego 8.5 ICs
Antisocial/	Negative Companion 6 ICs
Dangerous	Containing/expressing forbidden emotions 5.5 ICs

Note. If an IC shared two functions then each function would receive a .5 of a point, other wise each
function was tallied as 1 point.
Excluded from the totals include the function of the ICs in cases numbered 2, 3, 12, 10 ICs in case 14,
and case 19 in Table 1.

A Functional Method of Regarding ICs

Now that the IC phenomena has been examined from the perspective of associated
clinical disorders and personality features, the various functions of an adult's IC can be
explored. According to Ball et al. [26] various functions have been identified that the IC can
have including for control, companionship, nurturance, emotional outlet, alter ego guidance
and facilitating fantasy.

As identified in Table 3, the various functions of the identified ICs in the 20 presented
cases can be summarized as follows:

· In summarizing the findings in Table 3, adaptive aspects (i.e. assets) of adults having ICs
include for the purpose of companionship, for guidance, to help contain and/or express
difficult emotions, for a positive alter ego and for nurturance and love. However, three
maladaptive functions of having negative alter egos (a mean, hostile IC for a passive
individual), having negative companions (i.e. children if you have pedophilia), and having
ICs contain/express forbidden emotions (such as rage, hatred) were also evident. Relatively
speaking, given that a total of 16 ICs weren't included since the function of their IC's weren't
identified, a relative total of 20 ICs served a negative function while 13.5 ICs were positive
for the adult creator; the 53 persons with Down's Syndrome in Patti [14] were identified as
having primarily adaptive functions such as for planning, rehearsing, debriefing, self-calming,
and problem solving.

However, when the function of the ICs is examined, for the three primary clinical
disorders in adults with ICs, such as in Table 2, an interaction effect is observed. In particular,
Down's Syndrome was the most prevalent disorder and primarily the functions of the ICs
were adaptive according to Patti et al.(personal communication, February 2, 2010). When a
Dissociative Disorder was diagnosed, the function of the ICs were adaptive and maladaptive
with about equal frequencies (i.e. adaptive= 2 ICs that were companions, 2ICs
containing/expressing difficult emotions, 2ICs for guidance/support, and 2 ICs for
nurturance/love versus 4 ICs for negative companions, 2.5 ICs for negative alter ego
functions, and 2.5 ICs for containing/expressing forbidden emotions). Furthermore, if a
Schizophrenic Spectrum Disorder was diagnosed, then the reported ICs were primarily

maladaptive (i.e. 3 ICs that were negative companions, 1 IC as a negative alter ego, and 1IC that contained/expressed forbidden emotions versus 1 IC that served as a positive alter ego). In summary, the functions of the ICs are primarily regarded as adaptive and positive for adults with Down's Syndrome, about equally adaptive and maladaptive for adults with Dissociative Disorders, and primarily negative for adults with Schizophrenic spectrum disorders.

CONCLUSION

In conclusion, the adult experience of ICs can be thought of as a voluntary process of creating imaginary beings, both inside or outside, of one's body. They are created voluntarily by one's imagination, serve a specific purpose for the person, and can be destroyed through an act of will when the disadvantages of having it outweigh the advantages. From a phenomological perspective, ICs have been described as ill defined, with no substance, and all emotion; this differs from the experience of an alter personality which is described as similar to a person, with ideas, a name, and associated with a color swirl or strong colors. Cases were presented where an adult IC coexisted with various dissociative disorders, clinical disorders and personality disorders. However, cases were also identified were an adult IC was the sole part of the clinical presentation. The importance of making a proper diagnosis was stressed given that the presence of an adult IC could be mistaken for an alter personality, a dissociative disorder then suspected and a case made for a Not Criminally Responsible plea in forensic cases. However the current gap in how to conceptualize and diagnose these cases doesn't help the clinician or forensic examiner. Several possibilities, maybe over-simplistic, included coding for Adult Antisocial Behavior (under Axis I of the DSM IV-TR), Impulse Control Disorder, NOS with an IC influence parenthetical qualifier, or to identify a stressful IC under the DSM IV-TR Axis IV psychosocial problems section were presented. Another option of the Fantasy Prone Personality "Disorder" was also presented and reviewed due to its overlap with the IC experience, and similarities in mediating mechanisms, and the use one's extraordinary imaginations. In addition, the function of the Adults' ICs were both serving adaptive and maladaptive ways of coping, depending on the disorders that were present. However, all of the presented options, including the Functional Method, were not considered adequate to assist the clinician or forensic examiners conceptualize or diagnose adult IC cases. Continued research and dialogue between clinicians, forensic examiners and researchers should lead to better applicable diagnostic possibilities.

REFERENCES

[1] Svenden, S. (1934). Children's imaginary companions. *Archives of Neurology and Psychiatry, 32*, 985-999.
[2] Allison, R. (1997). *The Case of Alter-Personalities v. Imaginary Playmates.* www.dissociation.
[3] Hawksworth, H. & Schwartz, T. (1997). *The Five of Me: The Autobiography of a Multiple Personality.* Chicago: Henry Regnery Company.

[4]   Allison, R. (1999). Multiple Personality Disorder, Dissociative Identity Disorder and Intended Imaginary *Companions. Hypnos, 25(3)*, 125-133.

[5]   Lewis, D. O., Yeager, C. A., Swica, Y., Pincus, J. H. & Lewis, M. (1997). Objective Documentation of Child Abuse and Dissociation in 12 Murderers with DID. American *Journal of Psychiatry, 154(12)*, 1703-1710.

[6]   Faccini, L. & Tucker, J. (2009). The Return of Koro and the Companions: Follow Up Assessment and Analysis. *Sexuality and Disability*, www.springerlink.com.

[7]   Sawa, T., Oae, T., Abiru, T., Ogawa, T. & Takahashi, T. (2004). Role of Imaginary Companion in Promoting the Psychotherapeutic Process. *Psychiatry and ClinicalNeurosciences, 58*, 145-151.

[8]   Allison, R. (2006). *Criminals and Imaginary Companions*. www.disscoaition.com.

[9]   Dierker, L., Davis, K. F. & Sanders, B. (1995). The Imaginary Companion Phenomenon: An Analysis of Personality Correlates and Developmental Antecedents. *Dissociation, 8(4)*, 220-228.

[10]   Dierker, L. (unpublished study) cited in: Holcomb, N. (2007) *Imaginary Companions and Dissociation*. http://faculty.mckendree.edu/scholars/summer2007/holcomb.htm.

[11]   Bonne, O., Cancetti, L., Bachar, E., De-Nour, A. & Shalev, A. (1999). Childhood imaginary companions and mental health in adolescence. *Child Psychiatry and HumanDevelopment, 29*, 277-286.

[12]   Sanders, B. (1992). The Imaginary Companions Experience in Multiple Personality Disorder. *Dissociation, 5(3)*, 160-163.

[13]   Allison, R. (1998). *Differentiating Intended Imaginary Companions from Alter-Personalities*. www.dissociation.

[14]   Patti, J. P., Andiloro, N. & Gavin, M. (2009). Parent/Carer Ratings of Self-Talk Behavior in Children and Adults with Down Syndrome in Canada and the United Kingdom. *Down Syndrome Research and Practice. Volume12*, Issue 3, February.

[15]   Millon, T. (1981). *Disorders of Personality DSM-III: Axis II*. New York: John Wiley & Sons.

[16]   Long, P. W. (2001). *Schizoid Personality Disorder Treatment*. www.mentalhelp.net.

[17]   Southern Poverty Law Center (2003). *The Cop-Shooter Harold Ray Redfeairn*. www.splcenter.org/intel/intelreport/article.com.

[18]   Stone, M. (2009). *The Anatomy of Evil*. New York: Prometheus Books.

[19]   Posters, S. M. (1991). Fantasy Proneness, Amnesia, and the UFO Abduction Phenomena. *Dissociation, 6(1)*, 46-54.

[20]   Merritt, R. D. & Waldo, T. G. (2000). MMPI Code Types and the Fantasy Prone Personality. *Assessment, 7(1)*, 87-95.

[21]   Sanchez-Bernardos, M. L. & Avia, M. D. (2006). The Relationship Between Fantasy Proneness and Schizotypy in Adolescents. *The Journal of Nervous and Mental Disease, 194(6)*, 411-414.

[22]   Waldo, T. G. (1998). *Fantasy Proneness, dissociation, and personality disorders: A psychometric investigation*. http://proquest.uni.com.

[23]   Spiegel, H. & Spiegel, D. (1978) *Trance and Treatment: Clinical Uses of Hypnosis*. New York: Basic Books.

[24]   Lynn, S. J. & Rhue, J. W. (1986). The fantasy-prone person: hypnosis, imagination, and creativity. *Journal of Personality and Social Psychology, 51(2)*, 404-408.

[25] Aleman, A. & deHaan, E. H. F. (2004). Fantasy proneness, mental imagery and reality monitoring. *Personality and IndividualDifferences.*, *36(8)*, 1747-1754.

[26] Ball, L., Wright-Cassidy, K. & Lalonde, C. (1998). *Virtual research on Imgainary Companions: Using the Internet to Gather Adult Retrospective Accounts of Imaginary Companions in Childhood.* Paper presented at the 28th Annual Symposium of the Jean Piaget Society, Chicago, Ill., June 11-13.

In: Personality Traits: Theory, Testing and Influences
Editor: Melissa E. Jordan

ISBN: 978-1-61728-934-7
© 2011 Nova Science Publishers, Inc.

Chapter 4

SCHIZOTYPAL PERSONALITY TRAITS: AUDITORY HALLUCINATION-LIKE EXPERIENCES AND ATYPICAL HEMISPHERIC LATERALIZATION

Tomohisa Asai*, Eriko Sugimoriand YoshihikoTanno
Department of Cognitive and Behavioral Science,
Graduate School of Arts and Sciences, The University of Tokyo, Japan

ABSTRACT

Individual differences in schizotypal personality traits (schizotypy), which might be the predisposition to schizophrenia, have commonly been explored as a means of examining the nature and structure of schizophrenia symptoms. Research on schizotypal personality in the general population may provide a particular opportunity to study the biological and cognitive markers of vulnerability to schizophrenia without the confounding effects of long-term hospitalization, medication, and severe psychotic symptoms (Raine & Lencz, 1995).

A systematic review of general-population surveys indicated that the experiences associated with schizophrenia and related categories, such as paranoid delusional thinking and auditory hallucinations, are observed in an attenuated form in 5–8% of healthy people (Os et al., 2009). These attenuated expressions could be regarded as the behavioral marker of an underlying risk for schizophrenia and related disorders, just as high blood pressure indicates high susceptibility for cardiovascular disease in a dose–response fashion (Os & Kapur, 2009).

Auditory hallucination (AH) refers to the perception that one's own inner speech originates outside the self. Patients with AH make external misattributions of the source of perceived speech. Recent studies have suggested that auditory hallucinations in patients with schizophrenia might occur in the right hemisphere, where they might produce irregular and unpredicted inner speech, which their auditory and sensory feedback processing system does not attribute to themselves.

* Corresponding author: Department of Cognitive and Behavioral Science, Graduate School of Arts and Sciences, University of Tokyo, 3-8-1 Komaba, Meguro-ku, Tokyo 153-8902, JAPAN. Tel: +81-3-5454-6259 Fax: +81-3-5454-6979 as@beck.c.u-tokyo.ac.jp

In the present study, general participants judged self–other attribution in speech subjectively in response to on-line auditory feedback presented through their right, left, and both ears. People with high auditory-hallucination-like experiences made external misattributions more frequently under the right- and left-ear only conditions compared with the both-ears condition. We interpreted this result as suggesting that people with a high degree of proneness to AH might have disorders in both the right and left hemispheric language-related areas: speech perception deficit in the left hemisphere and prediction violation in speech processing in the right hemisphere.

A perspective that situates schizophrenia on a continuum with general personality variations implies that this disorder constitutes a potential risk for everyone and, thus, helps to promote understanding and correct misunderstandings that contribute to prejudice.

INTRODUCTION

Many people with schizophrenia describe a sense of passivity to their experiences, in that their actions, thoughts, or emotions are experienced as created for them by some external agent rather than by their own will. These positive symptoms of schizophrenia are included among Schneider's first-rank symptoms for the diagnosis of schizophrenia (Mellors, 1970; Schneider, 1959). In most cases, the actions carried out when people feel that they are being controlled by alien forces are not discrepant with their intentions (Frith, Blakemore & Wolpert, 2000a, 2000b). In other words, people with schizophrenia have an abnormal sense of agency, that is, of the feeling of causing our own actions (Gallagher, 2000). Phenomena such as delusions of control, auditory hallucinations, and thought insertion may all be caused by an abnormal sense of agency (Frith et al., 2000a; Gallagher, 2004; Lindner, Their, Kircher, Haarmeier & Leube, 2005). For example, one's own speech could seem to be auditory hallucinations (McGuigan, 1966). The activation of Broca's area, which can produce but cannot listen to speech, has been associated with auditory hallucinations (McGuire, Shah & Murray, 1993). Therefore, these people might produce speech but not think that they actually spoke. As a result, they may hear their own voices as the voices of others.

The abnormal sense of agency in schizophrenia has been shown empirically. Some studies reported that when required to make judgments about the origin of hand actions or movements based upon biased feedback (self-action recognition task), people with schizophrenia were more likely than normal controls to misattribute their own actions (Daprati et al., 1997; Franck et al., 2001), which might be interpreted as delusions of control. As well, schizophrenic patients with auditory hallucinations tend to misattribute their own speech (self-speech recognition task: e.g., Johns et al., 1999; 2001). It was recently suggested that psychopathological models of schizophrenia that include the sense of agency may also apply to schizotypal personality traits (schizotypy). Cyhlarova and Claridge (2005) indicated that schizotypal people, identified by questionnaires or semi-structured interviews, might have a predisposition to schizophrenia. Although schizotypal people can have schizophrenic-like experiences, many can live normal lives. The traits of schizophrenia are generally considered to span a continuum. By applying the paradigms of the previous studies (Johns et al., 1999; 2001; Franck et al., 2001; Sato and Yasuda, 2005), Asai and Tanno (2007, 2008) found that people high in schizotypy also tend to have an abnormal sense of agency in their actions including speech both on the explicit and implicit measures (Asai et al., submitted).

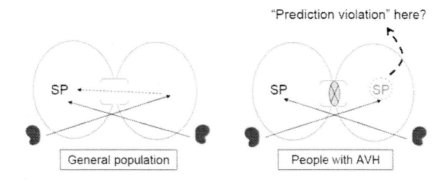

Figure 1. Schematic of speech perception paths of intra- and interhemispheric information transfer in general population and people with AVH (altered from Asai et al., 2009).

Note: SP, area for speech perception; solid lines, direct links between areas; dashed line, transmission through corpus callosum.

Individual differences in schizotypal personality have commonly been explored as a means of examining the nature and structure of schizophrenia symptoms. Research on schizotypal personality in the general population may provide a particular opportunity to study the biological and cognitive markers of vulnerability to schizophrenia without the confounding effects of long-term hospitalization, medication, and severe psychotic symptoms (Raine & Lenez, 1995). Relatives of schizophrenia patients score significantly higher on measures of schizotypal personality, which suggests that within the spectrum of schizophrenia disorders there is a range in which schizotypal traits may be expressed, and that this range is at least partly genetic (Kremen, Faraone, Toomey, Seidman & Tsuang, 1998; Lenzenweger, 2006; Plated & Gallup, 2002).

Recent studies have suggested that in schizophrenia, an abnormal sense of agency might be caused by an abnormal action prediction system in the sense of the agency model (e.g., Frith et al., 2000a; 2000b; Blakemore et al., 2002; Seal, Alemam, & McGuire, 2004; Jones & Fernyhough, 2007. In this model, two information processing pathways are implicated (the action-predictive and the executive pathways), and the discrepancy between the predicted and actual sensations causes the misplaced sense of agency (the sense that"I am the one who generates the action."). With auditory hallucinations and self–other attributions in speech, patients with schizophrenia experiencing auditory hallucinations and those in the general population with high auditory-hallucination proneness do not attribute their own speech to themselves(e.g., Johns et al., 2001; Asai et al., submitted), and furthermore, they do not show sensory cancellationof self-produced speech, indicating that their implicit external misattributionoccurs on a neural level (Ford& Mathalon, 2004, 2005; Ford et al.,2001). How does abnormal prediction lead to the external misattribution in speech? One possibility is that abnormal hemispheric lateralization occurs in patients with schizophrenia.

Atypical cerebral lateralization may represent a risk factor fordeveloping schizophrenia (Crow, 2004). Patients withschizophrenia have shown differences in lateralization as measuredby handedness (Reilly et al.,2001), and schizotypal personality scores are increased among mixed-handed general participants (Annett & Moran, 2006; Somers, Sommer, Boks,

&Kahn, 2008) even in non-western cultures (Asai & Tanno, 2009).These results might implicate a relationship between schizophrenia or schizotypal personalityand non-lateralized cerebral functioning, at least with regardto motor ability. Furthermore, in schizophrenia, non-lateralization has been empirically suggested not only in motor skills, but also in language functions (e.g., Asai et al., 2009; Blyler, Maher, Manschreck,& Fenton, 1997; Hugdahl et al., 2008; Lenzenweger & Maher, 2002; Lohr & Caligiuri, 1997; Ngan et al., 2003; Tabarés-Seisdedos et al.,2003). Moreover, it has been suggested that the essential disconnection between the two hemispheres might equalize the two hemispheres, at least in relation to some motor and language functions (Asai et al., 2009). Patients with schizophrenia might have second language areas in the right hemisphere (e.g., "bicameral mind;" for a review, see Cavanna et al., 2007; Sher, 2000; Olin, 1999). Many studies have shown that the right homologues of the language-related areasare activated during auditory verbal hallucination (e.g., Sommer et al., 2007).

In line with this discussion, in considering the relationship between abnormal hemispheric lateralityin schizophrenia and external misattribution in speech, Sommer et al. (2003) suggested a challenging but important hypothesis that connected the major theories explaining schizophrenia. As mentioned above, the decreased cerebralasymmetry found in schizophreniahas been replicated using severaltechniques. In addition, functionalimaging studies have reporteddecreased lateralization oflanguage-related activation inpatients with schizophrenia comparedwith healthy controls (Sommer et al., 2001).Itcould be hypothesized that innerspeech, originating from rightcerebral homologues of the languageareas, is perceived asan auditory hallucination. In the right hemisphere, "prediction violation" might occur. Self-producedlanguage activity normallyleads to inhibition of the languageperception areas (McGuire et al., 1996) because self-produced sensation can be predicted accurately and filtered (e.g., Blackmore et al., 1998).Whenthis inhibitory mechanism fails,verbal thoughts may not berecognized as originating fromthe self and may beattributed erroneously to an external source.Indeed, inhibition of languageperception might be more proneto failure when language activityis derived from an unusual site(i.e., from contralateral homologueareas in the right hemisphere).These serial hypothesesaresummarizedin Figure 1. Patients with auditory hallucinations might have a second language area in the right hemisphere, but this irregular language processingmay not be predicted, and feedback sensations may not be filtered or attenuated. As a result of this prediction violation, individuals would perceive self-produced (inner) voices as originating externally. To examine this hypothesis, we administered a simple experiment assessing self–other speech attributionfor each ear (hemisphere) in relation to auditory-hallucination proneness in the general population, as with our previous studies (Asai et al., submitted; 2008).

METHODS

Participants

Fifty-one university students (aged 18–22 years, mean = 19.6; 30 men, 21 women) participated in theexperiment and completed the questionnaire. Participants were recruited from a pool of students in an introductory psychology class. We sent an e-mail describing the experiment and the questionnaire, to which interested participantsresponded voluntarily. None had a history of mental disease or hearing difficulties, and none reported anyhearing problems at the time of the experiments. We obtained written informed consent from all participantsbefore conducting the experiment.

Apparatus

The experiment was conducted in a soundproof room. The visual stimuli were created and the experimentsconducted using MATLAB (MathWorks, Natick, MA, USA) and Psychophysics Toolbox (Brainard, 1997; Pelli,1997). Participants spoke into a microphone attached to headphones (SENNHEISER HMD280PRO), and the auditory input was amplified(BEHRINGER MIC200). Auditory input below 1 kHz was filtered at +3 dB, and auditory input above 1kHz was filtered at -3 dB using an equalizer (BEHRINGER FBQ800) in order to obtain a subjectiveapproximation of each participant's own voice (Shuster & Durrant, 2003). Then, the pitch was either unchanged(no distortion) or raised by 1 (moderate) or 4 (severe) semi-tones using aneffecter (ZOOM RFX-2200) and fed back to the subjects through headphones (SENNHEISER HMD280PRO). These parameters were decided in accordance with our previous study (Asai et al., submitted). We predicted that participantswould attribute the fed-back voice to themselves about 50% of the time under the moderate-distortion condition but 0 % of the timeunder the severe condition.

Toreduce any effects of bone conduction and to prevent participants from hearing their own voices directly, pinknoise at 70 dB SPL was generated and mixed into the fed-back voice using a sound mixer (YAMAHA MW10C)(Toyomura et al., 2007). Their fed-back voice was presented to the right, the left,or both ears through headphones using the mixer (pan-pot function) so that the total signal levels were equal under each ear condition. Pink noise was also presented through the bone-conduction headphone (Golden Dance co., Ltd. MGD-701BK) to suppress the bone conduction sound of their speech. For example, under the right-ear condition, while pink noise was presented to both ears through the headphones, participants first read aloud the presented word and then listened as their voice was presented to the right ear only through the headphones. During this time, only pink noise was presented to the left ear. A few signals were sent from the right ear to the right auditory cortex (ipsilateral) through the preponderance of the contralateral auditorypathways (Rosenzweig, 1951). The noise from the contralateral ear was supposed to reduce this ipsilateral pathway relatively (Asai et al., 2009). Participants were briefly trained to speak aloud atapproximately 65–70 dB, as if murmuring. Under these conditions, each participant was able to clearly recognize theirvoice over the noise through the headphones.

Materials

We used 50 four-mora (the prosodic unit in Japanese) words as visual stimuli, selected from an established list ofwords for speech (Amano et al., 2009). This list was controlled for familiarity and phonological balance. We chose 50 of themost familiar words for the present experiment (five for the practice trials and 45 for the test trials).

Procedure

Participants read the presented words aloud into the microphone. They were required to finish reading withinapproximately 400 ms after the words were presented following a countdown from three to one, during which timethey could prepare for speech while viewing the presented words. After they heard the fed-back voice, participants were required to judge intuitively whether the voice they heard was their own, regardless of the feeling of distortion. That is, theycould answer, "This is my own voice," even when they could detect distortion, and vice versa (self-other attribution task). Nine conditions were used (three distortion conditions ×three ear conditions), and participants completed 45 trials (five repetitions for each of the nine conditions). The orders of the 45words and the three conditions were double randomized.

Questionnaire

After the participants finished the experiment, they completed a battery of questionnaires. We assigned a random number to each participant, and data from the questionnaires were crosschecked with experimental data using this randomly assigned number. The battery included the following questionnaires, all of which, except for the AHES-17 and SOAS, have been translated into Japanese and demonstrate good reliability and validity.

1. Auditory hallucination proneness: the Auditory Hallucination Experience Scale 17 (AHES-17, Asai et al., in press) is a brief version of the Auditory Hallucination Experience Scale (AHES, Sugimori, Asai, & Tanno, in press), which has been developed in Japan because a scale for directly measuring auditory hallucination-like experiences was needed. The Launay–Slade Hallucination Scale (LSHS; Launay & Slade, 1981) and its revised version (LSHS-R; Waters, Badcock, & Matbery, 2003) measure hallucination-like experiences, including auditory hallucinations, but do not focus on auditory hallucinations separately. The AHES-17 is a self-report 17-item questionnaire with responses based on a 5-point Likert scale (1–5) measuring the frequency of auditory hallucination-like experiences (e.g., "I heard someone's voice, but nobody was actually around."). The scores for this scale range from 17 to 85. Test–retest reliability ($r = 0.78$, $p < .0001$) and internal reliability ($\alpha = 0.84$) were adequate, and the investigation of criterion-related validity showed that the AHES-17 was highly correlated with scales measuring positive schizotypy, including auditory hallucination proneness (Asai et al., in press).
2. Positive schizotypal personality: the Oxford Schizotypal Personality Scale (STA; Claridge & Broks, 1984; Cyhlarova & Claridge, 2005; Gregory, Claridge, Clark, & Taylor, 2003) is a 37-item true–false self-report questionnaire based on the DSM-III diagnostic criteria for schizotypal personality disorder. It measures schizotypal traits, especially perceptual aberrations that are analogous to positive symptoms, such as auditory hallucinations, thought insertions, and delusions of control.
3. Schizotypal personality traits: the Schizotypal Personality Questionnaire Brief (SPQB: Raine & Benishay, 1995) is a shortened version of the Schizotypal

Personality Questionnaire (SPQ: Raine, 1991). SPQB is a 22-item true–false self-report questionnaire measuring schizotypal personality traits. Though it consists of three subscales: Cognitive–Perceptual (Cog: positive schizotypy), Interpersonal (Int: negative schizotypy), and Disorganization (Dis: disorganized schizotypy), resent studies have suggested that this three factor structures in SPQ(B) might be open to question (e.g., Compton et al., 2009; Fonseca-Pedrero et al., 2009). Furthermore, each subscale score ranges, for example, from 0 to 6 (Dis). So we didn't use these subscale scores and adopted total SPQB score as whole schizotypal personality.

4. Sense of agency: the Sense of Agency Scale (SOAS; Asai et al., in press) is a newly developed prototype measure for assessing the sense of agency. It includes 22 items that are related to an abnormal sense of agency in the general population according to previous experimental studies. The scale consists of three subscales: misattribution of the agent (Mental Self: e.g., "I sometimes turn around feeling as if someone called my name in a crowd."), uncontrollability of one's own body (Physical Self: e.g., "I sometimes feel I cannot move my body as I want."), and self-assertiveness in social situations (Social Self: e.g., "I sometimes feel my behavior has some effect on society."). Responses are based on a 4-point Likert scale. Test–retest reliability ($r = 0.73$, $p < .0001$) and internal reliability ($\alpha = 0.77$) were adequate.

5. Depression: the Self-rating Depression Scale (SDS; Zung, 1965) is a well-known self-report questionnaire comprised of 20 items; responses are based on a 4-point Likert scale measuring depressive tendencies.

6. Anxiety: the Trait Anxiety Inventory (STAI-T; Spielberger, Gorsuch, & Lushene, 1970) is a well-known self-report questionnaire consisting of 20 items; responses are based on a 4-point Likert scale measuring anxiety traits.

7. Handedness: the H.N. Handedness Scale (HNHS; Hatta & Kawakami, 1995; Hatta & Nakatsuka, 1975) is a revised version of the Edinburgh Inventory (Oldfield, 1971) for use with Japanese participants. Revisions were necessary because cultural differences render the original Edinburgh Inventory inappropriate for Japanese participants. The scale is often used in Japan to measure or control for handedness (e.g., Ogawa, Inui, & Sugio, 2006). Participants respond to this scale by indicating whether they use their right, left, or either hand for 10 common actions: handling an eraser; striking a match; thumb tacking; hammering; brushing their teeth; throwing; and using a pair of scissors, a knife, a screwdriver, and a shaver or lipstick. This scale ranges from -10 to +10; a "right" response is scored as +1, a "left" response is scored as -1 and a response of "either" is scored as zero.

Higher scores for all questionnaires indicate a stronger tendency on the relevant dimension. SDS and STAI were used as control measures; that is, we predicted that these scales would not be related to the present study although they might be related to schizotypal personality traits, especially to auditory hallucination proneness or abnormal experiences relating to the sense of agency (that is, "Mental Self").

RESULTS

At least two methods are available to examine the relationship between questionnaire scores and experimentalperformances: linear relationships between scores and performance (e.g., Asai et al., 2008) and comparisonsbetween groups according to questionnaire scores (e.g., Asai & Tanno, 2007). Multiple rather than single measures are most reliable (e.g., Asai et al., 2009). To examinethe relationship between auditory-hallucination proneness and self-attribution, first we selected theparticipants scoring highest (top third; 17 participants) and lowest (bottom third; 17 participants) on the AHES (see Table 1 for demographic data),in accordance with previous studies. Later, we examined the relationships of our data to other questionnaires andother methods (e.g., linear relationships) to examine the individual differences.

Figures 2 and 3 show the relationship between self-attribution in speech and ear condition in each group, as in Asai & Tanno's (2008) study. Repeated-measures analysis of variance (ANOVA) with pitchdistortion and the ear condition as the within-subject variables showed that only the main effect of pitch distortionwas statistically significant ($F(2, 32) = 39.6$, $p < .001$) in the low-AHES group (Figure2). In contrast, in the high AHESgroup, the main effects of pitch distortion ($F(2, 32) = 152.5$, $p < .001$) and of ear condition ($F(2, 32) = 4.01$, $p < .05$) were significant (Figure 3). Regarding the main effects of ear condition, multiple comparisonsusing Ryan's method (i.e., R-E-G-W's F test) for post-hoc analysis revealed that scores under the both-ears condition were significantly higher than under either one-ear condition (right or left) ($p < .05$). These results suggest a relationship between the AHES, self-attribution in speech, and ear (hemisphere) conditions. In the low AHES group, there was no difference between the ear conditions. In contrast, in the high AHES group, less feedback was attributed to participants' own voice under the one-ear conditions (right or left) than under the both-ears condition, regardless of the pitch distortion. To confirm these results, we then examined the linear relationship among these variables.

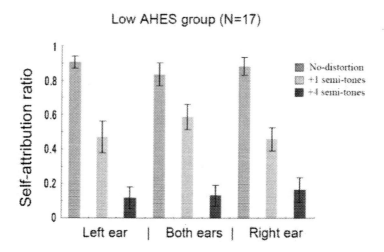

Figure 2. Schematic of speech perception paths of intra- and interhemispheric information transfer in general population and people with AVH (altered from Asai et al., 2009).

Note: SP, area for speech perception; solid lines, direct links between areas; dashed line, transmission through corpus callosum.

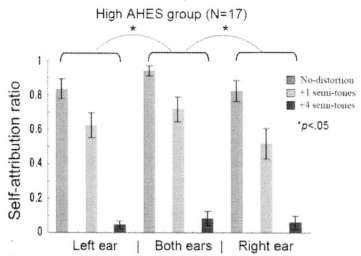

Figure 3. Schematic of speech perception paths of intra- and interhemispheric information transfer in general population and people with AVH (altered from Asai et al., 2009).

Note: SP, area for speech perception; solid lines, direct links between areas; dashed line, transmission through corpus callosum.

We calculated the two laterality indices under the both-ears conditions as baseline scores in accordance with the results of the group comparisons. The laterality index for the right ear (LIR) was calculated as follows: (self-attribution rate under the right-ear condition) − (self-attribution rate under the both-ears condition). Finally, these values were averaged across pitch distortion conditions. The laterality index for the left ear (LIL) was calculated in the same way. Negative LIR and LIL values meant that the participant attributed the fed-back voice to him or herself less under the one-ear condition (right or left) than under the both-ears condition. Table 2 shows the Pearson's correlation matrix for these laterality indexes and questionnaire scores. Not surprisingly, AHES and LIR or LIL showed a significant negative correlation, confirming the results of the group comparison analysis. Furthermore, this correlation matrix revealed that other schizotypal traits, including positive or whole schizotypy, and other mental traits, including anxiety and depression, might not related to the lateralized self-attribution pattern. Auditory-hallucination proneness might be specific to this phenomenon. On the sense of agency scale, the "Mental Self (misattribution of the agent)" subscale was significantly correlated with LIL. Although the self–other attribution task is supposed to relate to this factor, unlike AHES, "Mental Self" was only correlated with LIL. We had hypothesized that people with high AHES would attribute the fed-back voice to themselves less under the left-ear (right hemisphere) condition than under either the both-ears or the right-ear condition. The results, however, suggest that under the right-ear condition, they also attributed the speech to themselves less. Yet, according to the results of SOAS, external misattribution of the agent should be related to the left ear (right hemisphere) condition only, as we hypothesized above. These findings are discussed below.

Table 1. The demographical data (*Mean* and *Standard Deviation*) between the low and the high AHES groups.

	N (M/F)	Age	HNHS [left-hander]	AHES	STA	SPQB	SOAS Total	Mental	Physical	Social	SDS	STAI
Low AHES	17 (11/6)	19.6 (1.0)	8.3(1.7) [0]	42.4 (4.4)	6.9 (4.4)	5.9 (2.4)	39.5 (6.0)	13.5 (3.3)	15.6 (2.9)	10.4 (1.8)	39.2 (7.7)	44.9 (9.8)
High AHES	17 (8/9)	20.0 (1.0)	7.3(4.5) [1]	63.3 (4.2)	15.0 (4.8)	11.1 (3.3)	46.8 (5.0)	18.2 (2.8)	18.8 (1.9)	9.8 (2.2)	44.9 (8.6)	50.1 (8.5)
Significance				**	**	**	**	**	**		*	

$$*p<.05, **p<.01$$

Note: The significances were revealed by χ^2 tests for sex ratio and the number of left-handers (HNHS scores < -4), and MANOVA for Age-STAI. HNHS=Hatta and Nakatsuka Handedness Scale. AHES=Auditory Hallucination Experience Scale. STA=Schizotypal personality scale. SPQB=Schizotypal Personality Questionnaire Brief. SOAS=Sense Of Agency Scale. SDS= Self-rating Depression Scale. STAI= Trait anxiety inventory.

Table 2

Inter-correlations between the experimental laterality indexes and questionnaire scores.

	AHES	STA	SPQB	SOAS	Mental	Physical	Social	SDS	STAI
LIR	-.29*	-.04	-.11	-.03	-.21	.01	.20	-.01	-.03
LIL	-.25*	-.15	-.23	-.14	-.31*	.01	.08	-.08	.04

$$*p<.05$$

Note: N = 51. Values are Pearson's correlation coefficients. Correlations were tested for statistical significance using a one-tailed procedure based on a directional a priori hypothesis. LIR= (right ear)-(both ears). LIL=(left ear)-(both ears).

DISCUSSION

The objective in the present study was to examine self–other speech attribution in the right hemisphere in people with high proneness to auditory hallucination. First, in people with low AH, laterality of self–other speech attribution was not confirmed. They attributed the feedback voice to themselves with equal frequency regardless of ear condition. Fu et al. (2006) showed the relationship between bilateral temporal lobes and on-line self–other speech attribution: the speech information is sent to left language areas first and might then be returned to the bilateral temporal lobes. No effect of ear condition might indicate smooth transmission of these signals through the corpus callosum. In general, a laterality effect of ear condition in the general population would be observed only under specific experimental conditions, namely classic dichotic listening, in which participants hear a different auditory stimulusin each ear (e.g., Hugdahl et al., 2007) or a reaction time paradigm (e.g., Asai et al., 2009), because of the connection between the two hemispheres through the corpus callosum. Considering that the present study presented one speech stimulus and required participants to answer at their own pace, the absence of laterality effect in people with low AH was unsurprising.

On the other hand, the effect of ear condition appears in people with high AH. Because previous studies have suggested that external misattribution in speech (i.e., auditory hallucination) might occur in the right hemisphere (e.g., Sommer et al., 2007), we had hypothesized that, if an inter-hemispherical disconnection exists (e.g., Lohr et al., 2006)), under the left-ear condition, people with high AH would be more likelyto attributethe fed-back voice to an externalsource (i.e., to feel it is "the other's voice") than under the right-ear or both-ears conditions. Compared with the both-ears condition, under the left-ear condition, participants with high AH did misattribute the fed-back voice to an external source, as expected. According to the hypothesis of Sommer et al. (2003), speech processing may occur in the right hemisphere (cerebral homologues of the languageareas) in subjects with AH. This irregular language processing, however, cannot be predicted, and the feedback sensationcannot be filtered or attenuated (e.g., Ford et al., 2004). As a result of this prediction violation, subjects would hear the self-produced (inner) voices as the voices of others. The present study supports this view, providing the first data from a behavioral experiment in line with this challenging hypothesis, but from the viewpoint of the difference between the both-ears and left-ear conditions.

However, contrary to our expectation, the right-ear condition showed results similar to those for the left-ear condition. People with high AH made an equally high number of external misattributions under the right-ear conditioncompared with the both-ears condition. The"Mental Self" subscale in SOAS refers to the tendency for misattribution of the agent, including auditory hallucination. Participants with high Mental Self scores may also externally misattribute information reaching the right hemisphere. Given that AHES was highly correlated with Mental Self (r=.53, p<.001), this result seems inevitable. Under the right-ear condition, however, Mental Self was not correlated with LIR, indicating that the difference between the right-ear and both-ears condition may not have been the result of misattribution of the agent, but may have occurred for some other reason. Indeed, many studies have suggested that the language-related areas in the left hemisphere of patients with AH might be disordered.

Patients with AH might have a deficit in speech perception related to the left temporal lobe, regardless of whether the speech originates with the self or another (e.g., Hugdahl et al., 2007). In addition, Mechelli et al. (2007) suggested that when patients with AH appraisedtheir own speechafter the fact, they show impaired functional integration between the left superior temporal and anterior cingulate cortex. In a postmortem study, Allen et al. (2007) also showed that the misidentification of self-generated speech in patients with AH was associated with functional abnormalities in the anterior cingulate and left temporal cortex. These results suggested that patients with AH might have an abnormality in the left temporal cortex that leaves them deficient in a self-voice representation.This creates a disorder in speech perception when they identify their retrospectively rather than online. Therefore, it could be that not the on-line "prediction violation" but other reasons,perhaps including disorders of speech perception, explain the difference between the right-ear and both-ears condition. Further research should examine this possibility using brain-imaging techniques.

When taken together, our findings indicate that people with AH might have disorders in both the right and left language-related areas: speech perception deficit in the left hemisphere and prediction violation in speech processing in the right hemisphere. Indeed, Woodruff et al. (1997) have suggested that AH is associated with a reduced left and increased right temporal cortical response to auditory perception of speech. Patients with AH process speech stimuli less well in the left hemisphere but better in the right hemisphere. However, if speech stimuli are produced by the patients themselves, the speech being processed in the right hemisphere might be perceived as another's voice. Further research should focus on both right and left hemisphere language processing and self-other attribution in speech. Although the present study showed the effect of laterality on self–other speech attribution for the first time by behavioral experiment, some unavoidable limitations should be noted. Because we discussed brain abnormalities from behavioral data alone, speculative interpretations were inevitable. Although the dichotic listening paradigm (e.g., Hugdahl et al., 2008), which we applied in the present study, has been developed to provide non-invasive brain measurements, particularly regarding neural pathways, a follow-up brain imaging study should provide further insight on this topic. We could present a basic experimental methodology for the further research.

REFERENCES

Allen, P., Amaro, E., Fu, C.H., Williams, S.C., Brammer, M.J., Johns, L.C. & McGuire, P.K. (2007). Neural correlates of the misattribution of speech in schizophrenia. *British Journal of Psychiatry, 190*, 162-169.

Amano, S., Sakamoto, S., Kondo, T. & Suzuki, Y. (2009). Development of familiarity-controlled word lists2003 (FW03) to assess spoken-word intelligibility in *Japanese. Speech Communication, 51*, 76-82.

Annett, M. & Moran, P. (2006). Schizotypy is increased in mixed-handers, especially right-handed writers who use the left hand for primary actions. *Schizophrenia Research, 81*, 239-246.

Asai, T. & Tanno, Y. (2007).The relationship between the sense of self-agency and schizotypal personality traits.*Journal of Motor Behavior, 39*, 162-168.

Asai, T. & Tanno, Y. (2008). Highly schizotypal students have a weaker sense of self-agency. *Psychiatry and Clinical Neurosciences, 62*, 115-119.

Asai, T. & Tanno, Y. (2009). Schizotypy and handedness in Japanese participants revisited. *Laterality, 14*, 86-94.

Asai, T., Takano, K., Sugimori, E. & Tanno, Y. (in press). Development of the sense of agency scale and its factor structure.*The Japanese Journal of Psychology*. (in Japanese).

Bentler, P. M. & Bonnet, D. G. (1980). Significance tests and goodness of fit in the analysis of covariance structures.*Psychological Bulletin, 107*, 238-246.

Blakemore, S. J., Wolpert, D. M. & Frith, C. D. (1998).Central cancellation of self-produced tickle sensation.*Nature Neuroscience, 1*, 635-640.

Blakemore, S. J., Wolpert, D. M. & Frith, C. D. (1998).Central cancellation of self-produced tickle sensation.*Nature Neuroscience*, *1*, 635-640.

Blyler, C. R., Maher, B. A., Manschreck, T. C. & Fenton, W. S. (1997). Line drawing as a possible measure of lateralized motor performance in schizophrenia. *Schizophrenia Research*, *26*, 15-23.

Brainard, D. H. (1997).The psychophysics toolbox.*Spatial Vision*, *10*, 433-436.

Browne, M. W. & Cudeck, R. (1993). Alternative ways of assessing model fit. In: K. A. Bollen, & J. S. Long, (Eds.) *Testing Structural Equation Models*. Beverley Hills, CA: Sage, 132-162

Cavanna, A. E., Trimble, M., Cinti, F. & Monaco, F. (2007). The "bicameral mind" 30 years on: a critical reappraisal of Julian Jaynes' hypothesis. *Functional Neurology*, *22*, 11-15.

Cavanna, A. E., Trimble, M., Cinti, F. & Monaco, F. (2007). The "bicameral mind" 30 years on: a critical reappraisal of Julian Jaynes' hypothesis. *Functional Neurology*, *22*, 11-15.

Chapman, J. P., Chapman, L. J. & Allen, J. J. (1987).The measurement of foot preference.*Neuropsychologia*, *25*, 579-584.

Claridge, G. & Broks, P. (1984). Schizotypy and hemisphere function: I. Theoretical considerations and themeasurement of schizotypy. *Personality and Individual Differences*, *5*, 643-670.

Compton, M. T., Goulding, S. M., Bakeman, R. & McClure-Tone, E. B. (2009).Confirmation of a four-factor structure of the Schizotypal Personality Questionnaire among undergraduate students.*Schizophrenia Research*, *111*, 46-52.

Crow, T. J. (2004). Cerebral asymmetry and the lateralization of language: core deficits in schizophrenia as pointers to the gene. *Current Opinion in Psychiatry*, *17*, 97-106.

Cyhlarova, E. & Claridge, G. (2005).Development of a version of the Schizotypy Traits Questionnaire (STA) for screening children.*Schizophrenia Research*, *80*, 253-261.

Daprati, E., Franck, N., Georgieff, N., Proust, J., Pacherie, E., Dalery, J. & Jeannerod, M. (1997).Looking for the agent: An investigation into consciousness of action and self-consciousness in schizophrenic patients.*Cognition*, *65*, 71-86.

Fonseca-Pedrero, E., Paíno-Piñeiro, M., Lemos-Giráldez, S., Villazón-García, U. & Muñiz, J. (2009).Validation of the Schizotypal Personality Questionnaire-Brief Form in adolescents.*Schizophrenia Research*, *111*, 53-60.

Ford, J. M. & Mathalon, D. H. (2004).Electrophysiological evidence of corollary discharge dysfunction inschizophrenia during talking and thinking.*Journal of PsychiatricResearch*, *38*, 37-46.

Ford, J. M. & Mathalon, D. H. (2005). Corollary discharge dysfunction in schizophrenia: Can it explainauditory hallucination? *International Journal of Psychophysiology*, *58*, 179-189.

Ford, J. M., Mathalon, D. H., Heinks, T., Kalba, S., Faustman, W. O. & Roth, W. T. (2001).Neurophysiologicalevidence of corollary discharge dysfunction in schizophrenia.*American Journal of Psychiatry*, *158*,2069-2071.

Franck, N., Farrer, C., Georgieff, N., Marie-Cardine, M., Dalery, J., d'Amato, T. & Jeannerod, M. (2001).Defective recognition of one's own actions in patients with schizophrenia.*American Journal of Psychiatry*, *158*, 454-459.

Frith, C. (2005). The neural basis of hallucinations and delusions.*Comptes Rendus Biologies*, *328*, 169-175.

Frith, C. D., Blakemore, S. J. & Wolpert, D. M. (2000a). Explaining the symptoms of schizophrenia:Abnormalities in the awareness of action.*Brain Research Reviews*, *31*, 357-363.

Frith, C. D., Blakemore, S. J. & Wolpert, D. M. (2000b). Abnormalities in the awareness and control of action.Philosophical Transactions of the Royal Societyof London: *Biological Sciences*, *355*, 1771-1788.

Fu, C. H., Vythelingum, G. N., Brammer, M. J., Williams, S. C., Amaro, E., Jr, Andrew, C. M., Yágüez, L., van Haren, N. E., Matsumoto, K. & McGuire, P. K. (2006). An fMRI study of verbal self-monitoring: neural correlates of auditory verbal feedback. *Cereb Cortex*,*16*, 969-77.

Gallagher, S. (2000). Philosophical conceptions of the self: Implications for cognitive science. *Trends in Cognitive Science*, *4*, 14-21.

Gallagher, S. (2004). Neurocognitive models of schizophrenia: a neurophenomenological critique. *Psychopathology*, *37*, 8-19.

Gregory, A. M., Claridge, G., Clark, K. & Taylor, P. D. (2003). Handedness and schizotypy in a Japanese sample: an association masked by cultural effects on hand usage. *Schizophrenia Research*, *65*, 139-145.

Hatta, T. & Kawakami, A. (1995). Patterns of handedness in modern Japanese: a cohort effect shown by re-administration of the H.N. Handedness Inventory after 20 years. Canadian *Journal of Experimental Psychology*, *49*, 505-512.

Hatta, T. & Nakatsuka, Z. (1975).Handedness inventory. In: Ohno, D. (Ed.), Papers on Celebrating the 63rd Birthday of Prof. Ohnishi. Osaka City University, Osaka, Japan, 224-245.

Hu, Li-tze, & Bentler, P. M. (1999). Cutoff criteria for fit indexes in covariance structure analysis: Conventional criteria versus new alternatives. *Structural Equation Modeling*, *6*, 1-55.

Hugdahl, K., Løberg, E. M., Jørgensen, H. A., Lundervold, A., Lund, A., Green, M. F. & Rund, B. (2008). Left hemisphere lateralisation of auditory hallucinations in schizophrenia: a dichotic listening study. *Cognitive Neuropsychiatry*, *13*, 166-179.

Hugdahl, K., Løberg, E. M., Specht, K., Steen, V. M., van Wageningen, H. & Jørgensen, H. A. (2007). Auditory hallucinations in schizophrenia: the role of cognitive, brain structural and genetic disturbances in the left temporal lobe. *Frontiers in Human Neuroscience*,*1*, 6.

Johns, L. C. & McGuire, P. K. (1999).Verbal self-monitoring and auditory hallucinations in schizophrenia.*Lancet*, *353*, 469-470.

Johns, L. C., Rossell, S., Frith, C., Ahmad, F., Hemsley, D., Kuipers, E. & McGuire, P. K. (2001).Verbal self-monitoring and auditory verbal hallucinations in patients with schizophrenia.*Psychological Medicine*, *31*, 705-715.

Kremen, W. S., Faraone, S. V., Toomey, R., Seidman, L. J. & Tsuang, M. T. (1998). Sex differences in self-reported schizotypal traitsin relatives of schizophrenic probands. *Schizophrenia Research*, *34*, 27-37.

Launay, B. & Slade, P. D. (1981).The measurement of hallucinatory predisposition in male and female prisoners.*Personality and Individual Differences*, *2*, 221-234.

Lenzenweger, M. F. & Maher, B. A. (2002). Psychometric schizotypy and motor performance.*Journal of Abnormal Psychology*, *111*, 546-55.

Lenzenweger, M. F. (2006). Schizotaxia, schizotypy, and schizophrenia: Paul E. Meehl's blueprint for the experimental psychopathology and genetics of schizophrenia. *Journal of Abnormal Psychology*, *115*, 195-200.

Levy, J. (1974).Psychobiological implications of bilateral asymmetry.In S. J. Dimond, & G. Beaumont, (Eds.).*Hemispheric function in the human brain.* London: Elek Science.

Lindner, A., Their, P., Kircher, T. T. J., Haarmeier, T. & Leube, D. T. (2005). Disorders of agency in schizophrenia correlate with an inability to compensate for the sensory consequences of actions. *Current Biology*, *15*, 1119-1124.

Lohr, J. B. & Caligiuri, M. P. (1997). Lateralized hemispheric dysfunction in the major psychotic disorders: historical perspectives and findings from a study of motor asymmetry in older patients.*Schizophrenia Research*, *27*, 191-198.

McGuigan, F. J. (1966). Covert oral behaviour and auditory hallucinations.*Psychiatry*, *158*, 307-316.

McGuire, P. K., Shah, G. M. & Murray, R. M. (1993).Increased blood flow in Broca's area during auditory hallucinations in schizophrenia.*Lancet*, *342*, 703-706.

McGuire, P. K., Silbersweig, D. A., Wright, I., Murray, R. M., Frackowiak, R. S. & Frith, C. D. (1996). The neural correlates of inner speech and auditory verbal imagery in schizophrenia: relationship to auditory verbal hallucinations. *British Journal of Psychiatry*,*169*,148-159.

McGuire, P. K., Silbersweig, D. A., Wright, I., Murray, R. M., Frackowiak, R. S. & Frith, C. D. (1996). The neural correlates of inner speech and auditory verbal imagery in schizophrenia: relationship to auditory verbal hallucinations. *British Journal of Psychiatry*, *169*, 148-159.

Mechelli, A., Allen, P., Amaro, E. Jr, Fu, C. H., Williams, S. C., Brammer, M. J., Johns, L. C. & McGuire, P. K. (2007). Misattribution of speech and impaired connectivity in patients with auditory verbal hallucinations.*Human Brain Mapping*, *28*, 1213-22.

Mellors, C. S. (1970). First rank symptoms of schizophrenia.*British Journal of Psychiatry*, *117*, 15-23.

Ngan, E. T., Vouloumanos, A., Cairo, T. A., Laurens, K. R., Bates, A. T., Anderson, C. M., Werker, J. F. & Liddle, P. F. (2003).Abnormal processing of speech during oddball target detection in schizophrenia.*Neuroimage*, *20*, 889-897.

Ogawa, K, & Inui, T. (2007).Lateralization of the posterior parietal cortex for internal monitoring of self- versus externally generated movements.*Journal of Cognitive Neuroscience*, *19*, 1827-1835.

Oldfield, R. C. (1971). The assessment and analysis of handedness: the Edinburgh Inventory. *Neuropsychologia*, *9*, 97-113.

Olin, R. (1999). Auditory hallucinations and the bicameral mind.*Lancet*, *354*, 166.

Pelli, D. G. (1997). The video toolbox software for visual psychophysics: Transforming numbers into movies.*SpatialVision*, *10*, 437-442.

Plated, S. M. & Gallup Jr., G. G. (2002). Self-face recognition is affected by schizotypal personality traits. *SchizophreniaResearch*, *57*, 81-85.

Raine, A. & Benishay, D. (1995). The SPQ-B: A brief screening instrument for schizotypal personality disorder. *Journal of Personality Disorder*, *9*, 346-355.

Raine, A. & Lencz, T. (1995).Conceptual and theoretical issues in schizotypal personality research. In: A., Raine, T. Lencz, & A. Mednick, (Eds.), Schizotypal personality (3-15). New York: Cambridge University Press.

Raine, A. (1991). The SPQ: A scale for the assessment of schizotypal personality based on DSM-III-R criteria.*Schizophrenia Bulletin*, *17*, 555-564.

Reilly, J. L., Murphy, P. T., Byrne, M., Larkin, C., Gill, M., O'Callaghan, E. & Lane, A. (2001). Dermatoglyphic fluctuating asymmetry and atypical handedness in schizophrenia.*Schizophrenia Research*, *50*, 159-168.

Rosenzweig, M. R. (1951). Representations of the two ears at the auditory cortex. American *Journal ofPhysiology*, *167*, 147-214.

Sato, A. & Yasuda, A. (2005). Illusion of self-agency: Discrepancy between the predicted and actual sensory consequences of actions modulates the sense of self-agency, but not the sense of self-ownership. *Cognition*, *94*, 241-255

Schneider, K. (1959). *Clinical psychopathology*. New York: Grune & Stratton.

Sher, L. (2000).Neuroimaging, auditory hallucinations, and the bicameral mind.*Journal of Psychiatry Neuroscience*, *25*, 239-240.

Sher, L. (2000).Neuroimaging, auditory hallucinations, and the bicameral mind.*Journal ofPsychiatry Neuroscience*, *25*, 239-240.

Shuster, L. I. & Durrant, J. D. (2003).Toward a better understanding of the perception of self-produced speech.*Journal of CommunicationDisorders*, *36*, 1-11.

Somers, M., Sommer, I. E., Boks, M. P. & Kahn, R. S. (2009). Hand-preference and population schizotypy: A meta-analysis. *Schizophrenia Research*, *108*, 25-32

Sommer, I. E. C., Diederen, K. M. J., Blom, J. D., Willems, A., Kushan, L., Slotema, K., Boks, M. P. M., Daalman, K., Hoek, H. W., Neggers, S. F. W. & Kahn, R. S. (2008). Auditory Verbal Hallucinations Predominantely Activate the Right Inferior Frontal Area. *Brain*, *131*, 3169-3177

Sommer, I. E. C., Ramsey, N. F. & Kahn, R. S. (2001). Lateralization in schizophrenia: an fMRI study. *Schizophrenia Research*,*52*, 57-67.

Sommer, I. E. C., Slotema, C. W., de Weijer, A. D., Blom, J., Daalman, K., Neggers, S., Somers, M., Hoek, H., Aleman, A. & Kahn, R. (2007). Can fMRI-guidanceImprove the Efficacy of rTMS Treatment for Auditory Verbal Hallucinations? *Schizophrenia Research*, *93*, 406-408

Sommer, I. E., Aleman, A. & Kahn, R. S. (2003). Left with the voices or hearing right? Lateralization of auditory verbal hallucinations in schizophrenia.*Journal of PsychiatryNeuroscience*, *28*, 217-218.

Sommer, I. E., Aleman, A. & Kahn, R. S. (2003). Left with the voices or hearing right? Lateralization of auditory verbal hallucinations in schizophrenia.*Journal of Psychiatry Neuroscience*, *28*, 217-218.

Sommer, I., Ramsay, N., Kahn, R., Aleman, A. & Bouma, A. (2001). Handedness, language lateralisation and anatomical asymmetry in schizophrenia: meta-analysis. *British Journal ofPsychiatry*, *178*, 344-351.

Spielberger, C. D., Gorsuch, R. L. & Lushene, R. E. (1970). In cursive: STAI. Manual for the state-trait anxietyinventory. Palo Alto, CA: *Consulting Psychologist*.

Sugimori, E., Asai, T. & Yoshihiko, T. (in press). Reliability and validity of the Auditory Hallucination-like Experience Scale. *The Japanese Journal ofPsychology*. (in Japanese)

Tabarés-Seisdedos, R., Salazar-Fraile, J., Selva-Vera, G., Balanzá-Martinez, V., Ballester-Sánchez, F., Cózar-Santiago, R., Leal-Cercós, C. & Gómez-Beneyto, M. (2003). Abnormal motor asymmetry only during bimanual movement in schizophrenic patients compared with healthy subjects. *Schizophrenia Research*, *61*, 245-253.

Toyomura, A., Koyama, S., Miyamaoto, T., Terao, A., Omori, T., Murohashi, H. & Kuriki, S. (2007). Neuralcorrelates of auditory feedback control in human. *Neuroscience, 146,* 499-503.

Waters, F. A. V. , Badcock, J. C. & Maybery, M .T. (2003). Revision of the factor structure of the Launay –Slade Hallucination Scale LSHS-R.*Personality and Individual Differences, 35,* 1351-1357.

Woodruff, P. W. R., Wright, I. C., Bullmore, E. T., Brammer, M., Howard, R. J., Williams, S. C. R., Shapleske, J., Rossell, S., David, A. S., McGuire, P. K. & Murray, R. M. (1997). Auditory Hallucinations and the Temporal Cortical Response to Speech in Schizophrenia: A Functional Magnetic Resonance Imaging Study. *American Journal of Psychiatry, 154,* 1676-1682.

Zung, W. (1965).A self-rating depression scale.*Archives of General Psychiatry, 12,* 63-70.

In: Personality Traits: Theory, Testing and Influences
Editors: Melissa E. Jordan

ISBN: 978-1-61728-934-7
©2011 Nova Science Publishers, Inc.

Chapter 5

GENETICS OF PERSONALITITY DISORDERS

Gonzalo Haro[1], Ernesto Tarragón[2], César Mateu[3], Ana Benito[3] and Cecilio Álamo[5]

[1]Patología Dual Grave. Hospital Provincial de Castellón. Comunidad Valenciana, España
[2]Departamento de Psicobiología. Universidad Jaume I de Castellón, España
[3]Grupo TXP de Investigación. Comunidad Valenciana, España
[4]Catedrático de Farmacología. Comunidad de Madrid, España

1. INTRODUCTION

Talking about addiction genetics and its most common comorbid disorders, Personality Disorders (PD), one of the concepts that first should be clarified is the importance of the studies logic chronology on psychiatric genetics. Thus, it should be noted that for molecular genetic techniques to be justified in any study, a substantial role of genetics in the etiology of this disorder has to be demonstrated first by epidemiological data. Genetic epidemiological studies which here is referred to are mainly three: family, twin and adoption studies. So, if these studies do not raise doubts about whether or not one disorder is inherited, it is better to focus on the environmental causes and drop molecular studies determined to "grab" some related gene. Once the genetic implication has been demonstrated in some disorder's etiology, it is time to mathematical and molecular genetic studies. By means of these studies, detecting which gene or combination of genes causes the disorder is a matter of try. This is not easy, though, considering that only 2% of the 3 billion base pairs of DNA are genes.

Once in the field of molecular genetics, difficulties manifest. The first genes isolated and characterized are either Mendelian or monogenic characters, hereditary diseases or somatic malignancies mostly, in which there is a major gene involved. The Mendelian scheme fulfills the "one gene / one disease" rule. Thus, one single-locus mutations cause one specific disease, e.g. sickle cell anemia, cystic fibrosis, phenylketonuria and Huntington's disease. Non-Mendelian characters either depend on a small number of loci (oligogenic characters) or gene plots (polygenes), with each of them showing a small effect with an environmental factor varied contribution. All these possibilities are included within the term multifactorial character.

However, unlike one might suspect, monogenic characters are not exempt of complexity. Many of them either have "reduced penetrance", meaning that not all individuals with the conferring disease genotype develop it; "variable expression", meaning that there is a huge variability on disease's severity; or "pleiotropy", when the gene has more than a single appreciable effect on the body. On the other hand, different genes may promote a single phenotype in different families. In this case is called "genetic" or "locus heterogeneity". Even more, different mutations in the same gene can cause distinguishable clinical diseases. Hence, there is an enormous genetic complexity, even through simple Mendelian characters, which are only governed by one gene. This suggests that there is a few purely Mendelian biological characters, and that may be extend to purely polygenic also.

Studies on the role of genetic factors in biopsychosocial diseases in humans have to confront many problems. Among them, the polygenic and multifactorial nature of inheritance stands out by itself, so that multiple genes and environmental factors interact in each subject in very different ways and degrees.

2. ABOUT PERSONALITY AND ITS DISORDERS

The importance of talking about the genetics of PD lays on the fact that mental illness is most often presented comorbidly in patients with addictive disorders, as recently demonstrated by Haro et al (2004). There are a variety of definitions that try to define the concept "personality", reflecting the diversity of "personality theory" advocated by the multiple schools of psychology. Since the beginning of civilization, mankind has been preoccupied with understanding itself. In 372 BC, Theophrastus proposed 30 different types of human beings, and Hippocrates developed his theory of humors years later, whereby for each body fluid a temperament-regulating affective disposition was corresponded, resulting a person's temperament in four types of personalities: the *blood* (optimistic and outgoing), the *melancholic* (gloomy, sad) the *phlegmatic* (impassive) and *angry* (bitter and irritable). Many were the traditional constitutionalists who proposed different types of personality trait based on this concept (Galen, Jung, Kretschmer, Sheldon, etc).

Personality has been studied from different approaches. Dimensional approach for instance, considers personality as a continuum from normal to pathological (speak of quantitative differences), whereas the categorical perspective (which include psychiatric classifications such as DSM or ICD) provides taxonomies on what is pathological (qualitative differences between normal and abnormal). The dimensional perspective has the advantage of providing a more realistic view of psychopathology, allowing a more accurately fit to the functioning of the human personality. Still, the attempt to find breakpoints in which split normality from pathologic it is a problem. For its part, the categorical approach serves a useful purpose to clinicians, who must make rapid diagnoses with relatively large numbers of patients in a short space of time.

A fairly complete and current definition of personality is that from Millon's, who considers personality as *"a complex pattern of deeply embedded psychological characteristics, mostly unconscious and difficult to change, and are expressed automatically in almost all areas of individual functioning. These intrinsic and general features arise from a complicated matrix of biological determinants and learning, and ultimately comprise the idiosyncratic pattern of perceiving, feeling, thinking, coping and behaving of an individual".*

For DSM-IV-TR, a PD is a *"permanent and inflexible pattern of inner experience and behavior that deviates markedly from the expectations of the individual's culture, has its onset in adolescence or early adulthood, is stable over time and involves discomfort or injury to the subject".*

Latest revision of the American Psychiatric Association DSM groups PD into three broad groups of generic features, including a total of 10 diagnostic categories established on the basis of strict criteria:

1. **Group A.** Characterized by its inability to establish and maintain relationships because of their marked introversion or lack of harmony and warmth, and a striking difficulty learning elementary social skills. They are considered odd or eccentric personalities. Includes single individuals who lack a sense of humor and feelings of affiliation. They are usually cold, expressionless, and vulnerable to mental pathology. Includes 3 categories:

    Schizoid PD: mainly characterized by a pervasive pattern of detachment from social relationships and restricted emotional expression in interpersonal settings. Individuals are indifferent to interpersonal relations and tend to be isolated.

    Paranoid PD: general distrust and suspicion since the beginning of adulthood, so that the intentions of others are interpreted as malevolent. They are suspicious, hypersensitive and skeptics.

    Schizotypal PD: the most rare among this group. Besides the general pattern of social and interpersonal deficits associated with acute discomfort, they tend to cognitive or perceptual distortions and eccentricities of behavior.

2. **Group B.** Characterized by emotional lability and a peculiar emotion that is associated with uncontrolled or undesirable social behaviors. It is the immature group. They are dramatic and emotional personalities. Includes 4 categories:

    Antisocial PD: characterized by a persistent pattern of disregard and violation of the rights of others occurring since age of 15. There is evidence of Conduct Disorder prior to age 15, though. It seems very early gestation and is expressed by conflicts with the rules since childhood. They are cold and are not afraid of danger. They often engage in illegal or destructive activities.

    Borderline PD: persistent pattern of instability in interpersonal relationships, self-image and affects, and marked impulsivity. They range from a need for attention to a rejection of intimate relationships. The mood switches easily from normality to depression or irritability. They are impulsive and have little control over anger. Chronic feelings of emptiness, self-identity disorders and suicide attempts or threats are common.

    Histrionic PD: general pattern of excessive emotionality and attention seeking. They are warm, seductive, issuing wrong signals that give rise to misunderstandings. Hypersensitive, they tend to theatricality, superficial and childish behavior.

Narcissistic PD: persistent pattern of grandiosity (in fantasy or behavior), need for admiration and lack of empathy. Tendency to be self-importance and hypersensitive to other's assessment. Are egocentric, dismissive and insensitive for the rights of others. They consider that deserve a special kind of treatment.

3. **Group C.** This is a group of disorders characterized by people extremely sensitive to signals of punishment. They are the group of fearful. They are anxious and frightened individuals. Includes 3 categories:

Avoidant PD: general pattern of social inhibition, feelings of inferiority and hypersensitivity to negative evaluation. They tolerate neither criticism nor ridicule, and they need assurance of unconditional approval in their relationships. They have no close friends or confidants, and avoid activities and social contact. They have low self-esteem and are excessively timid.

Dependent PD: general and excessive need for others to address one, which causes a submission, adherence behavior and fears of separation. They are afraid of loneliness and hypersensitive to disapproval. Are considered incapable of living on their own.

Obsessive-Compulsive PD: pervasive pattern of preoccupation with orderliness, perfectionism and mental and interpersonal control, at the expense of spontaneity, flexibility and efficiency. Are persevering, policy and parsimonious personalities. Concerned about perfectionism and yields. Meticulous. They do not tolerate uncertainty.

3. PERSONALITY DISORDER AND GENETICS

Among the genetic characters, the most interesting and controversial are those dealing with human personality and behavior. It is clear that these are not simple characters, but framed under the rubric of complexes. Virtually, all the work done in this area supports the idea of the existence of a hereditary component in temperament and personality shaping, which explain between 30 and 60% of the observed variance. However, has been not possible yet to identify a single gene responsible for the observed variability in human personality. However, for several reasons this result should not be surprising: a) the high genetic complexity of these characters, that have a large multifactorial component; b) genetic analysis methods used so far have been successful in the simplest characters; and c) is necessary to start from a definition of character in terms of biological entities that are useful for genetic studies.

There have been several approaches to the subject of study in an attempt to elucidate the genetic basis of personality. Based on a given phenotype, a first approach tries to discover the allelic variations of genes that influence the presence of this behavioral pattern. From this approach, the difficulty in genetic research of PD lies in first place on how to choose the most appropriate phenotype. It is therefore essential to lay the groundwork for what is an appropriate phenotype. Personality Disorders described in DSM-IV-TR are complex and poorly defined constructs, even clinically.

Another approach is to focus on the study of how allelic variations of a gene affect measurably changes in behavior. To some extent, the phenotypes proposed by the biosocial theory of personality integrated in Cloninger's model meet these requirements. Cloninger defines three basic dimensions, largely inheritable: novelty seeking, harm avoidance, and reward dependence. At the same time, these key figures would be influenced by the activity of certain neurotransmitters: the first dimension could be explained by genetic variability in the dopaminergic systems, the second by serotonin, and third, by noradrenergic.

Under these assumptions we have studied the polymorphisms of genes encoding receptors and transporters of neurotransmitters in the brain.

3.1. Personality Disorders Cluster A and Genetic Studies

Almost all research on these disorders rotates also around schizophrenia. And is from these findings when has been possible to start to analyze the genetic characteristic of each syndrome, and the role of genetic markers in vulnerability increase to suffer any of them. Of the three PD that contains cluster A, the schizotypal personality disorder (SPDD) and its relation to schizophrenia have been the nucleus that has most of the research. Hence, there is a considerable lack of research to analyze the genetic influences of both disorders in both paranoid personality disorder (PPD) and schizoid personality disorder (SPD).

3.2. Heritability

Torgensen (1984) was the first to glimpse that SPDD could have genetic determinants by itself. This author came to this conclusion from a study in which 7 co-identical twins of 25 subjects with SPDD, taken from a register of non-psychotic patients, also had SPDD, compared with only 1 of 34 dizygotic co-twins (28% vs. 3%). Subsequently, another study suggested that two dimensions of SPDD on genetic factors exerted their influence to varying degrees. Both studies are not without drawbacks and methodological biases, however, and pointed to a small proportion of heritability of SPDD.

There are three genetic-epidemiological designs commonly used to analyze the possible relationship between SPDD and schizophrenia.

Main among these designs consist in estimate the risk of SPDD amongst relatives of subjects with schizophrenia. A study of these characteristics was conducted by *Kety et al.* in 1968 with Danish population, showing that schizophrenia and its related disorders had an incidence of 20% in biological relatives of individuals with the disease, while in control was about 6%.

Since then, seven studies of families and twins with numerous samples have confirmed that although SPDD rates differ significantly between studies (probably due to diagnostic methods used in personality analysis), both SPDD and PPD rates are significantly higher among relatives of subjects with schizophrenia compared with control subjects.

In addition, some studies report specificity in the familial transmission because the incidence of SPDD and / or PPD is significantly higher in relatives of subjects with schizophrenia than in relatives of subjects with mood disorders. This hypothesis remains to be seen, and the results of studies are controversial.

A second method of analysis is evaluating the relationships between SPDD and schizophrenia, assuming SPDD as a sort of moderate schizophrenia phenotype. This method requires analyzing the proportion of relatives having a severe phenotype of the disease (chronic schizophrenia) among relatives of subjects with a milder phenotype (SPD). According to a review of Battaglia and Torgensen, there were 12 studies with this method until 1996, including those carried out by the same authors. These studies point out clearly that the familial risk of schizophrenia varies between 0% and 8.4%. However, until 1996, most studies that took SPDD as a starting point carried out established a lower relative risk of developing schizophrenia than those using relatives of subjects with schizophrenia indeed. This would be compatible with a polygenic model of schizophrenia that predicts that the risk of suffering the most severe form of the disease is lower among relatives of subjects with a milder form than those relatives who have the severe form. Controlled family studies have indicated an increased risk for schizophrenia in relatives of subjects with SPDD than in control subjects, or schizophrenia plus some PD of cluster A. However, when subjects with SPD conducted the family inquiry themselves, data from twin and adoption studies showed no relationship between SPDD and schizophrenia, probably because of samples size and genetic heterogeneity.

The third type of heritability analysis encompasses family, twin and adoption studies by analyzing the presence of the disorder in relatives of individuals who suffer it. The goal is to determine whether SPDD is more concentrated in families with an increased risk of schizophrenia. It is therefore important to determine whether relatives themselves may transmit SPDD, and how much of this transmission would be due to genetic factors.

Taken together, all these studies suggest that SPDD is transmitted familiarly, and that genetic factors contribute significantly to the transmission. Nevertheless, results also point out the possibility of only transmit a part of the disorder, not the disorder in its entirety.

At the same time, some authors believe that there are no strong family studies on assessing phenotypic markers of SPDD vulnerability, relative risk, or heritability of these traits. For them, it is possible that SPDD is genetically identical to some variety of schizophrenia, but with a weaker phenotype, due to a combination of reduced penetrance, greater number of protective factors, or lack of non-genetic factors, viral or toxic agents. What seems possible is that only a subset of subjects with SPDD is genetically identical or closely related to the various forms of schizophrenia, and this marker-associated genetic vulnerability could help to clearly define this subgroup.

3.3. Neuropsychological Markers

On a different plane to what has been outlined, a number of specific neuropsychological indicators related to schizophrenia have been studied over the years, and have been also analyzed for SPDD recently. Neuropsychological indicators can be very useful as phenotypic indicators in genetic linkage analysis. Based on these indicators, three endophenotypes that may be useful for understanding the genetic liability in the SPD arose:

Prepulse Inhibition (PPI): repeated presentation of weak stimuli before a strong stimulus reduces the magnitude of the blink reflex. Schizophrenic patients show a lower response inhibition than normal subjects. Even clinically unaffected relatives of schizophrenic subjects show a deficit in inhibitory response similar to that found in affected individuals. Compared with normal subjects, patients with SPDD show this deficit also. There has been no definitive analysis of the inheritance pattern of PPI in twins, but the modulation of this response using affective stimuli seems, at least in part, that is under genetic control, since monozygotic twins (but not dizygotic) show similar changes in the amplitude of this response.

Suppression of P50 evoked potential: multiple studies have found that there is a normal suppression of the second P50 potential, possibly due to activation of the inhibitory process caused by the first P50. In normal individuals, the second P50 shows a decrease of 80% compared to the first, detected from the final stage of adolescence to age 65. Schizophrenic patients, their first-degree relatives and subjects with SPDD show all reduced P50 suppression compared with normal subjects. Still, more studies are needed to provide genetic data regarding this matter.

Antisacer Paradigm: Saccadic reflex (rapid redirection of gaze to a place of interest) is a good measure to differentiate schizophrenic patients from those who are not. Close relatives of non-psychotic subjects with schizophrenia and SPDD generate a higher proportion of Antisacer errors. For instance, in a sophisticated work of this kind, 75% of schizophrenic patients and 25-50% of their families generated more errors than the worst performer of the control subjects.

Recent studies have noted an interaction between genetic risk for schizophrenia and schizotypal symptoms on many neurocognitive functions. Schizotypal symptoms among individuals with high genetic risk for developing schizophrenia are typically associated with deficits in verbal and visuo-spatial memory, complex attention and executive functions. These symptoms, together with a family history of schizophrenia, seem to place the subject in an increased risk position for developing certain cognitive deficits. This suggests that some neurocognitive functions may be sensitive to sub-psychothic symptoms within the schizophrenia spectrum. This would be consistent with a model where genetic locations would intervene in both schizotypal symptoms and neurocognitive deficits.

3.4 Studies of Molecular Genetics

Some studies show that personality characteristics of cluster A are associated with a low density of dopamine D2 receptors. It has been hypothesized that this receptor deficit may raise blood pressure through a deficient inhibition in catecholamine release. There are also attempts to clarify whether a length polymorphism of exon 6 of dopamine D2 receptor gene (DRD2) obtained with NcoI restriction factor, is associated with a low density of dopamine D2 receptors. Results from this study showed that homozygous men for the T allele had higher blood pressure and more cluster A PD, compared to other alleles.

One study found a strong association between the Taq A1 allele of the dopamine D2 receptor and a schizoid / avoidant behavior. A weaker association was found between 480-bp VNTR allele 10/10 dopamine transporter gene DAT1 and schizoid / avoidant behavior.

One could timidly argue that personalities of cluster A seem to have a different distribution of DRD2 genotypes obtained with NcoI, suggesting that the DRD2 polymorphism is potentially associated with this category of PD, ie, paranoid, schizoid and schizotypal.

4. CLUSTER B PERSONALITY DISORDERS AND GENETIC STUDIES

Antisocial Personality Disorder (ASPD) and Borderline Personality Disorder (BPD) are the only PD investigated on their heritability and genetics in this cluster.

C.3.2.1. Antisocial Personality Disorder

Antisocial behavior is so diverse that even its etiology may be different. We found evidence of this among property and violent crimes, where genetic influences were significant in the property but not violent ones associated with alcoholism. Cloninger studied this phenomenon attending Danish twins, and concluded that there was no genetic match between the two antisocial behaviors mentioned above, suggesting a different etiology for both.

Heritability

Development of antisocial behavior often begins in childhood. These individuals often manifest earlier antisocial behaviors, and have less verbal and spatial memory, more negative emotionality, greater familial transmission of antisocial behavior and greater genetic influence on phenotype. It seems that genetic component on behaviors persistence may influence behavioral disinhibition, being this factor responsible for the earliness and stability of antisocial behaviors through life. There is evidence of a progression from Oppositional Defiant Disorder (ODD) to personality disorder with the years, but should be pointed that although many children with conduct disorder show a history of ODD, many with ODD do not evolve into a subsequent conduct disorder (CD). CD affects more often boys than girls, but there are no consistent data to support that case in ODD. Studies with adults diagnosed with CD show that one to two thirds of subjects have psychiatric disorders, personality disorders or significant criminal behavior. CD shows a moderate comorbidity with anxiety and mood disorders, but a strong one with attention deficit / hyperactivity disorder (ADHD). About one third of cases of ADHD develop a significant criminal behavior. However, there are no studies that indicate the proportion of adults with ASPD and a history of ADHD.

Thus, can be concluded that behavioral disorders in childhood is not a necessary indicator of developing ASPD when adults.

Single-adoption studies suggest a lower family influence on antisocial behavior than those using twins and adopted siblings. However, difference between these two types is none. This fact, thought, may be due to a lack of precision in the measurement. Heritability levels vary from 7% to 81%, which makes extremely difficult to reach any firm conclusions. Three of the studies with larger samples suggest that most measures of antisocial behavior in childhood show a 50% (or even slightly above) of heritability.

Studies of Molecular Genetics

Current research in molecular genetics is majorly developed on ADHD and antisocial personality disorders in adults, in relation to alcohol and / or substance abuse. In concern to ADHD, it has been appreciated a clear contribution of dopaminergic system and an influence of the dopamine D4 receptor gene (DRD4) and dopamine transporter (DAT1) in numerous studies. Because of the high comorbidity between both disorders, it would be interesting to further explore the relationship of these findings with antisocial behavior. Genetic work on alcohol abuse have followed two strands: one related to the genes involved in alcohol metabolism, which is unlikely to shed some light on antisocial behavior in childhood; and a second that tries to explore the genes of monoamines, which may be more revealing. By the time, genetic associations that include alcohol dependence tendency suggest a link between D4S244 and D4S2393 genetic markers. In one family, which showed a mild mental retardation and unpredictable aggression so far, a mutation of the monoamine oxidase gene on males X chromosome was observed. In spite of this, no MAO-A disfunction could be pointed by a replica study, perhaps because the patient sample was statistically small. Two consecutive studies showed significant differences in specific alleles, comparing groups of alcoholics with antisocial controls and non-antisocial alcoholics.

Genetic analysis carried out in a Finnish population and a large American Indians family suggest a vulnerability located in 5HT1B receptor gene, compared to low levels of serotonin metabolites shown by impulsive and aggressive individuals. Nevertheless, differences regarding the neurotransmitter transporter gene cannot be appreciated. Slutske came out with results that suggested at least one genetic locus that would be enhancing vulnerability to suffer ASPD with pathological gambling, pathological gambling disorder, adult antisocial behavior and pathological gambling. Associations between dopamine receptor gene D5 and substance dependence propensity and the BN were observed, resulting stronger in women. The D5 receptor shows ten times more affinity for dopamine than D1 receptor. Plus, it is important to note that a high density of the D5 receptor in brain structures of the limbic system is found, which may suggest a role of this system in emotional regulation.

5. BORDERLINE PERSONALITY DISORDER

Although multifactorial etiology of BPD and complex interaction of genetic and environmental factors is generally recognized, the genetic substrates of this disorder have not been yet extensively investigated. Heritability of BPD as a diagnosis is well supported by the whole family studies, but genetic basis of some dimensions (e.g. impulsivity / aggressiveness and emotional instability) may be stronger than for the entire diagnostic itself. Impulsiveness is considered a fundamental dimension in BPD, and may represent a heritable *endophenotype* that significantly contribute to increase likelihood to developing BPD.

Some studies have investigated ·the correlations between the 'Big Five personality factors' model and BPD, concluding that the 'Big Five' model explains almost half of the variance in BPD. Thus, genetic analysis of the 'Big Five' factors may help to clarify the genetic basis of BPD.

Two studies with Norwegian twin yielded different results. The first study identified the environment as the most important factor in BPD development. The second study, which counted with a larger sample, noted a significant effect from genetic load, stating near 0.70 the total proportion of explained variance. Studies with twins reared together and apart reveal a strong genetic influence on personality dimensions, such as neuroticism and extraversion.

Some reports assert that individuals with a higher score on neuroticism (or equivalent) tend to have a short variant of the serotonin reuptake encoding gene. This polymorphism accounts for 3% to 4% of total variance, and 7% to 9% of inherited variance. A similar study found a gene that influences high scores on novelty seeking and low awareness. Although very little percentage of the total variance is explained by these studies, they are a first step in unravel the gene mapping of those responsible of PD. In a research conducted by Livesley, 18 personality dimensions that justified many of the anomalies in the PD were described. Among those dimensions, the following aspects are very similar to the ones shown in BPD (subtraits in parentheses): emotional lability (emotional instability, overreactions, generalized hypersensitivity, anger and irritability), cognitive distortion (depersonalization, schizotypal cognition and brief stress-addressed-psychosis), identity problems (anhedonia, feelings of emptiness, self-changing and pessimism), commitment of insecurity (low tolerance to separation, loss of fear, proximity search and inability to tolerate solitude) and autolysis (suicidal attempts and ideas). Affective lability, problems of identity and commitment of insecurity, characteristic features of BPD, belonged to a higher order factor called 'emotional lability' or *dysregulation*. In that investigation, higher heritability of 0.4 to 0.5 for traits and subtraits was found. Because most of the variance appears to be due to this dysregulation factor, Livesley proposes it as the core dimension of BPD. In turn, Siever studies suggest a relation between noradrenergic system and risk taking, irritability and impulsivity behaviors, all of which seems to lead the individual into a stronger reaction to the environment. Noradrenergic system would be regulatating this reaction, and together with an increased propensity for impulsive aggression, regulated by the serotonergic system, may be combined to create the problematic behavior pattern typical of patients with BPD.

Heritability of Impulsivity

Given the elevated harm potential that high impulsivity entails in relation to suicide attempts and mortality in these patients, determine heritability factors is a must. In this sense, a polymorphism on chromosome 11, that is manifested by lower 5-HIAA levels in the cerebrospinal fluid in subjects with a history of suicide attempts and high levels of impulsivity and aggression in their lifetime, has been discovered while studying the serotonin gene encoding precursor. However, the lowest levels have been found in depressive suicidal without comorbid BPD pathology. This may suggest that suicide in major depression may be more genetically influenced than comorbidity with BPD. Nearly all information indicates a lower serotonergic activity in patients with BPD. A study using Positron Emission Tomography (PET) and F-deoxyglucose, found a significant inverse correlation between aggressive-impulsive problems and glucose metabolism in the frontal cortex. This sheds light on the importance of the frontal cortex in mediating the aggressive impulses. Yet, it is curious to see how this glucose metabolism decrease was not found in murderers who planned their crimes, and only appreciated in impulsive murderers. Low levels of serotonin together with dopaminergic system deficiencies are related to autolytic behaviors in patients with borderline personality disorder and depression. Evidence of genetic risk factors of suicide has been found on both family and twin and adoption studies.

6. PERSONALITY DISORDERS CLUSTER C AND GENETIC STUDIES

Specific personality genetics studies on current scientific literature are scarce. There are few about cluster C, though. Cluster C includes Avoidant Personality Disorder (APD), Dependent Personality Disorder (DPD) and Obsessive-Compulsive Personality Disorder (OCPD).

In a recent epidemiological work, OCPD was the more prevalent disorder in general population, ranking the APD and DPD at fifth and seventh place, respectively.

Two papers (1996) established an association between exon III VNTR in dopamine D4 receptor gene and novelty seeking. Since then, numerous studies have explored this relationship with mixed results. Some have examined the relationship between the DRD4 exon III VNTR and other addictive and impulsive disorders, but results are inconsistent. Other DRD4 polymorphisms have been discovered, including single nucleotide -521 C> T polymorphism, associated with novelty seeking, yet results are again inconsistent. Two recent meta-analysis have concluded that no relationship exists between the exon III VNTR polymorphism of D4 receptor and novelty seeking, whereas may be a weak relation between novelty seeking and the -521 C> T polymorphism. Dopamine D3 receptor gene is located on chromosome 3q13.3. A polymorphism on two alleles called Ser9Gly has been identified, and its genotypic variants may be associated with schizophrenia, search and sense of novelty in bipolar European population, and with alcohol and opiate dependency and neurotic personality traits in Australian population, but this has not been possible to replicate yet.

In a study conducted by Joyce et al., DRD4, 521 C> T, and DRD3 polymorphisms were analyzed. Subjects who expressed the DRD4 exon III polymorphism with repeated allele showed more obsessive and avoidant symptoms than other groups (three, four, six, seven, eight and ten repetitions). When analyzing data according to PD, APD and OCPD percentage was statistically significant for five groups that held the polymorphism, although higher rates were observed in the two repeat allele group. Significant statistical differences were found on the -521 C> T polymorphism, regarding avoidant and obsessive personality features, and further post-hoc tests showed that 30% of subjects with genotype C had a OCPD, whereas only occurred on 4% of individuals without this genotype. Regarding DRD3 genotypes and Gly9 genotype, Gly9 was associated with more obsessive symptoms and OCPD. It is appropriate to note that a study of the same year but prior to Joyce's found no association between variants of DRD3 and personality traits, measured by five psychometric tests.

Association evidence of DRD4 and DRD3 polymorphisms presence and clinical values of traits with obsessive-compulsive and avoidant personality disorders field, suggest that associations between dopamine genotypes and personality disorders of cluster C could be mediated by dopamine receptors.

An allelic variation found in the role of the serotonin transporter (5-HTT) could represent 8% of the personality traits inherited variance, related to anxiety and depression. A single copy gene (SLC6A4) located on chromosome 17q12, which transcription is modulated through a 44-bp length change called 5-HTTLPR (whose alleles can be short or long), encodes this serotonine transporter. Recent research found neither differences on the 5-HTTLPR genotype distributions among control subjects, subjects diagnosed with PD of cluster B nor subjects diagnosed with PD of cluster C. Individuals diagnosed with PD of cluster C presented higher scores in neuroticism than controls and cluster B subjects. Among cluster C diagnosed subjects, those with the short version of the 5-HTTLPR allele showed higher levels of neuroticism and harm avoidance than the rest. Anxiogenic stimuli may cause an excitability enhancement in amygdala, as well as in the control performed by prefrontal cortical circuits, due to an increased neurotransmission in those low-activity 5-HTTLPR alleles carriers diagnosed with a cluster C PD.

REFERENCES

Agrawal, A; Lynskey, MT.The genetic epidemiology of cannabis use, abuse and dependence.*Addiction*., 2006, 101(6), 801-812.

Allende, S. Impacto de la genética en el alcoholismo.Un enfoque desde la lógica difusa. *Rev hanan cienc méd LaHabana*., 2009, VIII(1).

American Psychiatric Association.DSM-IV-TR. Manual diagnóstico y estadístico de los trastornos mentales.*Barcelona:Masson*.

Ball, D. Addiction science and its genetics.*Addiction*., 2008, 103(3), 360-367.

Bart, G; Heiling, M; LaForge, KS; Pollack, L; Leal, SM; Ott, J; et al. Substantial attributable risk related to a functional mu-opioid receptor gene polymorphism in association with heroin addiction in Central Sweden. *Mol Psychiatry*, 2004, 9, 547-549.

Battaglia, M; Torgersen, S. Schizotypal disorder: at the crossroads of genetics and nosology. *Acta Psichiatrica Scandinavica*,1996, 94, 303-10.

Bevilacqua, L; Goldman, D. Genes and addictions.*Clin.Pharmacol.Ther.*, 2009, 85(4), 359-361.

Cloninger, CR. A unified biosocial theory of personality and its role in the development of anxiety states.*Psychiatric developments*, 1986, 3, 167-226.

Connor,J; Young,R; Saunders,J; Lawford,B; Ho,R; Ritchie,T; Noble.E.The A1 allele of the D2 dopamine receptor gene region, alcohol expectancies and drinking refusal self-efficacy are associated with alcohol dependence severity. *Psychiatry Research*,2008, 160(1), 94-105.

Curling, HMD; Psych, MRC; Grant, S; Dangl, J. The genetic and cultural transmission of alcohol use, alcoholism, cigarette smoking and coffee drinking: A review and an example using a log linear cultural transmission model. *Addiction*., 1985, 80(3), 269–279.

Edenberg, HJ; Foroud, T. The genetics of alcoholism: identifying specific genes through family studies. *Addiction biology*., 2006, 11(3), 386-396.

Edenberg, HJ; Foroud, T; Koller, DL; Goate, A; Rice, J; Van Eerdewegh, P; et al. A family-based analysis of the association of the dopamine D2 receptor (DRD2) with alcoholism.*Alcoholism: Clinical and experimental Research*, 1998, 22, 505-12.

Enoch, MA; Goldman, D. Genetics of alcoholism and substance abuse.*Psychiatric Clinics of North America*., 1999, 22(2), 289-299.

Faraone, SV; Tsuang, MT; Tsuang, DW.Genetics of Mental Disorders.A guide for students, clinicians, and researchers.*The Guilford Press ed. Nueva York*, 1999, 272.

Haro, G, Mateu, C; Martínez-Raga, J; Valderrama, JC; Castellano, M; Cervera, G.The role of personality disorders on drug dependence treatment outcomes following inpatient detoxification.*European Psychiatry.*, 2004, 9(4), 187-92.

Hemby, SE. Assessment of genome and proteome profiles in cocaine abuse. *Prog. Brain Res.,* 2006, 158, 173-195.

Hoenicka, J; Ampuero, I; Ramos, JA. Aspectos genéticos del alcoholismo. *Trastornos Adictivos.*, 2003, 5(3), 213-22.

Joyce, PR; Rogers, GR; Miller, AL; Mulder, RT; Luty, SE; Kennedy, MA. Polymorphisms of DRD4 and DRD3 and risk of avoidant and obsessive personality traits and disorders.*Psychiatry Research.*, 2003, 119, 1-10.

Kety, SS; Wender, PH; Jacobsen, B; Ingraham, LJ; Jansson, L; Faber, B; Kinney, DK. Mental illness in the biological and adoptive relatives of schizophrenic adoptees. Replication of the Copenhagen study in the rest of Denmark.*Archives of General Psychiatry.*, 1994, 51, 442-55.

Kreek, MJ. Role of a functional human gene polymorphism in stress responsivity and addictions.*Clin.Pharmacol.Ther.*, 2008, 83(4), 615-618.

Kreek, MJ; Nielsen, DA; LaForge, KS. Genes associated with addiction: alcoholism, opiate, and cocaine addiction. *Neuromolecular Med.,* 2004, 5, 85-108.

Lyons, MJ; True, WR; Eisen, SA; Goldberg, J; Meyer, JM; Faraone, SV; et al. Differential heritability of adult and juvenile antisocial traits. *Archives of General Psychiatry.*, 1995, 52, 906-13.

Meana, JJ; Ballesteros, J. Investigación básica y genética en drogodependencias. En: Consellería de benestar social (eds). Trastornos adictivos. Drogodependencias: clínica y tratamientos psicobiológicos.Generalitat Valenciana (ed). *Valencia*, 2001, 47-83.

Persico, AM. Contribución genética a la neurobiología de la vulnerabilidad a la adicción a drogas. En: Meana JJ (eds). *Herencia genética en drogodependencias.* Universidad de Deusto (ed). Bilbao, 1996, 69-95.

Phillips, TJ; Kamens, HM; Wheeler, JM.Behavioral genetic contributions to the study of addiction-related amphetamine effects.*Neurosci Biobehav Rev.*, 2008, 32(4), 707-759.

Schuckit, MA. Genetics of the risk for alcoholism.*American Journal on Addictions.*, 2000, 9(2), 103-112.

Siever, LJ; Silverman, JM; Hovarth, TB; Klar, H; Coccaro, E; Keefe RS et al. Increased morbid risk for schizophrenia-related disorders in relatives of schizotypal personality disordered patients. *Archives of General Psychiatry.*1990, 47: 634-40.

Tsuang, MT; Lyons, MJ; Doyle, T; Eisen, SA; Goldberg, J; True, W; et al. Co-occurrence of abuse of different drugs in men: the role of drug-specific and shared vulnerabilities. *Archives of General Psychiatry.*, 1998, 55, 967-72.

Uhl, GR. Molecular genetics of addiction vulnerability.*NeuroRx.*, 2006, 3(3), 295-301.

Uhl, GR; Drgon, T; Johnson, C; Li, C; Contoreggi, C; Hess, J; et al. Molecular genetics of addiction and related heritable phenotypes: genome-wide association approaches identify "connectivity constellation" and drug target genes with pleiotropic effects. *Ann. N. Y. Acad. Sci.*, 2008, 1141, 318-381.

Uhl, GR; Liu, QR; Drgon, T; Johnson, C; Walther, D; Rose, JE. Molecular genetics of nicotine dependence and abstinence: whole genome association using, 520, 000 SNPs. *BMC genetics.* 2007, 8(1), 10

von der Pahlen, B; Santtila, P; Johansson, A; Varjonen, M; Jern, P; Witting, K; Kenneth, Sandnabba, N. Do the same genetic and environmental effects underlie the covariation of alcohol dependence, smoking, and aggressive behaviour?(2008). *Biol Psychol.*, 78(3), 269-77.

Wodarz,N.; Bobbe,G.; Eichhammer,P.; Weijers, H. G; Wiesbeck, G. A. and Johann M. The candidate gene approach in alcoholism: are there gender-specific differences, 2003, *Arch. Women Ment. Healt*, 6(4), 225-30.

Wong, CCY; Schumann, G. Review. Genetics of addictions: strategies for addressing heterogeneity and polygenicity of substance use disorders. *Philos. Trans. R. Soc. Lond., B, Biological Science.*, 2008, 363(1507), 3213-3222.

In: Personality Traits: Theory, Testing and Influences   ISBN: 978-1-61728-934-7
Editor: Melissa E. Jordan   © 2011 Nova Science Publishers, Inc.

Chapter 6

STRUCTURAL AND FUNCTIONAL NEUROIMAGING STUDIES OF THE ANXIETY-RELATED PERSONALITY TRAIT: IMPLICATIONS FOR THE NEUROBIOLOGICAL BASIS OF HUMAN ANXIOUS PERSONALITY

Yuko Hakamata [1,2] *and Toshiya Inada* [3*]

[1]Department of Clinical Psychology, The University of Tokyo,
Graduate School of Education, Tokyo, Japan
[2]The Japan Society for the Promotion of Science, Tokyo, Japan
[3]Seiwa Hospital, Institute of Neuropsychiatry, Tokyo, Japan

1. ANXIETY-RELATED PERSONALITY TRAITS: HISTORICAL BACKGROUND, REPRESENTATIVE THEORETICAL MODELS, AND HYPOTHESES FOR THE BIOLOGICAL BASIS

Personality is a specific pattern of individual behavioral, emotional, and thought processesthatremain relatively stable throughout life. The pattern that is characterized by ready elicitation and maintenance of a high anxiety level is referred to as the "anxious personality". Although many researchers have proposed theoretical models of the anxious personality trait, the most influential have been "Neuroticism (vs. Emotional Stability)" developed by Eysenck (1967), the "Behavioral Inhibition System" developed byGray (1972), "Neuroticism" developed by Costa and McCrae(1985), and "Harm Avoidance" developed by Cloninger (1986).

Research on personality can be originally traced back to the "personality trait theory", which attempted to account for human personality as several measurable "traits" (Allport 1936, Cattell 1943, Fiske 1949). Such studies have been based on factorial analysis in which many adjectival termswere adopted to describe individual behavioral, emotional, or

---

[*] Corresponding author: Vice President, Seiwa Hospital, Institute of Neuropsychiatry, Benten-cho 91, Shinjuku-ku, Tokyo 162-0851, Japan, Tel+81-3-3260-9171, Fax+81-3-3235-0961, E mailhan91010@rio.odn.ne.jp

thoughtcharacteristics,and converged into several fundamental components (i.e. traits). Although researchers in this field have not reached a consensus on the number of such personality traits, they have commonly found that one of themis closely related to an increased level of anxiety. In an attempt to settle this lingering controversy over the number of traits by proposing that human personality consists of five basic ones, mostly derivedfrom systematic factorial analysis, Costa and McCrae (1985)adopted the term "Neuroticism" for that related to anxiety. They considered that individuals with a high Neuroticism (N) score tend to exhibit worry, nervousness, emotionality, insecurity, inadequacy, or hypochondria.[1]

The original adoption of N can be seen in "Neuroticism (vs. Emotional Stability)" proposed by Eysenck (1967). Showing considerable similarity to N, this Neuroticism is associated with anxiety, depression, tension, feelingsof guilt, low self-esteem, lack of autonomy, moodiness, hypochondria, and obsession. However, Eysenck's theory was of distinct importance in the history of personality research because it specificallymentioned the biological basis of personality, whereas most traditional studies based on factorial analysis had made every endeavor to derive a minimum number of traitscapable of describing human personality.[2]As with the anxiety-related personality trait, he explained that individual differences in Neuroticism are based on activation thresholds in the sympathetic nervous system or visceral brain, which is also referred to as the limbic system, including the amygdala, hippocampus, septum, and hypothalamus(Eysenck, 1990).

Subsequent to Eysenck's model (Eysenck, 1967), Gray (1976, 1981) attempted to integrate it into his two basic theoretical dimensions: the "Behavioral Inhibition System" and the "Behavioral Activation System". As Eysenck assumed that an individual with high Neuroticism accompanied by strong Introversion would be much more likely to manifest anxiety symptoms(Eysenck 1969), he simply clarified that such an individual would have a highly sensitive or reactive Behavioral Inhibition System (BIS) (Gray 1981). The BIS is a system activated by warnings of punishment or non-reward, novel stimuli, and innate fear stimuli as inputs, thereby triggering behavioral inhibition, increased arousal, and increased attention as outputs. This means that strong susceptibilityto the BIS is associated with increased anxiety. In addition, he assumed the BIS to have a biological basis in the septo-hippocampal system, pointing out the similarity between the behavioral effects of hippocampal lesions and those of anxiolytic drugs. However, instead of this system, the amygdala is now considered to play a central role in the BIS (Gray and McNaughton, 2000), since its critical involvement in both fear and anxiety has become widely recognized(LeDoux 1994).

In contrast to the ideas of Eysenck and Gray, whose workcreated a rough map of the biological basis of an anxiety-related personality, Cloninger tried to determine the neurophysiological properties responsible for it. Based on various findings from studies in the fields of neuroscience, genetics, and biochemistry, he advocated that an anxiety-related

---

[1] Additionally, this trait is composed of 6 sub-facets: Anxiety, Hostility, Depression, Self-consciousness, Impulsiveness, and Vulnerability.

[2] In Eysenck's model, human personality is assumed to consist of 3 dimensions: "Neuroticism (vs Emotional Stability)", "Extraversion (vs Introversion), and "Psychoticism". In 1967, he proposed that behavioral differences between individuals with high extraversion (extraverts) and individuals with high introversion (introverts) occur from innate drive to compensate for overactive and underactive reticulo-thalamo-cortical pathways (Eysenck, 1967).

temperament[3], "Harm Avoidance", is basically regulated by the serotonin neurotransmitters that are richly distributed in the hypothalamus, basal ganglia, and raphe nuclei(Cloninger 1986).Harm Avoidance (HA) is a tendency characterized by behavioral inhibition such as pessimistic worry in anticipation of future problems, passive avoidance behavior such as fear of uncertainty and shyness of strangers, and rapid fatigability(Cloninger, Svrakic and Przybeck 1993). This theoretical hypothesis was supported by a subsequent genetic study by Lesch, Heils and Riederer (1996),which found that HA is significantly associated with the serotonin-related gene polymorphism regulating expression of the serotonin transporter gene (5HTTLPR), thus accelerating further investigation of the biological correlates of HA. HA, N developed by Costa and McCrae (1985), Neuroticism developed by Eysenck (1967), and BIS developed by Gray (1976) are similar to one another, and all reflect individual differences in the behavioral inhibition associated with increased anxiety (Morgan 2006). Because of these similarities, scientists have frequently used these anxiety-related personality traits in an attempt to elucidate the biological basis of anxious personality. To date, a significant relationship between an anxiety-related personality trait and specific genetic variation (i.e. 5HTTLPR) has been repeatedly confirmed(Munafò et al. 2009, Sen, Burmeister and Ghosh 2004, Schinka, Busch and Robichaux-Keene 2004, Munafò, Clark and Flint 2005).

Despite the accumulation of findings pertaining to genetic correlates, the neural basis of an anxiety-related personality trait (i.e. brain regions and circuits) has not been extensively investigated. Although several neuroimaging studies have so far examined relationshipsbetween the anxiety-related personality trait and brain structures or activities, no study has attempted to integrate the findings in a meaningful way.Since the anxiety-related personality trait has become widely recognized as one of the representative predisposing factors for mood and anxiety disorders (Clark, Watson and Mineka 1994), an understanding of its neurobiological basis is very much needed for clarifying the etiology of mood and anxiety disorders and for establishing better methods of intervention or prevention.

In this chapter, to derive a picture of the neurobiological basis of the anxious personality, we will first take a detailed look at the findings of structural and functional neuroimaging studies of the anxiety-related personality trait in healthy individuals. With regard to functional neuroimaging modalities such as positron emission tomography (PET) and functional magnetic resonance imaging (fMRI), we specifically focus on studies that have examined brain activitiesin a resting state,assuch activities have been examined relatively extensively. We then attempt to identify brain regions and possible neural networks considered to play an important role in the anxiety-related personality trait, not only by summarizing the above-mentioned findings but also by referring to fMRI studies during the processing of cognitive or emotional tasks. Lastly, we discuss the functional aspectsthat may contribute to anxious personality via such brain regions or networks.

---

[3] The term "temperament" has been historically defined as an individual difference particularly in emotional responses associated with physiological reactivity such as occurs in the autonomic or endocrine system and is assumed to have some neurobiological basis (Strelau, 1995).

Table 1. Structural neuroimaging studies examining an association with anxiety-related personality traits

Author	Year	Subject	Imaging apparatus	Measurment method	Questionnaire	Covariates	Regions of interest (ROI)	Statistical threshold	Results Positive correlation	Negative correlation
Blankstein et al.	2009	35 healthy adolescents (males=15, females = 20, age range = 16-17)	MRI (3Tesla)	VBM	Neuroticism (NEO-PI-R)	ICV	frontal lobe	uncorrected p = 0.001, k > 200	R subgenual ACC (BA24-25)	None
				CTA			limbic lobe			
							MFG	corrected p = 0.05 (FDR)	* Only in females	
							medial frontal gyrus			
							subgenial ACC			
Gardini et al.	2009	85 healthy adults (males = 58, females = 27, mean age ±SD = 32.69±6.5)	MRI (3Tesla)	VBM	HA (TPQ)	age	None	corrected p = 0.05 (FDR)	None	R cuneus (BA19)
						sex				L precuneus (BA31)
						education (years)				L MOG (BA19)
						NS score				L IFG (BA9 & 46)
						RD score				R IFG (BA46 & 47)
						P score				L MFG (BA8)
										R IPL (BA7 & 40)
Cherbuin et al.	2008	430 healthy adults (males = 197, females = 233, mean age ±SD = 46.68±1.4) * Of total of subjects, 399 were depression medication naive	MRI (1.5Tesla)	mannual tracing method	BIS (BIS/BAS)	age	amyglada	p = 0.01	-	None
						sex	hippocampus	by Pearson corelational analysis	hippocampus	
						education (years)				
						total brain volume				
						ICV				

Table 1. (Continued)

Author	Year	Subject	Imaging apparatus	Measurment method	Questionnaire	Covariates	Regions of interest (ROI)	Statistical threshold	Results: Positive correlation	Results: Negative correlation
Yamasue et al.	2008	183 healthy adults (males = 117, females = 66, age range = 21-40)	MRI (1.5Tesla)	VBM	HA (TCI)	ICV	amygdala	corrected p = 0.05 (FDR)	None	R hippocampus *Common to both genders
							hippocampus			L anterior PFC *Only in females
							PFC			
Wright et al.	2007	29 healthy elderly (males = 12, females = 17, age range = 61-84)	MRI (1.5Tesla)	VBM	Neuroticism (NEO-PI-R)	age	lateral PFC (including SFG and MFG and their adjacent sulcus)	p = 0.001 *as a correction within ROI	R anterior temporal cortex (BA38)	R SFG (BA6)
						sex	inferior PFC (including IFG and its adjacent sulci) *For amygdala, mannual tracing method was applied.	For other regions, uncorrected p = 0.0001		R IFG (BA44)
Barros-Loscertales et al.	2006	63 healthy undergaraduates (All males, age range = 18-34)	MRI (1.5Tesla)	VBM	SP (SPSRQ)	total brain volume	None	corrected p = 0.05, k > 80	L parahippocampal gyrus	None
									R parahippocampal gyrus (including amygdala and hippocampus)	

Table 1. (Continued)

Author	Year	Subject	Imaging apparatus	Measurment method	Questionnaire	Covariates	Regions of interest (ROI)	Statistical threshold	Results — Positive correlation	Results — Negative correlation
Iidaka et al.	2006	56 healthy adults (males = 30, females = 26, mean age ±SD = 22.3±3.1)	MRI (3Tesla)	VBM	HA (TCI)	age, sex, BDI, gray matter total volume	None	uncorrected p = 0.001, k > 100. When any regions detected at this level, SVC was applied for the regions.	L amygdala; L OFG; R MTG; R angular gyrus; *Regions other than amygdala did not survive SVC	None
Wright et al.	2006	28 healthy adults (males = 11, females = 17, age range = 20-34)	MRI (1.5Tesla)	VBM / CTA	Neuroticism (NEO-PI-R)	age; sex	PFC; amyglada *For amygdala, manual tracing method was applied.	p = 0.00031 (as a correction within PFC); For other regions, p = 0.00013 (as a correction for all areas outside PFC); uncorrected p = 0.025 (as a correction within bilateral amygdala)	None	L OFC (BA10/11); *However, this correlation became non-significant when age and sex were controlled.
Omura et al.	2005	41 healthy adults (males = 19, females = 22, mean age ±SD = 23.8±5.4)	MRI (3Tesla)	VBM	Neuroticism (NEO-PI-R)	age	amygdala	corrected p = 0.01 (FWE)	None	R amygdala

Table 1. (Continued)

Author	Year	Subject	Imaging apparatus	Measument method	Questionnaire	Covariates	Regions of interest (ROI)	Statistical threshold	Results Positive correlation	Results Negative correlation (R)	Results Negative correlation
Rauch et al.	2005	14 healthy adults (males = 8, females = 6, age range = 21-34)	MRI (1.5Tesla)	CTA	Neuroticism (NEO-PI-R)	sex		For other regions, uncorrected p = 0.001, k > 200		R	SPL
										R	angular gyrus
						None	medial OFC	p = 0.05 by regression analysis	None	R	medial OFC
Gündel et al.	2004	100 healthy adults (males = 49, females = 52, age range = 20-43)	MRI (1.5Tesla)	mannual tracing method	HA (TCI)	total brain volume	ACC	p = 0.05 by ANOVA	R ACC (BA24-25)	None	
							PCC (including precuneus)		* Only in females		
Pujol et al.	2002	100 healthy adults (males = 50, females = 50, age range = 20-40)	MRI (1.5Tesla)	mannual tracing method	HA (TCI)	total brain volume	ACC	p = 0.05 by ANOVA	R ACC	None	
							PCC (including precuneus and medial parietal cortex)				

Abbreviations:

BIS/BAS: Behaviral Inhibition Scales and Behavioral Activation Scales (Carver & White, 1994)

MRI: magnetic resonance imaging

BDI: Beck's Depression Inventory (Beck & Steer, 1987)

VBM: voxel-based morphometry

TCI: Temperament and Character Inventory (Cloninger et al., 1993)

CTA: cortical thickness analysis

TPQ: Tridimensional Personality Questionnaire (Cloninger, 1987)

ICV: intracranial volume

NEO-PI-R: Revised NEO Personality Inventory (Costa and McCrae, 1985)

SVC: small volume correction

SPSRQ: Sensitivity to punishment and sensitivity to reward questionnaire (Torrubia et al., 2001)
FDR: false discovery rate
HA: Harm Avoidance scale in TCI
FWE: family wise error correction
NS: Novelty Seeking scale in TCI
BA: Brodmann's area
RD: Reward Dependence scale in TCI
PFC: prefrontal cortex
MTG: middle temporal gyrus
OFC: orbitofrontal cortex
PCC: posterior cingulate cortex
IFG: inferior frontal gyrus
ACC: anterior cingulate cortex
SFG: superior frontal gyrus
MOG: middle oocipital gyrus
MFG: middle frontal gyrus
IPL: inferior parietal lobule
OFG: orbitofrontal gyrus
SPL: superior parietal lobule

2. STRUCTURAL AND FUNCTIONAL NEUROIMAGING STUDIES OF THE ANXIETY-RELATED PERSONALITY TRAIT

Structural differences in the anxiety-related personality trait have been examined, to our knowledge,in 12 studies using magnetic resonance imaging (MRI) (Table 1). With regard to functional differences, 2 studies using single photon emission tomography (SPECT) and 18 studies using positron emission tomography (PET) have examined the relationship between an anxiety-related personality trait and brain activities in a resting state (Tables 2 and 3, respectively). In such functional studies, brain activities in a resting state (i.e. lying with the eyes closed but not sleeping) are considered to represent an individual's personality state resulting from specific patterns of thoughts or feelings experienced frequently in daily life. Brain regions shown by these structural and functional imagingstudies to have a significant relationship with the anxiety-related personality trait are summarized in Table 4.

Amygdala

Of theoretical relevance, the amygdala is considered to be one of the critical regions involved in the anxiety-related personality trait, as mentioned above.

One PET study found that DRD2 receptor binding potential in the amygdalahad a significant negative correlation with HA (Yasuno ct al. 2001). However, no other PET studies havcdemonstrateda significant difference in the amygdala. This is partly because most of those studies did not include the amygdala as a region of interest (ROI) among the hypothetical regions considered (Farde et al. 1997, Laakso et al. 2000, Kestler et al. 2000, Tauscher et al. 2001, Kaasinen et al. 2002, Rabiner et al. 2002, Borg et al. 2003), although no significant correlations were found in studies employing voxel-based analysisthat makes it possible to examine likely correlations with the anxiety-related personality trait throughout the brain(Hakamata et al. 2006, Hakamata et al. 2009, Schreckenberger et al. 2008, Frokjaer et al. 2008, Deckersbach et al. 2006, Van Laere et al. 2009, Youn et al. 2002). Given the relatively low spatial resolution of PET in comparison with MRI,itmay bepossible to attribute the failure to detect any significant difference in the amygdala to the small size of this brain structure. This also applies to the results of studies using SPECT (Sugiura et al. 2000, Turner et al, 2003), which has a lower spatial resolution than PET. On the other hand, a few MRI studies have found that the volume of gray matter in the amygdala became larger (Barrós-Loscertales et al. 2006, Iidaka et al. 2006) or a smaller (Omura, Aron and Canli 2005) as the anxiety-related personality score increased. In contrast, other studies failed to find any significant structural difference in the amygdala in relation to anxiety-related personality score (Blankstein et al. 2009, Gardini, Cloninger and Venneri 2009, Cherbuin et al. 2008, Wright et al. 2006, Wright et al. 2007, Yamasue et al. 2008).

Table 2. SPECT studies examining an association with Anxiety-related personality trait

Study	Year	Subjects	Ligand	Target	Questionnaire	Results	
						Positive associations	Negative associations
Sugiura et al.	2000	21 healthy subjects (all males, age range=20-33)	Tc-99m-HMPAO	rCBF	HA (TCI)	None	Left parahippocampal gyrus Right orbitoinsular junction Right precentral gyrus Right postcentral gyrus Right superior frontal gyrus Left fusiform gyrus Left inferior temporal gyrus
Turner et al.*	2003	30 healthy subjects (males=13, females=17, age range=26-61)	Tc-99m-HMPAO	rCBF	HA (TCI)	Right fusiform gyrus Right middle temporal gyrus Right superior temporal gyrus Parahippocampal gyrus Right superior occipiral gyrus Cuneus	None
						* 4 groups (25 percentile increment: 0-25, 26-50, 51-75, 76-100) were compared using a non-linear model. The upper section is the result of a comparison between 0-25 vs 50-75. The lower section is the result of a comparison between 25-50 vs 50-75.	

Abbreviations:
SPECT: single photon emission tomography
rCBF: regional cerebral blood flow
TCI: Temperament and Character Inventory (Cloninger et al., 1993)
HA: Harm Avoidance scale in TCI

Table 3. PET studies examining an association with Anxiety-related personality trait

Study	Year	Participants	Ligand	Target	Quantification method	Questionnaire	Covariates	Regions of interest (ROI)	Statistical threshold	Results — Positive correlation		Results — Negative correlation	
Breier et al.	1998	18 healthy subjects (males=14, females=4, mean age = 33.1±7.3)	[11C] Raclopride	DR2	Binding potential	HA (TCI)	sex, age, race	striatum	p = 0.05 by Pearson correlational analysis		None		
Hakamata et al.	2006	31 healthy adults (males = 21, females = 10, age range = 34-70)	18F-FDG	Glucose metabolic rate	Uptake	HA (TCI)	NS score, RD score, P score	None	p = 0.005 (uncorrected), k > 100 by voxel-based correlation analysis	R	mediodorsal nucleus (thalamus)	R	PCC
												L& R	MTG (BA21)
												L	MTG (BA39)
												L	parahippocampal gyrus
													fusiform gyrus (BA19)
												L	MFG (BA11)
												R	CG (BA31)
Hakamata et al.	2009	102 healthy adults (males = 65, females = 37, age range = 34-73)	18F-FDG	Glucose metabolic rate	Uptake	HA (TCI)	NS score, RD score, P score, age, sex	None	p = 0.005 (uncorrected), k > 100 by voxel-based correlation analysis		None	R	medial frontal gyrus (BA10)
Deckersbach et al.	2006	20 healthy adults (All females, mean age = 25.26±3.66)	18F-FDG	Glucose metabolic rate	Uptake	Neuroticism (NEO-FFI)	E score	medial PFC including ACC and OFC	p = 0.005, k > 5 within ROI		None	L	insula
								insula	p = 0.001, k > 5 (corrected) for other regions			L	STG (BA22)

Table 3 (Continued)

Study	Year	Sample	Tracer	Target	Measure	Trait scale	Covariates	Brain regions	Statistics	Result	Notes
Farde et al.	1997	24 healthy adults (males = 14, females = 10, age range = 18-38)	[11C]Raclopride	DR2	Binding potential	Anxiety-related scales (KSP)	None	putamen excluding the most ventral part	$p = 0.01$ by Pearson correlational analysis	None	-
Laakso et al.	2003	33 healthy adults (males = 22, females = 11, age range = 20-59)	[18F]fluorodopa	DA synthesis capacity	Uptake	Anxiety-related scales (KSP)	age / sex	caudate putamen occipital cortex	$p = 0.05$ by linear regression analysis	None	caudate / * Of Anxiety-related scales, Somatic anxiety facet / Muscular tension facet showed significance, respectively.
Ketsler et al.	2000	18 healthy adults (males = 15, females = 3, age=35.4±6.3)	[11C]Raclopride	DR2	Binding potential	Neuroticism (NEO-PI-R)	age / sex	striatum	$p = 0.05$ by Pearson correlational analysis	- / striatum	None
Van Laere et al.	2009	47 healthy adults (males = 23, females = 24, age range = 18-69)	[18F]MK 9470	cannabinoid receptor I	Uptake	HA (TCI)	age / sex	None	$p = 0.001$ (uncorrected, $k > 100$) by voxel-based correlation analysis	None	
Schreckenberger et al.	2008	23 healthy adults (all	[18F]fluoroe	opioid receptor	Binding potential	HA (TCI)	None	None	$p = 0.001$ (uncorrecte	None	

Study	Year	Subjects	Tracer	Receptor	Outcome measure	Personality measure	Covariate	Brain regions examined	Statistical threshold	Direction	Significant region
		...males, age range = 25-54)	...thyldiprenorphine						...d), k > 100 by voxel-based correlation analysis		None
Frokjaer et al.	2008	83 healthy adults (males = 53, females = 31, age range=18-76)	[18F]altanserin	5HT2AR	Binding potential	Neuroticism (NEO-PI-R)	age	frontolimbic regions (including OFC, medial inferior frontal cortex, superior frontal cortex, ACC, PCC, hippocampus, and entorhinal cortex)	p = 0.05 (uncorrected) by linear regression analysis	-	PCC
										-	medial inferior frontal cortex
										-	superior frontal cortex
										-	entorhinal cortex
							sex	None	p = 0.001 (uncorrected, k > 10) by voxel-based correlation analysis	L	insula
										R	parahippocampal gyrus
Yasuno et al.	2001	16 healthy subjects (all males, age range=21-35)	[11C]FLB 457	DR2	Binding potential	HA (TCI)	None	ACC, thalamus, PFC, temporal cortex, hippocampus	p = 0.05 by Pearson correlational analysis		None
										-	amygdala

Table 3 (Continued)

Study	Year	Tracer	Target	Measure	Personality measure	Covariates	Regions examined	Statistics	Positive correlation	Negative correlation	
Takano et al.	2007	[11C] DASB	5HTT	Binding potential	Nueroticism (NEO-PI-R)	None	amygdala, ACC, thalamus, PFC, striatum, hippocampus	p = 0.008 by Pearson correlational analysis	thalamus * Within Neurotisicm dimension, only Depression facet was significant.	-	None
Tauscher et al.	2001	[11C] WAY-100635	5HTR1A	Binding potential	Nueroticism (NEO-PI-R)	age	amygdala, dorsolateral PFC, ACC, parietal cortex, occipital cortex	p = 0.05 by Pearson correlational analysis	None	-	ACC
										-	parietal cortex
Kaasinen et al.	2002	[18F] fluorodopa	DA synthesis capacity	Uptake	HA (TCI)	age, sex	head of caudate nucleus, putamen, occipital regions	p = 0.05 by Pearson correlational analysis	None		
Rabiner et al.	2002	[11C] WAY-100635	5HTR1A	Binding potential	HA (TPQ) & Neuroticism (EPQ) & STAI	age, sex, height, weight, body surface area	21 regions throughout the brain	p = 0.05 by Pearson correlational analysis	None		
Moresco et al.	2002	[18F]FESP	5HTR2A	Binding potential	HA (TCI)	age, other regions	frontal cortex, ACC, temporal cortex, parietal	p = 0.05 by Spearman correlational analysis	None	-	frontal cortex
										L	occipital cortex

Subject details:
- Takano et al. (2007): 31 healthy adults (all males, age range=20-30)
- Tauscher et al. (2001): 19 healthy adults (males = 11, females = 8, age range = 22-53)
- Kaasinen et al. (2002): 25 healthy subjects (males=13, females=12, mean age = 60.2±7.0)
- Rabiner et al. (2002): 66 healthy subjects (all males, age range=24-53)
- Moresco et al. (2002): 11 healthy subjects (males=8, females=3, mean range =22-32)

Author	Year	Subjects	Tracer	Measure	Parameter	Scale	Correlates	ROI	Threshold	Neg.	Side	Region
Youn et al.	2002	19 healthy subjects (males=13, females=6, mean age = 26.3±9.8)	18F-FDG	Glucose metabolic rate	Uptake	HA (TPQ)	age / NS score / RD score	cortex / basal ganglia — None	p = 0.05 (uncorrected) by voxel-based correlation analysis	None	L&R	MTG (BA21)
											L	MTG (BA39)
											R	fusiform gyrus (BA19)
											R	ITG (BA37)
											-	hypothalamus
											L	inferior frontal cortex (BA6)
											R	inferior frontal cortex (BA45)
											L	IFG (BA45)
											L	postcentral gyrus (BA1,2)
											-	ACC
Borg et al.	2003	15 healthy subjects (all males, age range=20-45)	[11C] WAY-100635	5HTR1A	Binding potential	HA (TCI)	None	neocortex / hippocampus / dorsal raphe nucleus	p = 0.005 (uncorrected), k > 100 by voxel-based correlation analysis	None	L&R	ITG
											R	ACC
									p = 0.05 by Pearson correlational analysis	None	L	MTG

Abbreviations:

PET: positron emission tomography

BIS/BAS: Behaviral Inhibition Scales and Behavioral Activation Scales (Carver & White, 1994)

HA: Harm Avoidance scale in TCI

DR2: Dopamine Receptor 2

BDI: Beck's Depression Inventory (Beck & Steer, 1987)

NS: Novelty Seeking scale in TCI

5HTR1A: Serotonin Receptor 1A

TCI: Temperament and Character Inventory (Cloninger et al., 1993)

RD: Reward Dependence scale in TCI

5HTR2A: Serotonin Receptor 2A

TPQ: Tridimensional Personality Questionnaire (Cloninger, 1987)

P: Persitstence scale in TCI

DA: dopamine

KSP: Karolinska Scales of Personality (Schalling et al., 1987)

E: Extraversion scale in NEO

5HT: serotonin transporter

NEO-PI-R: Revised NEO Personality Inventory (Costa and McCrae, 1985)

NEO-FFI: NEO-Five Factor Inventory (a short form of NEO-PI-R; Costa and McCrae, 1992)

EPQ: Eysenck Personality Questionnaire (Eysenck, 1975)

STAI: Spielberger Trait & State Anxiety Inventory (Spielberger, 1970)

PFC: prefrontal cortex

PCC: posterior cingulate cortex

OFC: orbitofrontal cortex

ACC: anterior cingulate cortex

IFG: inferior frontal gyrus

CG: cingulate gyrus

MFG: middle frontal gyrus

Table 4. Summary of significant correlations between specific brain regions and anxiety-related personality trait reported in previous structural or functional neuroimaging studies during a resiting state

Imaging apparatus / Brain regions		Structure MRI	Function PET	Function SPECT
Frontal cortex				
not specified	not specified		↓	
superior frontal gyrus	R	↓(BA6)		↓
middle frontal gyrus	not specified		↑	
	L	↓(BA8)	↓(BA11)	
inferior frontal gyrus	R	↓(BA44)↓(BA46 & 47)	↓(BA45)	
	L	↓(BA9 & 46)	↓(BA6)↓(BA45)	
not specified			↑(medial part)	
		Structure MRI	**Function PET**	**Function SPECT**
medial frontal gyrus	R		↓(BA10)	↓
Precentral gyrus	R			
orbito frontal gyrus	R	↓(medial part)		
	L	↑↓(BA10/11)		
orbitoinsular junction	R			↓
Temporal cortex				
anterior temporal cortex	L	↑(BA38)		
superior temporal gyrus	R			↑
	L		↓(BA22)	
middle temporal gyrus	R	↑	↓↓(BA21)	↑
	L		↓↓(BA21)↓↓(BA39)↓	
inferior temporal gyrus	R		↓(BA37)↓	
	L		↓	
angular gyrus	R	↑↓		↓
fusiform gyrus	R		↓(BA19)	↑
	L		↓(BA19)	↓
not specified	not specified		↓	

Table 4. (Continued)

Imaging apparatus			Structure	Function	
			MRI	PET	SPECT
Parietal cortex	postcentral gyrus	R			↓
		L		↓(BA1,2)	
	precuneus	L	↓(BA31)		
	superior parietal lobule	R	↓		
		L			
	inferior parietal lobule	R	↓(BA7&40)		
		L			
Occipital cortex	not specified	L		↓	
	cuneus	R	↓(BA19)		
	middle occipital gyrus	L	↓(BA19)		
Para limbic system	cingulate gyrus	R		↓(BA31)	
	anterior cingulate gyrus	R	↑↓(BA24-25)↑	↑↓	
		not specified		↑↓	
	posterior cingulate gyrus	R		↓	
		not specified		↑	
	insula	L		↑	
	putamen	not specified		↑	
	caudate	not specified		↑↓	
	entorhinal cortex	not specified		↑	
	parahippocampal gyrus	R	↑	↑	
		L	↑	↓	
		not specified			
Limbic system	hippocampus	R	↑↓		
		not specified	↑		
	amygdala	R	↑↓		
		L	↑		
		not specified			
Thalamus	thalamus	R		↑(mediodorsal nuclei)	↑
		not specified		↓	↓
Hypothalamus	hypothalamus	not specified		↓	

↓ : negative correlation
↑ : positive correlation

A clue for resolving this inconsistency may be drawn from the findings of fMRI studies. For example, Etkin et al. (2004) reported that exaggerated amygdala activity during unconscious processing of fearful stimuli was predicted by trait anxiety. Subsequent studies also confirmed the presence of a significant relationship between amygdala activity and an anxiety-related personality trait: a significant correlation between increased amygdala activity and higher N during viewing of morally unpleasant images(Harenski, Kim and Hamann 2009), greater amygdala activation in individuals with high N compared to those with low N during a face emotion assessment task (Stein et al. 2007), a positive correlation between N and activities in the amygdala and subgenual anterior cingulate cortex (ACC) during an emotional conflict task (Haas et al. 2006), and a positive correlation between N and activities in the amygdala and hippocampus during observational fear learning(Hooker et al. 2008). What is intriguing here is that the amygdala, together with the fusiform cortex, which comprises an area responding specifically to face (Kanwisher and Yovel 2006), exhibited greater activation during processing of ambiguous fearful faces in the high-N group than in the low-N group (Chan et al. 2009). This indicates that individuals with a high anxiety-related personality trait tend to respond over-emotionally to an outside stimulus, even if its emotional intensity is not salient.

Furthermore, a seminal study employing both MRI and fMRI demonstrated not only a lower volume of gray matter in the amygdala and ventral ACC but also a reduction of functional connectivity between them during the processing of fearful stimuli in individuals with the shortallele of 5HTTLPR (Pezawas et al. 2005), which was revealed to be associated with an anxiety-related personality trait (Munafò et al. 2009, Sen et al. 2004, Schinka et al. 2004, Munafò et al. 2005). A noteworthy feature is that the magnitude of the coupling inversely predicted almost 30% of the variation in HA, suggestingthat the stronger the connectivity between the amygdala and the ACC, the weaker the anxiety-related personality trait becomes. Moreover, tight coupling between the amygdala and the ventral ACC has been implicated in the magnitude of the extinction of negative affect (Shin, Rauch and Pitman 2006). Thus, the amygdala, together with the ventral ACC, is likely to be critically involved in the formation of an anxiety-related personality trait, particularly from the aspect of cognitive regulation of negative emotion induced by a stimulus.

Ventral Part of the Anterior Cingulate Cortex (ACC)

As indicated by the above-mentioned fMRI study (Pezawas et al. 2005), the ACC is also an important region for formation of the anxiety-related personality trait.

Several PET studies have demonstrated a significant relationship between the ACC and an anxiety-related personality trait: higher HA and lower 5HT2A receptor binding potential around the genu(Moresco et al. 2002), higher N and lower 5HT1A receptor binding potential in the whole ACC as a ROI(Tauscher et al. 2001), and higher HA and lower glucose metabolism in the perigenual area(Youn et al. 2002). In addition, several MRI studies have found a larger volume of gray matter in the ACC, particularly its subgenual area(Blankstein et al. 2009, Gündel et al. 2004, Pujol et al. 2002). These findings confirm the importance of the ACC, particularly its ventral part (i.e. rostral to subgenual area or perigenual area), in the anxiety-related personality trait.

Table 5. Gender difference of specific cortical regions with Harm Avoidance in the PET study (Hakamata et al., 2009)

Cortical regions (Brodmann's area)[*1]	males (n=65) Laterality	Talairach Coordinates			k	Z	Cortical regions (Brodmann's area)[*1]	females (n=37) Laterality	Talairach Coordinates			k	Z
		x	y	z					x	y	z		
Positive correlation with HA							*Positive correlation with HA*						
None							None						
Negative correlation with HA							*Negative correlation with HA*						
None							superior frontal gyrus	L	-34	58	-11	1866	4.10
							medial frontal gyrus (BA11)	L	-6	46	-11		
							medial frontal gyrus (BA11)	L	-10	58	-13		

[*] Age and other temperament dimensions' scores were incorporated as covariates of interest.

The ventral ACC, together with the ventromedial prefrontal cortex (vmPFC), encompassing a medial part of the orbitofrontal cortex (mOFC), constitutes anatomically an extended network formed by their neural projections with the amygdala, hippocampus, superior and medial temporal gyri, ventral striatum, mid- and posterior cingulate cortex (PCC), hypothalamus, periaqueductal gray, and habenula (Ongür, Ferry and Price 2003). This network has been implicated in regulation of the evaluative, expressive, and experimental aspects of emotion, and has been shown to be disrupted in patients with mood and anxiety disorder who score quite highly on anxiety-related personality scales(Drevets, Savitz and Trimble 2008, Shin and Liberzon 2010). Consistent with the findingsof Pezawas et al. (2005), a subsequent fMRI study reported a decrease of functional connectivity between the amygdala and the ACC when N was increased during the processing of images of emotional faces, suggesting a diminished function of the ACC in regulating the amygdala (Cremers et. al. 2010). This loss of ability of the ACC to control excessive amygdala activity in response to emotional stimuli is considered to result in emotional over-reactivity such as hyperarousal and hypertension(Shin et al. 2006).

Ventromedial Prefrontal Cortex (vmPFC) Encompassing the Medial Orbitofrontal Cortex (mOFC)

In addition to the amygdala and ventral ACC, the importance of the vmPFC,through its extended anatomical network, has also been emphasized by Ongür et al. (2003). Our previous study, which examined the possible correlation between HA and glucose metabolism throughout the brain using [18F]FDG-PET in 31 healthy adults, found lower glucose metabolism in the vmPFC, encompassing parts of the ACC and the OFC, as a function of HA (Hakamata et al. 2006). This significant relationship with the vmPFC was later replicated in astudy involving a larger sample size (n = 102, see Figure 1) (Hakamata et al. 2009). Moreover, interestingly, we found this significant negative correlation only in females when the participants were divided by gender (Table 5). This is supported by the findings of two MRI studiesshowing a significant relationship between an anxiety-related personality trait and a lower gray matter volume in the vmPFC (Yamasue et al. 2008, Rauch et al. 2005). Notably, the study by Yamasue et al. (2008)demonstrated this relationship in females but not in males, indicating an important impact of gender on individual differences in the vmPFC. ·

Thus, the vmPFC, together with the ACC and the amygdala, may play a pivotal role in the anxiety-related personality trait. In contrast to the weaker coupling between the amygdala and the ACC during emotional processing as a function of anxiety-related personality trait (Pezawas et al. 2005, Cremers et al. 2010), another seminal fMRI study demonstrated that the vmPFC exhibited stronger coupling with the amygdala as a function of HA during a face-matching task (Buckholtz et al. 2008). It is important to note, however, that this stronger coupling was found only in males who showed lowexpression of a genetic variant of monoamine oxidase A (MAOA), which acts on noradrenaline, adrenaline, and serotonin as substrates. Again, this implies that the neural system underlying human anxious personality is very much influenced by gender and genetic variation. Moreover, the path analysis utilized in their study to parse the effective connectivity among the vmPFC, the rostral ACC, and the amygdala showed that the vmPFC regulated the amygdala indirectly by influencing the rostral

ACC (Buckholtz et al. 2008). Based on this result, they proposed a superordinate role of the vmPFC over the ACC and the amygdala in emotional regulation.

On the other hand, in studies employing different research approaches to those focusing on emotional regulation, the vmPFC has been implicated in autobiographical memory(Levine 2004). Autobiographical memory entails a complex set of operations, including episodic memory, self-reflection, emotion, visual imagery, attention, executive functions, and semantic processes (Svoboda, McKinnon and Levine 2006). The vmPFC is considered to be specifically engaged in this type of memory from the perspective of integration of sensory information with self-specific information (Levine 2004).

Taken together, these previous findings suggest that individual differences in anxious personality may originate from differences in emotional regulation, autobiographical memory recollection, or possibly functionsthat involve both, such as integrationof emotional experiences into autobiographical memory through self-relevant processing.

Hippocampal Regions

Hippocampal regions including the hippocampus and parahippocampal gyrus are known to have anatomically rich neural connections with the amygdala, the ACC, and the vmPFC (Ongür et al. 2003). Structural and functional alterations in these regions have been reported at relatively higher frequency in comparison with others (Table 4). Several functional imaging studies employing PET and SPECT in a resting state have demonstrated a significant relationship between the parahippocampal gyrus and an anxiety-related personality trait, although its direction was not consistent, being negative (Sugiura et al. 2000, Hakamata et al. 2006)or positive (Frokjaer et al. 2008, Turner et al. 2003). This inconsistency of direction has also been demonstrated in several MRI studies of the hippocampus (Yamasue et al. 2008, Barrós-Loscertales et al. 2006, Cherbuin et al. 2008). Conceivably, one of the reasons for these inconsistent findings may be related to gender difference or genetic variation. In fact, interaction between genetic variation and an anxiety-related personality trait has been shown to exert a striking influence on the volume of the hippocampal gray matter(Joffe et al. 2009). This MRI study found that a smaller hippocampal gray matter volume was associatedwith a higher N score only in individuals with a methionine type of genetic polymorphism, Val66Met, of brain-derived neurotrophic factor (BDNF), which is a neurotrophin expressed widely in the mature brain, particularly the hippocampus and the PFC, and is implicated in the process of hippocampal neurogenesis.

It has beenindicated that the hippocampal regions play a critical role in episodic memory[1] and help the mPFC by providing information about prior experiences in the form of memory (i.e. episodic memory) to construct self-relevant mental simulations for future planning, to navigate social interactions, and to maximize the utility of moments (Dickerson and Eichenbaum 2010, Buckner, Andrews-Hanna and Schacter 2008), corresponding to the

---

[1] Episodic memories consist of episodic elements, summary records of experience often in the form of visual images, associated to a conceptual frame that provides a conceptual context and are embedded in a more complex conceptual system in which they can become the basis of autobiographical memories (Conway, 2009).Thus, they can be discriminated from the autobiographical memories that are based on mental operations accompanied by such as emotional and self-relevant processing, as mentioned above (Subdova et al., 2006).

importance of its subdivision (vmPFC) in autobiographical memory integration from the perspective of self-relevant processing.

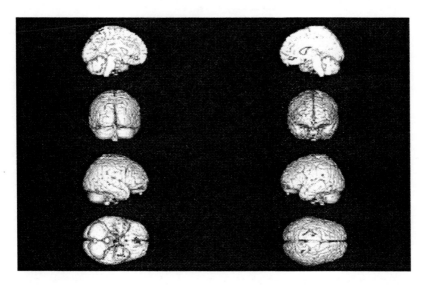

Figure 1. Significant negative correlation between brain cerebral glucose metabolism in the ventromedial prefrontal cortex and Harm Avoidance in 102 subjects (when a gender effect was excluded)

Although no study has so far investigated relationshipswithin the triad of an anxiety-related personality trait, brain structure or function such as that involving the mPFC and hippocampus, and memory function related to self-relevant processing, the possibility of biased autobiographical memory function associated with alteration in the vmPFC or hippocampal regions in highly anxious individuals has been indicated in several studies. For example, individuals with a high anxiety-related personality trait have been reported to have reduced ability to access specific memories of life events (i.e. overgenerality of autobiographical memory) (Chan, Goodwin and Harmer 2007). This overgenerality, in addition tothe anxiety-related personality trait, has also been shown to be a risk factor for emotional disorder in a prospective study (Bryant, Sutherland and Guthrie 2007). Moreover, overgenerality, as well as structural and functional alterations in the vmPFC and the hippocampus, have been reported in patients with mood and anxiety disorder(Williams and Moulds 2008, Kleim and Ehlers 2008, Rauch, Shin and Phelps 2006, Steele et al. 2007).

Therefore, individual differences in anxiety-proneness, by way of specific profile patterns of network connectivityamong the amygdala, ACC, vmPFC, and the hippocampal regions, may create individual differences in how perceived experience is incorporated into subjective experiences with personal or emotional meaning, which eventually becomes an individual's life story (i.e. autobiographical memory).

3. SUMMARY: IMPLICATIONS OF THE POSSIBLE NEUROBIOLOGICAL BASIS OF AN ANXIETY-RELATED PERSONALITY TRAIT

Through a detailed review of structural and functional neuroimagingin individuals with an anxiety-related personality trait, we have identified important roles of the amygdala, ACC, vmPFC, and hippocampal regions in the formation of an anxious personality. These regions have been revealed to work together through rich reciprocal neural connections, and are implicated to function in emotional regulation, memory, and self-relevant operations (Drevets et al. 2008, Levine 2004, Svoboda et al. 2006, Dickerson and Eichenbaum 2010, Buckner et al. 2008, Shin et al. 2006, Ongür et al. 2003). Above all, coupling of exaggerated amygdala activity and diminished ACC activity may contribute to strengthening of emotional sensitivity to an outside stimulus. Also, disruption of neural connectivityamong the vmPFC, hippocampal regions, and possibly the amygdaladuring the processing of prior emotional experiences may lead to the formation of biased autobiographical memories. Therefore, specific patterns of these brain activities are likely to create individual differences in various functional aspects reflected in the anxiety-related personality trait, although currently there areinsufficient data on the types of brain connectivity pattern that contribute to specific functional aspects of anxiety-related personality.

As mentioned earlier, these specific patterns are considered to be fairly dependent on gender difference and genetic variation (Pezawas et al. 2005, Buckholtz et al. 2008, Joffe et al. 2009). Given that personality is dependent not only on gender and genetic variation but also on a huge varietyof experiences and extremely complex interactionsamong them (Caspi et al. 2002), it will be necessary to incorporate a perspective of the "developing brain" into future research in this field. Clearly, the brains of children and adolescents,which are in the process of active and continuous development and exhibit enhanced neuronal plasticity, are distinct from those of adults (Johnston 2009). Therefore, to fully understand the neurobiological formation of an anxious personality in humans, prospective studies from infancy to adulthoodtaking account of gender and genetic variation will be essential.

REFERENCES

Allport, G. W., & Odbert, H. S. (1936) Trait names: A psycho-lexical study. *Psychological Monographs,47*, Whole.

Barrós-Loscertales, A., Meseguer, V., Sanjuán, A., Belloch, V., Parcet, M., Torrubia, R., & Avila, C. (2006). Behavioral Inhibition System activity is associated with increased amygdala and hippocampal gray matter volume: A voxel-based morphometry study. *Neuroimage,33*, 1011-5.

Blankstein, U., Chen, J., Mincic, A., McGrath. P, & Davis, K. (2009) The complex minds of teenagers: neuroanatomy of personality differs between sexes. *Neuropsychologia,47*, 599-603.

Borg, J., Andrée, B., Soderstrom, H, & Farde, L. (2003). The serotonin system and spiritual experiences. *Am J Psychiatry,160*, 1965-9.

Bryant, R., Sutherland, K, & Guthrie, R. (2007) Impaired specific autobiographical memory as a risk factor for posttraumatic stress after trauma. *J Abnorm Psychol,116*, 837-41.

Buckholtz, J., Callicott, J., Kolachana, B., Hariri, A., Goldberg, T., Genderson, M., Egan, M., Mattay, V., Weinberger, D. & Meyer-Lindenberg, A. (2008). Genetic variation in MAOA modulates ventromedial prefrontal circuitry mediating individual differences in human personality. *Mol Psychiatry,13*, 313-24.

Buckner, R., Andrews-Hanna, J. & Schacter, D. (2008). The brain's default network: anatomy, function, and relevance to disease. *Ann N Y Acad Sci,1124*, 1-38.

Caspi, A., McClay, J., Moffitt, T., Mill, J., Martin, J., Craig, I., Taylor, A. & Poulton, R. (2002). Role of genotype in the cycle of violence in maltreated children. *Science,297*, 851-4.

Cattell, R. B. (1943). The description of personality: Basic traits resolved into clusters. *Journal of Abnormal and Social Psychology,38*, 476-506.

Chan, S., Goodwin, G. & Harmer, C. (2007). Highly neurotic never-depressed students have negative biases in information processing. *Psychol Med,37*, 1281-91.

Chan, S., Norbury, R., Goodwin, G. & Harmer, C. (2009). Risk for depression and neural responses to fearful facial expressions of emotion. *Br J Psychiatry,194*, 139-45.

Cherbuin, N., Windsor, T., Anstey, K., Maller, J., Meslin, C. & Sachdev, P. (2008). Hippocampal volume is positively associated with behavioural inhibition (BIS) in a large community-based sample of mid-life adults: the PATH through life study. *Soc Cogn Affect Neurosci,3*, 262-9.

Clark, L., Watson, D. & Mineka, S. (1994). Temperament, personality, and the mood and anxiety disorders. *J Abnorm Psychol,103*, 103-16.

Cloninger, C. (1986). A unified biosocial theory of personality and its role in the development of anxiety states. *Psychiatr Dev,4*, 167-226.

Cloninger, C., Svrakic, D. & Przybeck, T. (1993). A psychobiological model of temperament and character. *Arch Gen Psychiatry,50*, 975-90.

Costa, P. T., Jr. (1985). *The NEO personality inventory manual.* Odessa, FL. Psychological Assessment Resources.

Costa, P. T. & McCrae, R.R. (1992). *Revised NEO Personality Inventory and five-factor inventory professional manual.* Odessa, FL.: Psychological Assessment Resources.

Cremers, H., Demenescu, L., Aleman, A., Renken, R., van Tol, M., van der Wee, N., Veltman, D. & Roelofs, K. (2010). Neuroticism modulates amygdala-prefrontal connectivity in response to negative emotional facial expressions. *Neuroimage,49*, 963-70.

Deckersbach, T., Miller, K., Klibanski, A., Fischman, A., Dougherty, D., Blais, M., Herzog, D. & Rauch, S. (2006). Regional cerebral brain metabolism correlates of neuroticism and extraversion. *Depress Anxiety,23,* 133-8.

Dickerson, B. & Eichenbaum, H. (2010). The episodic memory system: neurocircuitry and disorders. *Neuropsychopharmacology,35,* 86-104.

Drevets, W., Savitz, J. & Trimble, M. (2008). The subgenual anterior cingulate cortex in mood disorders. *CNS Spectr,13,* 663-81.

Etkin, A., Klemenhagen, K., Dudman, J., Rogan, M., Hen, R., Kandel, E. & Hirsch, J. (2004). Individual differences in trait anxiety predict the response of the basolateral amygdala to unconsciously processed fearful faces. *Neuron,44,* 1043-55.

Eysenck, H. J. (1967). *The biological basis of personality.*Springfield, IL: Charles C. Thomas.

Eysenck, H. J. (1990). Biological dimensions of personality. In *Handbook of personality: Theory and research,* ed. L. A. Pervin. New York: Guilford.

Eysenck, H. J. E. S. B. G. (1969). *Personality Structure and Measurement.* London: Routledge.

Farde, L., Ginovart, N., Ito, H., Lundkvist, C., Pike, V., McCarron, J. & Halldin, C. (1997). PET-characterization of [carbonyl-11C]WAY-100635 binding to 5-HT1A receptors in the primate brain. *Psychopharmacology (Berl),133,* 196-202.

Fiske, D. W. (1949). Consistency of the factorial structures of personality ratings from different sources. *The Journal of Abnormal and Social Psychology,44,* 329-344.

Frokjaer, V., Mortensen, E., Nielsen, F., Haugbol, S., Pinborg, L., Adams, K., Svarer, C., Hasselbalch, S., Holm, S., Paulson, O. & Knudsen, G. (2008). Frontolimbic serotonin 2A receptor binding in healthy subjects is associated with personality risk factors for affective disorder. *Biol Psychiatry,63,* 569-76.

Gardini, S., Cloninger, C. & Venneri, A. (2009). Individual differences in personality traits reflect structural variance in specific brain regions. *Brain Res Bull,79,* 265-70.

Gray, J. A. (1972). The psychophysiological basis of introversion-extraversion: A modification of Eysenck's theory. In *The biological bases of individual behaviour,* ed. V. D. Nebylitsyn, & Gray, J. A., 128-205. San Diego, CA: Academic Press.

Gray, J. A. (1976). The psychophysiological basis of introversion-extraversion: A modification of Eysenck's theory. In *Biological bases of individual behavior.,* ed. V. D. G. Nebylitsyn, J. A., 182-205. New York: Academic.

Gray, J. A. (1981). A critique of Eysenck's theory of personality. In *A model for personality.,* ed. H. J. Eysenck, 246-277. Berlin: Springer.

Gündel, H., López-Sala, A., Ceballos-Baumann, A., Deus, J., Cardoner, N., Marten-Mittag, B., Soriano-Mas, C. & Pujol, J. (2004). Alexithymia correlates with the size of the right anterior cingulate. *Psychosom Med,66,* 132-40.

Haas, B., Omura, K., Amin, Z., Constable, R. & Canli, T. (2006). Functional connectivity with the anterior cingulate is associated with extraversion during the emotional Stroop task. *Soc Neurosci,1,* 16-24.

Hakamata, Y., Iwase, M., Iwata, H., Kobayashi, T., Tamaki, T., Nishio, M., Kawahara, K., Matsuda, H., Ozaki, N., Honjo, S. & Inada, T. (2006). Regional brain cerebral glucose metabolism and temperament: a positron emission tomography study. *Neurosci Lett,396,* 33-7.

Hakamata, Y., Iwase, M., Iwata, H., Kobayashi, T., Tamaki, T., Nishio, M., Matsuda, H., Ozaki, N. & Inada, T. (2009). Gender difference in relationship between anxiety-related personality traits and cerebral brain glucose metabolism. *Psychiatry Res,173,* 206-11.

Harenski, C., Kim, S. & Hamann, S. (2009). Neuroticism and psychopathy predict brain activation during moral and nonmoral emotion regulation. *Cogn Affect Behav Neurosci,9,* 1-15.

Hooker, C., Verosky, S., Miyakawa, A., Knight, R. & D'Esposito, M. (2008). The influence of personality on neural mechanisms of observational fear and reward learning. *Neuropsychologia,46,* 2709-24.

Iidaka, T., Matsumoto, A., Ozaki, N., Suzuki, T., Iwata, N., Yamamoto, Y., Okada, T. & Sadato, N. (2006). Volume of left amygdala subregion predicted temperamental trait of harm avoidance in female young subjects. A voxel-based morphometry study. *Brain Res, 1125,* 85-93.

Joffe, R., Gatt, J., Kemp, A., Grieve, S., Dobson-Stone, C., Kuan, S., Schofield, P., Gordon, E. & Williams, L. (2009). Brain derived neurotrophic factor Val66Met polymorphism, the five factor model of personality and hippocampal volume: Implications for depressive illness. *Hum Brain Mapp,30,* 1246-56.

Johnston, M. (2009). Plasticity in the developing brain: implications for rehabilitation. *Dev Disabil Res Rev,15,* 94-101.

Kaasinen, V., Nurmi, E., Bergman, J., Solin, O., Kurki, T. & Rinne, J. (2002). Personality traits and striatal 6-[18F]fluoro-L-dopa uptake in healthy elderly subjects. *Neurosci Lett,332,* 61-4.

Kanwisher, N. & Yovel, G. (2006). The fusiform face area: a cortical region specialized for the perception of faces. *Philos Trans R Soc Lond B Biol Sci,361,* 2109-28.

Kestler, L., Malhotra, A., Finch, C., Adler, C. & Breier, A. (2000). The relation between dopamine D2 receptor density and personality: preliminary evidence from the NEO personality inventory-revised. *Neuropsychiatry Neuropsychol Behav Neurol,13,* 48-52.

Kleim, B. & Ehlers, A. (2008). Reduced autobiographical memory specificity predicts depression and posttraumatic stress disorder after recent trauma. *J Consult Clin Psychol,76,* 231-42.

Laakso, A., Vilkman, H., Kajander, J., Bergman, J., paranta, M., Solin, O. & Hietala, J. (2000). Prediction of detached personality in healthy subjects by low dopamine transporter binding. *Am J Psychiatry,157,* 290-2.

LeDoux, J. (1994). Emotion, memory and the brain. *Sci Am,270,* 50-7.

Lesch, K., Heils, A. & Riederer, P. (1996). The role of neurotransporters in excitotoxicity, neuronal cell death, and other neurodegenerative processes. *J Mol Med,74,* 365-78.

Levine, B. (2004). Autobiographical memory and the self in time: brain lesion effects, functional neuroanatomy, and lifespan development. *Brain Cogn,55,* 54-68.

Moresco, F., Dieci, M., Vita, A., Messa, C., Gobbo, C., Galli, L., Rizzo, G., Panzacchi, A., De Peri, L., Invernizzi, G. & Fazio, F. (2002). In vivo serotonin 5HT(2A). receptor binding and personality traits in healthy subjects: a positron emission tomography study. *Neuroimage,17,* 1470-8.

Morgan, B. (2006). Behavioral inhibition: a neurobiological perspective. *Curr Psychiatry Rep,8,* 270-8.

Munafò, M., Clark, T. & Flint, J. (2005). Does measurement instrument moderate the association between the serotonin transporter gene and anxiety-related personality traits? A meta-analysis. *Mol Psychiatry,10,* 415-9.

Munafò, M., Freimer, N., Ng, W., Ophoff, R., Veijola, J., Miettunen, J., Järvelin, M., Taanila, A. & Flint, J. (2009). 5-HTTLPR genotype and anxiety-related personality traits: a meta-analysis and new data. *Am J Med Genet B Neuropsychiatr Genet,* 150B, 271-81.

Omura, K., Aron, A. & Canli, T. (2005). Variance maps as a novel tool for localizing regions of interest in imaging studies of individual differences. *Cogn Affect Behav Neurosci,5,* 252-61.

Ongür, D., Ferry, A. & Price, J. (2003). Architectonic subdivision of the human orbital and medial prefrontal cortex. *J Comp Neurol,460,* 425-49.

Pezawas, L., Meyer-Lindenberg, A., Drabant, E., Verchinski, B., Munoz, K., Kolachana, B., Egan, M., Mattay, V., Hariri, A. & Weinberger, D. (2005). 5-HTTLPR polymorphism impacts human cingulate-amygdala interactions: a genetic susceptibility mechanism for depression. *Nat Neurosci,8,* 828-34.

Pujol, J., López, A., Deus, J., Cardoner, N., Vallejo, J., Capdevila, A. & Paus, T. (2002). Anatomical variability of the anterior cingulate gyrus and basic dimensions of human personality. *Neuroimage,15,* 847-55.

Rabiner, E., Messa, C., Sargent, P., Husted-Kjaer, K., Montgomery, A., Lawrence, A., Bench, C., Gunn, R., Cowen, P. & Grasby, P. (2002). A database of [(11)C]WAY-100635 binding to 5-HT(1A) receptors in normal male volunteers: normative data and relationship to methodological, demographic, physiological, and behavioral variables. *Neuroimage,15,* 620-32.

Rauch, S., Milad, M., Orr, S., Quinn, B., Fischl, B. & Pitman, R. (2005). Orbitofrontal thickness, retention of fear extinction, and extraversion. *Neuroreport,16,* 1909-12.

Rauch, S., Shin, L. & Phelps, E. (2006). Neurocircuitry models of posttraumatic stress disorder and extinction: human neuroimaging research--past, present, and future. *Biol Psychiatry,60,* 376-82.

Schinka, J., Busch, R. & Robichaux-Keene, N. (2004). A meta-analysis of the association between the serotonin transporter gene polymorphism (5-HTTLPR) and trait anxiety. *Mol Psychiatry,9,* 197-202.

Schreckenberger, M., Klega, A., Gründer, G., Buchholz, H., Scheurich, A., Schirrmacher, R., Schirrmacher, E., Müller, C., Henriksen, G. & Bartenstein, P. (2008). Opioid receptor PET reveals the psychobiologic correlates of reward processing. *J Nucl Med,49,* 1257-61.

Sen, S., Burmeister, M. & Ghosh, D. (2004). Meta-analysis of the association between a serotonin transporter promoter polymorphism (5-HTTLPR) and anxiety-related personality traits. *Am J Med Genet B Neuropsychiatr Genet,127B,* 85-9.

Shin, L. & Liberzon, I. (2010). The neurocircuitry of fear, stress, and anxiety disorders. *Neuropsychopharmacology,35,* 169-91.

Shin, L., Rauch, S. & Pitman, R. (2006). Amygdala, medial prefrontal cortex, and hippocampal function in PTSD. *Ann N Y Acad Sci,* 1071, 67-79.

Steele, J., Currie, J., Lawrie, S. & Reid, I. (2007). Prefrontal cortical functional abnormality in major depressive disorder: a stereotactic meta-analysis. *J Affect Disord,101,* 1-11.

Stein, M., Simmons, A., Feinstein, J. & Paulus, M. (2007). Increased amygdala and insula activation during emotion processing in anxiety-prone subjects. *Am J Psychiatry,164,* 318-27.

Sugiura, M., Kawashima, R., Nakagawa, M., Okada, K., Sato, T., Goto, R., Sato, K., Ono, S., Schormann, T., Zilles, K. & Fukuda, H. (2000). Correlation between human personality and neural activity in cerebral cortex. *Neuroimage,11,* 541-6.

Svoboda, E., McKinnon, M. & Levine, B. (2006). The functional neuroanatomy of autobiographical memory: a meta-analysis. *Neuropsychologia,44,* 2189-208.

Tauscher, J., Bagby, R., Javanmard, M., Christensen, B., Kasper, S. & Kapur, S. (2001). Inverse relationship between serotonin 5-HT(1A) receptor binding and anxiety: a [(11)C]WAY-100635 PET investigation in healthy volunteers. *Am J Psychiatry,158,* 1326-8.

Turner, R., Hudson, I., Butler, P. & Joyce, P. (2003). Brain function and personality in normal males: a SPECT study using statistical parametric mapping. *Neuroimage,19,* 1145-62.

Van Laere, K., Goffin, K., Bormans, G., Casteels, C., Mortelmans, L., de Hoon, J., Grachev, I., Vandenbulcke, M. & Pieters, G. (2009). Relationship of type 1 cannabinoid receptor availability in the human brain to novelty-seeking temperament. *Arch Gen Psychiatry,66,* 196-204.

Williams, A. & Moulds, M. (2008). Negative appraisals and cognitive avoidance of intrusive memories in depression: a replication and extension. *Depress Anxiety,25,* E26-33.

Wright, C., Feczko, E., Dickerson, B. & Williams, D. (2007). Neuroanatomical correlates of personality in the elderly. *Neuroimage,35,* 263-72.

Wright, C., Williams, D., Feczko, E., Barrett, L., Dickerson, B., Schwartz, C. & Wedig, M. (2006). Neuroanatomical correlates of extraversion and neuroticism. *Cereb Cortex,16,* 1809-19.

Yamasue, H., Abe, O., Suga, M., Yamada, H., Inoue, H., Tochigi, M., Rogers, M., Aoki, S., Kato, N. & Kasai, K. (2008). Gender-common and -specific neuroanatomical basis of human anxiety-related personality traits. *Cereb Cortex,18,* 46-52.

Yasuno, F., Suhara, T. Y. Sudo, Yamamoto, M., Inoue, M., Okubo, Y. & Suzuki, K. (2001). Relation among dopamine D(2) receptor binding, obesity and personality in normal human subjects. *Neurosci Lett,300,* 59-61.

Youn, T., Lyoo, I., Kim, J., Park, H., Ha, K., Lee, D., Abrams, K., Lee, M. & Kwon, J. (2002). Relationship between personality trait and regional cerebral glucose metabolism assessed with positron emission tomography. *Biol Psychol,60,* 109-20.

In: Personality Traits: Theory, Testing and Influences
Editor: Melissa E. Jordan

ISBN: 978-1-61728-934-7
© 2011 Nova Science Publishers, Inc.

Chapter 7

TOO MUCH OF A GOOD THING?: OPTIMISTIC OR PESSIMISTIC PERSONALITY TRAITS

Francine Conway and Laura Kelly

Adelphi University, Derner Institute of AdvancedPsychological Studies,
Garden City, NY, USA

The 'mind-body connection' has become a new buzz phrase that has served a variety of purposes including validating the practice of clinical psychology amongst the medical professionals.The results from a myriad of studies within this century have provided empirical evidence for the relations between the mind and body.Central to this connection are personality differences in one's world view, specifically optimistic versus pessimistic dispositions.Featured prominently in this body of literature is the beneficial role of optimism in physical health outcomes.More careful examination of the relations between optimism and health has begun to differentiate between the benefits associated with physical health and those circumscribed to psychological health.Researchers have made several additional distinctions regarding research on optimism: some studies have elaborated on whether the relations between optimism and health are linear or curvilinear and others have highlighted the differences between optimism and pessimism.

Since personality differences account for the variation of emotional experiences from one person to the next, it shapes how one regulates their emotional experiences which in turn influence health (Brickman, Coates, & Janoff-Bulman, 1978). Emotion regulation, as defined by Gross (1998) is the process by which people influence the emotions they have and how they experience and express these emotions. These processes can be automatic or controlled and conscious or unconscious (Gross, 1998).These emotion processes are largely influenced by individual differences in personality. Personality differences in dispositional factors such as optimism have attracted the interest of researchers as well as lay persons.The culture is littered with the pursuit of happiness and ways of training oneself to adopt a more optimistic view of life.Spurring the discussion has been the synchronicity between optimism and the very human condition to desire pleasurable emotional experiences and perhaps equally strongly shun painful ones.This chapter examines the optimism discourse occurring in the spheres of both empirical research and popular culture.We introduce a different perspective on the matter that is influenced by a parallel discourse which has not yet become a part of the lexicon of optimism although the evidence already exists, that of balance achieved through mindfulness.

THE BENEFICIAL ROLE OF OPTIMISM IN HEALTH OUTCOMES

Research studies have shown that pessimism rather than optimism seems to be more predictive of poor physical health outcomes (Irvine & Ritvo, 1998; Milam, Richardson, Marks, Kepmer, & McCutchan, 2004).Pessimism has an adverse effect on blood pressure (Räikkönen, Matthews, Flory, Owens & Gump, 1999) and exacerbates the progression of HIV virus to AIDS (Milam et al., 2004). However, the relation of health to dispositional traits appears to be age dependent.Physical health seems to be related to pessimism among older adults, but in younger adults optimism is a better predictor of physical health outcomes (Brenes, Rapp, Rejeski, & Miller, 2002; Lai, 1994; Robinson-Whelen, Kim, MacCallum, & Kiecolt-Glaser, 1997; Mroczek, Spiro, Aldwin, Ozer, & Bosse, 1993; Schulz, Bookwala, Knapp, Scheier, & Williamson, 1996).

In contrast to pessimism, optimism is generally associated with positive physical health outcomes.Optimists tend to have a lower death ratio (Giltay, Geleijnse, Zitman, Hoekstra & Schouten, 2004), lower rates of heart attack (Kubzansky, Sparrow, Vokonas & Kawachi, 2001), and improved likelihood of cancer survival (Carver, Pozo, Harris, Noriega, Scheier, Robinson, Ketcham, Moffat, & Clark, 1993; Greer, Morris, & Pettingale, 1979) and surgical recovery (Scheier, Matthews, Owens, Magovern, Lefebvre, Abbott, & Carver, 1989).

While a pessimistic outlook is associated with negative physical health outcomes, optimism has been mostly associated with favorable psychological outcomes (Carver & Gaines, 1987; Scheier & Carver, 1985). For example, optimists experience shorter bereavement periods following cancer loss (Kurtz, Kurtz, Stommel, Given, & Given, 1997) and seem to be immune from burnout when working with Parkinson patients (Lyons, Stewart, Archbold, Carter & Perrin, 2004). Optimism also impacts psychological adjustments to non-medical situations, such as experiences among law students (Segerstrom, Taylor, Kemeny & Fahey, 1998), black college students (Mosher, Prelow, Chen & Yackel, 2006), college in general (Aspinwall & Taylor, 1992), and academic and professional successes reflecting an individual's orientation towards achievement (Curry, Snyder, Cook, Ruby, & Rehm, 1997; Peterson, 2000; Peterson & Park, 1998).Psychological benefits associated with optimism include anxiety reduction, which allows the individual to attend to daily living tasks (Perloff, 1983).The empirical literature has found that highly optimistic individuals tend to have less negative affective symptoms (such as anger, anxiety, and depression) and improved life satisfaction and psychological well-being (Cederblad, Dahlin, Hagnell, & Hanson, 1995; Fry, 1995; Nelson, Karr, & Coleman, 1995; Plomin, Scheier, Bergeman, Pederson, Nesselroade, & McClean, 1992).

The studies evidencing the health benefits associated with optimism and pessimism have lead those in the helping professions, as well as those wishing to be helpful, to encourage an optimistic point of view and avoid a pessimistic one when ever adverse life events arise.However, the limits of optimism and the potential gains associated with pessimism must also be considered.

IS THERE SUCH A THING AS TOO MUCH OPTIMISM AND NOT ENOUGH PESSIMISM?

Research findings have supported the generally held belief that the more optimistic one is, the better one's health and well-being.The linear relationship between disposition and health is supported by Carver and Scheier's (1981) self-regulation of behavior theory.According to this theory, positive expectations, such as those commonly held by optimists, result in engagement in with goal attainment during times of conflict and occurrences of events that may interrupt achievement of one's goal. In contrast, individuals who have negative expectations, such as pessimists, are more likely to disengage from their goals and avoid goal attainment.In other words, the accepted belief is that optimists are more likely to work towards achieving their positive health outcomes relative to pessimists.

While a pessimistic outlook is associated with negative physical health outcomes, some research has found that the more pessimistic a person is, the more difficulty they encounter in regulating negative emotional experiences (Seligman, 1991).Similarly, a smaller, yet just as important vein of research studies have found that too much optimism can actually be negative and harmful. Schwarzer (1994) refers to this phenomenon as defensive optimism.He posits that optimism can imply "a defensive orientation that could sustain risk behaviors or, inversely, it can also imply a functional orientation that would assist in the adoption of preventive measures" (161). Defensive optimism refers to a type of optimism that prevents people from accurately assessing the risk inherent in certain situations, interferes with the acceptance of negative circumstances, and ultimately functions as a type of denial.As Schwarzer (1994) mentioned, being able to realize that we are vulnerable to negative life events, even when there is a low probability that we will encounter them, is necessary in order to motivate us to counteract threats and to avoid risks.

There are two predominant types of defensive optimism that tend to occur.The temporal comparison bias describes individual's belief that because an event occurred once, it is less likely to reoccur.Where as, the social comparison bias characterizes individuals who believe that though negative events happened to others, they are immune from these events.Defensive optimists appear to favor certain information that makes them appear less vulnerable (Van der Velde, van der Pligt, & Hooykaas, 1994).For example, "We are functional optimists when we know the right means to counteract threat, and we are defensive optimists when we are oblivious to the actual risks in our environment" (Schwarzer, 175, 1994).

What about individuals who do recognize the risks in their environment?These individuals are referred to as defensive pessimists.According to Cantor and Norem (1989) defensive pessimists are people who have negative expectations toward future.These negative expectations function to both prepare them for possible failure and to motivate them to work hard to avoid the failure (Miceli & Castelfranchi, 2002).Defensive pessimists are able to conceive the possibility of failure quite vividly tend to indulge in the idea of failure.This focus on the potential for failure does not cripple them nor does it lead them to become avoidant.Their acknowledgement of and indulgence in the realistic chance for failure motivates them to engage in behavior that minimizes their chance of failure.Unlike optimists, defensive pessimists do not take any outcome for granted and in fact tend to focus on the negative outcomes which, they believe,if manifested, are more challenging and stress inducing.The aversive thoughts and feelings that the possibility of experiencing the negative outcome induces motivates the defensive pessimists to work toward achieving a more beneficial outcome.Miceli & Castelfranchi (2002) argue that defensive pessimists actually achieve more satisfaction from achieving positive outcomes than do optimists because the defensive pessimists do not necessarily expect the positive outcome to occur, they simply work toward it knowing that they may have to face negative life circumstances.

Culture

Desired emotional responses to specific situations, as well as which emotions are valued are significantly influenced by cultural contexts.For instance, the norm in culture, like the United States of America, is happiness (D'Andrade, 1984; Wierzbicka, 1994).Happiness is not only often our goal (to be happy), but is also a measure of well-being (unhappiness leads to various psychological disorders).However, happiness is far from the norm in other cultural contexts, such as in Pacific Island and East Asian cultures (Mesquita & Albert, 2007).While Americans tend to emphasize accomplishment of positive outcomes, East Asians and Russians tend to avoid failures to meet cultural norms (Mesquita & Albert, 2007).In addition, the way people appraise a situation, and consequently, how they respond to it emotionally is dependent on the cultural context in which they are operating. As stated by Mesquita & Albert (2007), "Appraisal is meaning making and meaning making is always cultural" (p.495). One of the ways in which culture influences appraisal formation is by providing the schemas against which situations are appraised (Mesquita & Albert, 2007). Culture provides a backdrop against which events are meaningful and specifies the source of meaning for events (Mesquita & Albert, 2007).Because individuals operate in a social system, they in turn operate under the influence of the specific cultural context to which they belong.Emotional expression and emotion regulation is significantly influenced by these cultural contexts.Culture therefore, supports the notion that an optimistic attitude is good and a pessimistic one is disadvantageous.

Achieving Balance

Few studies have considered the question of whether too high or low levels of either optimism or pessimism matters.Studies finding beneficial effects of moderate levels of both optimism and pessimism on health relative to lower or higher levels offer support for those who may argue against an overly optimistic point of view (DeRidder, Schreurs, & Bensing, 2000; Janice, 1958 in Milam et al, 2004; Sergestrom, 2001).According to Milam and colleagues (2004) low and high optimism scores may increase health risks and moderate optimism scores predict good health outcomes.In disorders such as chronic fatigue syndrome, optimism scores are lowest amongst participants with the more medically severe conditions (Jason, Witter, & Torres-Harding, 2003).However, in patients coping with HIV (Cohen,

Kearney, Zegans, Kemeny, Neuhas, & Stites,1999), Multiple Sclerosis, and Parkinson's disease (De Ridder et al., 2000), high levels of optimism are not a protective factor against the evolution of the disease since it is associated with poor health care and increased health risk behaviors (Milam et al., 2004). Similar findings were reported in Perkins, Leserman, Murphy, and Evans (1993) study where they found that in a population of 53 HIV-negative gay men, those who were high in optimism tended to engage in more high risk behaviors including inconsistent condom use and increased sexual partners and scoring higher on the risk index than those low in optimism. A study by Goodman, Chesney, and Tipton (1995) found that in a group of adolescent girls at risk for HIV contraction, those higher in optimism were less likely to seek information about HIV testing and were less likely to get an HIV test than those lower in pessimism.Moderate levels of optimism have been found to benefit students' immune system (Stergerstrom, 2001) and those with Parkinson's disease and Multiple Sclerosis (De Ridder et al., 2000).

Moderate amounts of pessimism have been shown to be beneficial to well-being and too much optimism decreases well-being. Conway, Magai, Springer, & Jones (2008) assessed optimism and pessimism in grandmothers who are primary caregivers of their grandchildren.They found that optimism in the older grandmothers correlated with less depression and hostility and optimism in younger grandmothers correlated with less sleep disturbance.However, the researchers found a non-linear relationship between pessimism and obsessive-compulsive symptoms and hypertension.In other words a moderate level of pessimism was correlated with the least amount of hypertension and obsessive-compulsive symptoms, whereas too much or too little pessimism equally correlated with the highest degree of hypertension and obsessive-compulsive symptoms.Conway et al's (2008) findings replicated a previous study's finding that a moderate level of pessimism is protective (Janis, 1958 in Milam et al., 2004)

The empirical evidence exists in support of moderate levels of optimism and pessimism, but these findings have not yet been accepted by most lay persons as evidenced by a recent New York Times article by Ellin (2009) entitled *Seeking a Cure for Optimism.* Citing a study "Think Negative!" by Joseph Forgas. published in the November-December issue of *Australasian Science* Ellin puts forward both the point of view regarding the benefits of optimistic and pessimistic perspectives. Forgas' study found that people who are in a negative mood are more critical of and pay more attention to their surroundings than happier people. Whereas positive moods may produce more creativity, flexibility, cooperation, and reliance on mental shortcuts, negative moods trigger more attentive and careful thinking and help people pay greater attention to the external world.

The arguments become polarized even between those who have written extensively on the topic including Barbara Ehrenreich and Martin Seligman. "Ultimate pessimism" (Seligman, 1991), is another name for depression or major depressive disorder (MDD), a crippling mental illness characterized by lack of motivation to do much of anything.Seligman, who runs the Positive Psychology Center at the University of Pennsylvania and has written extensively on the benefits of optimism, finds himself at odds with Barbara Ehrenreich, another prominent author, but skeptic of the claim that optimism is a cure-all for life's difficulties.Ehrenreich's best-selling book, "Bright-Sided: How the Relentless Promotion of Positive Thinking Has Undermined America," promotes her idea that thinking positively not only does not improve overall well-being, but in the long run, may cause harm.In her article, "Overrated Optimism: The Perils of Positive Thinking" found in Time (October, 2009),

Ehrenreich claims, "Americans have long prided themselves on being positive and optimistic — traits that reached a manic zenith in the early years of this millennium... Optimism wasn't just a psycho-spiritual lifestyle option; by the mid-'00s it had become increasingly mandatory." Ehrenreich stresses the point that optimism has become an almost threatening and fearful stance.There is a great deal of pressure for people to be optimistic under even the most adverse of circumstances, "or else".Also, our overly-positive society seems to shun any person who shakes optimistic ideals out of fear that these realists or pessimists may bring them down.

Although the temptation to pick one disposition over the other is strong, a more moderate position that allows one to have a balanced view of life is recommended.This balance is sometimes attained when one grows older and is able to benefit for life's experiences.Age consideration introduces to the discussion the role of perspective or. balance.Conway et al (2009) found that the diversity of older adults world view have placed them in a position to re-examine their beliefs and expectation in a manner that benefits them (Herzberg, Glaesmer, & Hoyer, 2006).It is also possible that given their perspective on life and experiences, their goals in life has been re-oriented towards valuing relationships (Carstensen, 1993) and they are more likely to adopt positive attitudes in the service of maintaining what is more important to them, i.e. relationships.This is an example of balance.It is not that the older adults in the Conway et al (2009) study did not acknowledge the negative aspects of their relational world, but that they may weight those against the potential gains the relationship offers and adopt a more balanced perspective.However, waiting until one age or practicing positive thinking may not prove prudent.

Based on the research evidence reviewed, moderate levels of either optimism or pessimism have been shown to be beneficial.A position that results in clinging defensively to optimism or avoiding more pessimistic realities is one that begs for a balanced approach to life.Balance refers to the ability to "keep one's consciousness alive to the present reality" (Hanh, 1999, p.11) through a mindful awareness of our emotions. Germer (2005) describes mindfulness as "an awareness. . .of present experience. . .with acceptance (p. 7).The practice of mindfulness enables an individual to observe the process of how thoughts and emotions occur in the mind. Typically, our experiences are sifted through previously sculpted emotions and thought patterns. This sieve is constituted from our accumulated experiences resulting in our worldview. Viewing the world through the lens of past experiences can result in a lack of clarity in our perceptions.In contrast, a mind that is attuned and receptive to the present is in a state of mindfulness or awareness. Siegel (2007) explains that thoughts and emotions are part of human experience, however; they can and often do interfere with sensory awareness. In an "awakened" state of mindfulness one is able discern that internal distress often is a product of preconceived ideas and emotional reactions (Siegel, 2007, p.78).

Siegel's argument in support of mindfulness offers the promise of assisting individuals in regulating their emotional experiences that can transcend biological control.From a neuropsychological perspective, research on emotion relies heavily on findings from brain damaged patients, and tends to focus on associations between different areas of the brain and their relation to various behaviors and emotions.Neuropsychological research suggests that brain areas such as the temporal lobes, the amygdala, the frontal lobes, and the anterior cingulated are all involved in processes involving emotion regulation by influencing us to choose or create rewarding situations in favor of punishing situations (Beer & Lombardo, 2007).

The anterior and medial temporal lobes have been found to help people to recognize and avoid threatening situations by our ability to evoke anger and fear when in these situations.Individuals with damage to these areas of the temporal lobes, those with Kluver-Bucy syndrome, tend to show significantly less anger and fear in situations that call for these emotions to be expressed as a mode of protection (Beer & Lombardo, 2007).Damage to the amygdala has led researchers to conclude that it functions in the perception of emotional face perception in others as well as is involved in enabling us to use positive and negative emotions to select situations and responses to those situations which increase reward and decrease punishment (Beer & Lombardo, 2007).Damage to the frontal lobes results in impaired preference for reward over punishment as well as the failure to take into account the degree of risk associated with different actions.Individuals with frontal lobe damage also tend to have difficulty reducing interpersonal conflict quickly and have difficulty accomplishing goals (Beer & Lombardo, 2007).The anterior cingulated is associated with directing people away from punishment.Damage to this area results in decreased experience of pain, tension, and anger (Beer & Lombardo, 2007).From this research on brain damaged patients, we have discovered the portions of the brain most active in particular emotional responses.Mindfulness practitioners embrace the notion that contemplative practices such as mindfulness meditation can affect these emotion centers of the brain and result in better regulation of emotions.

Neuroscience has begun to provide evidence for the connection between the mind and body.Changes in neural pathways suggest the neural pathways of individuals who are attuned to their present circumstances-- such as is evident amongst moderate optimist and pessimist, are distinct. Siegel points out that a wide array of research suggests that the self-regulatory prefrontal regions of the brain, especially the middle prefrontal areas, are dependent upon proper experiences with caregivers for their development (2007, p.191). Siegel's research explores the theory that internal and interpersonal attunements are related and share common neural correlates (p.192). In this theory, attunement between parent and child mirrors the internal attunement proposed for mindfulness (p.205). Neural circuits involved in attunement would include the middle prefrontal regions, insula, superior temporal cortex, and the mirror neuron system. These circuits are also hypothesized by Siegel to be the neuronal mechanisms for attuning one's mind to its own internal processes (2007, p.191).

Dan Siegel is one of the primary researchers pioneering the work on mindfulness. In his book, *The Mindful Brain* (2007) Siegel explores how mindfulness relates to attachment and well-being and further highlights how the mind and body are connected. For Siegel mental well-being is defined by flexibility, adaptability, coherence, energy, and stability (FACES) (Siegel, 2007, p.78).Mindful awareness is a quality of attunement that is thought to facilitate FACES.Siegel believes the ability to attune to the external world, the somatic world, the mental world of self and of others brings a reverberant quality that is both coherent and stabilizing (2007, p.78). This balanced acceptance of present reality mirrors the argument that a moderate degree of pessimism and optimism is ideal in order to deal with life events most openly and in a way that promotes the greatest amount of both short-term and long-term well-being.

Mindfulness theory and research promotes that approaching each moment with insight and acceptance, even those moments that are the most painful, can increase well-being and help us decrease the degree of suffering we experience as we try to distract ourselves or avoid pain (Kabat-Zinn, 1994).Mindfulness can be used to relieve the suffering inherent in psychological disorders such as anxiety and depression.As noted by Morgan (2005), those suffering from depression withdraw into themselves in order to avoid emotional pain.Mindfulness can help counter this depressive stance by teaching depressed individuals to turn toward their experiences, bringing them closer to the source of their pain and making in more likely that they will be able to work through this pain rather than to continually avoid it and suffer.Anxiety, too, is a psychological disorder that can only be overcome with treatments that directly or indirectly address patient's adversarial relationship to anxiety symptoms (Germer, 2005).Siegel (2005) extends upon these ideas by explaining how mindfulness techniques can also be used for psychophysiological disorders.Principles derived from mindfuless practice, including relaxing control, tolerating discomfort, staying with negative emotions, and returning attention to the present can be incredibly useful when treating psychophysiological disorders.

Mindfulness, then, seems to correlate with the balanced, accepting stance characteristic of a realistic outlook on life that contains a moderate amount of optimism and pessimism, and avoids extreme amounts of these two traits.As stated by the Dalai Lama (1998), in order to achieve happiness we need to be fully aware of our life circumstances and the pain we feel in order to gain the insight to overcome the intense pain related to various life stressors.He explains that similar to how knowing the fighting capability of one's opponents puts one in a better position when engaging in war, facing our difficulties puts us in a better position to deal with them.The Dalai Lama says of one's worldview, "...if your basic outlook is that suffering is negative and must be avoided at all costs and in some sense is a sign of failure, this will add a distinct psychological component of anxiety and intolerance when you encounter difficult circumstances, a feeling of being overwhelmed" (p. 141).However, a worldview that enables one to accept that suffering is a natural part of life will prepare one to be more tolerant of life's hardships.Without a certain amount of tolerance toward suffering, says the Dalai Lama, life can be miserable and hardships can seem never ending.Perhaps a moderate amount of optimism or pessimism is the "certain amount" of tolerance toward suffering that his Holiness speaks of.

REFERENCES

Aspinwall, L. G. & Taylor, S. E. (1992). Modeling cognitive adaptation: A longitudinal investigation of the impact of individual differences and coping on college adjustment and performance. *Journal of Personality and Social Psychology, 63,* 989-1003.

Beer, J.S. & Lombardo, M.V. (2007). Insights into emotion regulation from neuropsychology.In J.Gross(Ed.), *Handbook of Emotion Regulation,* (69-86). New York:Guilford.

Brenes, G., Rapp, S., Rejeski, W. J. & Miller, M. (2002). Do optimism and pessimism predict physical functioning? *Journal of Behavioral Medicine, 25,* 219-231.

Brickman, P., Coates, D. & Janoff-Bulman, R. (1978). Lottery winners and accidentvictims: Is happiness relative? *Journal of Personality and SocialPsychology,36,* 917-927.

Cantor, N. & Norem, J.K., (1989) Defensive pessimism and stress and coping, *Social Cognition, 7,* 92-112.

Carstensen, L. L. (1995).Evidence for a life-span theory of socioemotional selectivity.*Current Directions in Psychological Science, 4*, 151-156.

Carver, C.S. & Gaines, J.G. (1987).Optimism, pessimism, and post-partum depression,Cognitive *Therapy and Research, 11*, 449-462.

Carver, C.S. & Scheier, M.F. (1981).*Attention and self-regulation: A control-theoryapproach to human behavior*, New York: Springer.

Carver, C.S.,Pozo, C., Harris, S.D., Noriega, V., Scheier, M.F., Robinson, D.S.,Ketcham, A.S., Moffat, F.L. & Clark, K.C. (1993). How coping mediatesthe effect of optimism on distress: A study of women with early stage breastcancer. *Journal of Personality and Social Psychology, 65*, 375-390.

Cederblad, M., Dahlin, L., Hagnell, O. & Hansson, K. (1995).Coping with life span crises in agroup at risk of mental and behavioral disorders: From the Lundby study.*Acta Psychiatrica Scandinavica, 91*, 322-330.

Cohen, F., Kearney, K. A., Zegans, L. S., Kemeny, M. E., Neuhas, J. M. & Stites, D. P. (1999).Differential immune system changes with acute and persistent stress for optimists vs pessimists. *Brain Behavior and Immunity, 13*, 155-174.

Conway, F., Magai, C., Springer, C. & Jones, S.C. (2008). Optimism and Pessimismas predictors of physical and psychological health among grandmothersraising their grandchildren.*Journal of Research in Personality, 42*,1352-1357.

Curry, L. A., Snyder, C. R., Cook, D. L., Ruby, B. C. & Rehm, M. (1997). Role of hope in academic and sport achievement.*Journal of Personality and Social Psychology, 73*, 1257-1267.

Dalai Lama & Cutler, H.C. (1998). The Art of Happiness.New York: Riverhead Books. De Ridder, D., Schreurs, K. & Bensing, J. (2000). The relative benefits of beingoptimistic. Optimism as a coping resource in multiple sclerosis and Parkinson's disease.*British Journal of Health Psychology, 5*, 141-155.

D'Andrade, R.G. (1984). Culture meaning systems. In: R. A. Shweder,& R. A. Levine, (Eds.), *Culturetheory: Essays on mind, self, and emotion* (pp. 88-119). Cambridge: Cambridge University Press.

Ehrenreich, B. (2009). "Overrated Optimism: The Perils of Positive Thinking." *Time,* October, 2009.

Ellin, A. (2009). *"Seeking a Cure for Optimism."*The New York Times, December.

Fry, P. S. (1995). Perfectionism, humor, and optimism as moderators of health outcomes anddeterminants of coping styles of female executives.*Genetic, Social & General Psychology, 121*, 211-245.

Germer, C.K. (2005). Anxiety Disorder: Befriending Fear. In *Mindfulness and Psychotherapy,*152-172.

Giltay, E. J., Geleijnse, J. M., Zitman, F. G., Hoekstra, T. & Schouten, E. G. (2004). Dispositional optimism and all-cause and cardiovascular mortality in a prospective cohort of elderly dutch men and women. *Archives of General Psychiatry, 61*, 1126-1135.

Goodman, E., Chesney, M.A. & Tipton, A.C. (1995).Relationship of optimism, knowledge, attitudes, and beliefs to use of HIV antibody test by at-risk female adolescents.*Psychosomatic Medicine, 57*, 541-546.

Greer, S. (1991). Psychological response to cancer and survival.*Psychological Medicine,21*, 43-49.

Gross, J.J. (1998). The emerging field of emotion regulation: An integrative review. *Review of General Psychology*, *2(3)*, 271-299.

Hanh, Thich Nhat (1999). *The Miracle of Mindfulness*.Beacon Press.

Herzberg, P. Y., Glaesmer, H. & Hoyer, J. (2006).Separating optimism and pessimism: A robustpsychometric analysis of the revised Life Orientation Test (LOT-R).*Psychological Assessment*, *18*, 433-438.

Irvine, J. & Ritvo, P. (1998).Health risk behaviour change and adaptation in cardiac patients.*Clinical Psychology and Psychotherapy*, *5*, 86-101.

Janis, I. L. (1958).*Psychological stress*. New York: Wiley.

Jason, L. A., Witter, E. & Torres-Harding, S. (2003). Chronic fatigue syndrome, coping, optimism, and social support.*Journal of Mental Health*, *12*, 109-118.

Kabat-Zinn, J. (1994). *Wherever you go, there you are: mindfulness meditation in everyday life*. New York: Hyperion.

Kubzansky, L. D., Sparrow, D., Vokonas, P. & Kawachi, I. (2001). Is the glass half empty or half full? A prospective study of optimism and coronary heart disease in the normative aging study.*Psychosomatic Medicine*, *63*, 910-916.

Kurtz, M. E., Kurtz, J. C., Stommel, M., Given, C. W. & Given, B. (1997). Loss of physical functioning among geriatric cancer patients: Relationships to cancer site, treatment, comorbidity, and age. *European Journal of Cancer*, *33*, 2352-2358.

Lai, J. C. L. (1994).Differential predictive power of the positively versus the negatively wordeditems of the Life Orientation test.*Psychological Reports*, *75*, 1507-1515.

Lyons, K. S., Stewart, B. J., Archbold, P. G., Carter, J. H. & Perrin, N. A. (2004). Pessimism andoptimism as early warning signs for compromised health for caregivers of patients with Parkinson's disease.*Nursing Research*, *53*, 354-362.

Mesquita, B. & Albert, D. (2007).The cultural regulation of emotions. In Gross, J. (Ed.), *Handbook of Emotion Regulation*, (486-503). New York: Guilford.

Miceli, M. & Castelfranchi, C. (2002). The Mind and the Future: The (negative) Power of Positive Thinking. *Theory Psychology, 12* (335).

Milam, J., Richardson, J., Marks, G., Kepmer, C. & McCutchan, A. (2004).The roles ofdispositional optimism and pessimism in HIV disease progression.*Psychology and Health*, *19*, 167-181.

Morgan, S.P. (2005). Depression: Turning Toward Life. In *Mindfulness and Psychotherapy*, 130-151.

Mosher, C. E., Prelow, H. M., Chen, W. W.& Yackel, M. E. (2006).Coping and social support asmediators of the relation of optimism to depressive symptoms among black college students.*Journal of BlackPsychology*, *32*, 72-86.

Mroczek, D. K., Spiro, A., Aldwin, C. M., Ozer, D. J. & Bosse, R. (1993). Construct validation ofoptimism and pessimism in older men: Findings from the normative aging study. *Health Psychology, 12,* 406-409.

Nelson, E. S., Karr, K. M. & Coleman, P. K. (1995). Relationships among daily hassles, optimism and reported physical symptoms.*Journal of College Student Psychotherapy*, *10*, 11-26.

Perkins, D.O., Leserman, J., Murphy, C.& Evans, D.L. (1993). Psychosocial predictors of high-risk sexual behavior among HIV-negative homosexual men.*AIDS Education and Prevention*, *5(2)*, 141-152.

Perloff, L. (1983). Perceptions of vulnerability to victimization.*Journal of Social Issues, 39,* 41-61.

Peterson, C. & Park, C. (1998).Learned helplessness and explanatory style. In D.F. Barone, V.B.Van Hasselt, & M. Hersen (Eds.), *Advanced Personality*(287-310). New York: Plenum.

Peterson, C. (2000). The future of optimism.*American Psychologist, 55,* 44-55.

Plomin, R., Scheier, M.F.,Bergeman, C.S., Pederson, N.L.,Nesselroade, J.R. & McClearn, G.E. (1992). Optimism, Pessimism, and Mental Health: A twin/ adoption analysis. *Personality and Individual Differences, 13,* 921-930.

Räikkönen, K., Matthews, K. A., Flory, J. D., Owens, J. F. & Gump, B. B. (1999).Effects of optimism, pessimism, and traitanxiety on ambulatory blood pressure and mood during everyday life.*Journal of Personality & Social Psychology, 76,* 104-113.

Robinson-Whelen, S., Kim, C., MacCallum, R. C. & Kiecolt-Glaser, J. K. (1997). Distinguishingoptimism from pessimism in older adults: Is it more important to be optimistic or not to be pessimistic? *Journal of Personality and Social Psychology, 73,* 1345-1353.

Scheier, M.F. & Carver, C.S. (1985). Optimism, coping, and health: Assessment and implications of generalized outcome expectancies. *Health Psychology, 4,* 219-247.

Scheier, M.F., Matthews, K.A., Owens, J.F., Magovern, G.J., Lefebvre, R.C., Abbott, R.A. & Carver, C.S. (1989). Dispositional optimism and recovery from coronary artery bypass surgery: The beneficial effects on physical and psychological well-being. *Journal of Personality and SocialPsychology, 57,* 1024-1040.

Schulz, R., Bookwala, J., Knapp, J. E., Scheier, M. & Williamson, G. M. (1996).Pessimism, age,and cancer mortality.*Psychology and Aging, 11,* 304-309.

Schwarzer, R. (1994). Optimism, vulnerability, and self-beliefs as health-relatedcognitions: A systematic overview. *Psychology and Health, 9,* 161-180.

Segerstrom, S. (2001).Optimism, goal conflict, and stressor-related immune change.*Journal ofBehavioral Medicine, 24,* 441-467.

Segerstrom, S. C., Taylor, S. E., Kemeny, M. E. & Fahey, J. L. (1998). Optimism is associatedwith mood, coping, and immune changes in response to stress. *Journal of Personality and Social Psychology, 74,* 1646-1655.

Seligman, M.E.P. (1991). *Learned optimism.*New York: Knopf. Siegel, D. (2005). Mindfulness training and neural integration: Differentiation of distinct streams of awareness and the cultivation of well-being. *Social Cognitive and Affective Neuroscience, 2(4),* 259-263.

Siegel, D. (2007). The Mindful Brain: Reflection and Attunement in the Cultivation of Well-Being.W.W. Norton.

Van der Velde, F.W., van der Pligt, J. & Hooykaas, C. (1994).Perceiving AIDS-related risk: Accuracy as a function in differences in actual risk. *Health Psychology, 13 (1),* 25-33.

Wierzbicka, A. (1994).*Emotion, language, and cultural scripts.* In S. Kitayama & H. R. Markus (Eds.), Emotion and culture: Empirical studies of mutual influence (133-196). Washington, DC: American Psychological Association.

In: Personality Traits: Theory, Testing and Influences
Editor: Melissa E. Jordan

ISBN: 978-1-61728-934-7
© 2011Nova Science Publishers, Inc.

Chapter 8

ILLNESS RECOGNITION AND BELIEFS ABOUT TREATMENT FOR SCHIZOPHRENIA IN A COMMUNITY SAMPLE OF MEXICO CITY: DIFFERENCES ACCORDING TO PERSONALITY TRAITS

*Ana Fresán[a]*and Rebeca Robles-García[b]*

[a]Subdirección de Investigaciones Clínicas. Instituto Nacional de Psiquiatría Ramón de la Fuente, Mexico City, Mexico
[b] Dirección de Investigaciones Epidemiológicas y Sociales. Instituto Nacional de Psiquiatría Ramón de la Fuente, Mexico City, Mexico

ABSTRACT

Previous studies have detected different variables influencing the attitude towards individuals with schizophrenia. It has been considered that individual's knowledge about schizophrenia has an important role in shaping attitudes about people diagnosed with the disorder, and that a lack of knowledge may increase prejudice and discrimination of these individuals. However, additional factors related to particular characteristics of the *perceiver*, such as personality traits, may have a direct influence in the recognition of schizophrenia as a mental disease and the subsequent attitudes related to the disorder.

Objective

To assess temperament and character features, based on Cloninger's biosocial model of personality, relating people's recognition and beliefs about schizophrenia. We also examined personality differences according to the subjects' belief about the most adequate treatment for symptoms.

* Corresponding author: Subdirección de Investigaciones Clínicas. Instituto Nacional de Psiquiatría Ramón de la Fuente, Mexico City, Mexico., Calz. México-Xochimilco No 101. Tlalpan, Mexico City, 14370, MEXICO., Tel: (5255) 41 60 50 69, Fax: (5255) 55 13 37 22, E-mail: a_fresan@yahoo.com.mx; fresan@imp.edu.mx

Method

A case vignette describing a patient with paranoid schizophrenia was used to assess subjects' recognition of the disorder and their belief about treatment options. Personality traits were assessed using the Temperament and Character Inventory-Revised (TCI-R). A total of 203 subjects who recognized symptoms as part of a mental disorder and 203 age-gender-and educational level-matched subjects who didn't recognize mental illness were included.

Results

A greater number of subjects recognizing mental illness considered psychiatric intervention – the use of medication and hospitalization – as the adequate treatment for the symptoms described in the vignette. Also, they exhibited higher scores in the temperament dimension "Persistence". When personality traits, were compared in terms of the belief about the most adequate treatment, subjects who considered non-psychiatric, non-restrictive interventions – such as talking – had higher "Reward Dependence" and "Cooperativeness" scores independently of their status in the recognition of mental illness.

Conclusions

Our results support the notion that individual differences may have a direct influence in the recognition and management of mental disorders, in particular schizophrenia, among the general population. Although additional studies are required, these results may have important implications for anti-stigma campaigns for schizophrenia, as it is possible that part of the knowledge, attitudes and behaviors related to stigmatization are deeply rooted in the subject's personality and may require an additional or different management in these campaigns.

INTRODUCTION

Schizophrenia, from the Greek roots *skhizein* (σχίζειν, "to split") and *phrēn, phren-* (φρήν, φρεν-; "mind") is a severe and persistent mental disorder characterized by the presence of hallucinations, delusions, or disorganized thinking and causes significant disability. Psychotic disorders are ranked as the third most disabling condition in general population (more than paraplegia or blindness) [1], and chronic schizophrenia accounts for 1.1% of the total *Disability-adjusted life years* (DALYs) and 2.8% of *Years of lived with disability* (YLDs) [2].

Nevertheless, few patients around the world are diagnosed and receive treatment at early stages of their illness, which results in long-term worse outcome [3, 4] and an increased risk of future episodes of illness [5]. Barriers to help seeking behavior include accessibility and availability of services, as well as the lack of knowledge about mental illness and its treatment, both in patients and general population [6] which increase prejudice and discrimination of these individuals. Unfortunately it is well documented that general public has trouble with recognition and management of mental disorders, particularly in the case of schizophrenia. Wright et al [7] reported that only a quarter of a randomly selected sample of 1207 individuals identified psychosis correctly, and almost half were able to identify depression; and data from Jorm et al [8] in a cross-sectional survey with a sample of 2031 respondents suggest that many standard psychiatric treatments were more often rated as harmful than helpful, and some non-standard treatments were rated highly appreciated (increased physical or social activity, relaxation and stress management, reading about people with similar problems).

We face a growing concern relating to *mental health literacy*, defined as "knowledge and beliefs about mental disorders which aid their recognition, management and prevention" [8]. Some studies have examined the role of *individual characteristics* in the way the *perceiver* conceptualize and treat mental disorders. One of such characteristics is gender. According to Farina [9, 10] both males and females have prejudicial attitudes toward people with mental disorders, but women tend to exhibit fewer discriminatory behaviours than men. Level of education and ethnicity are other sociodemographic variables that have been taken into account [11].

Another set of individual characteristics of the perceiver that may have a direct influence in the recognition of mental disorders and the subsequent attitudes toward its treatment include psychological factors (rather than sociodemographic ones) [12]. In fact, Jorm [6], one of the central researchers about mental health literacy, suggest that public's beliefs about mental disorders and its treatment reveal a number of factors representing general belief systems about health. From this argument, *personality traits*, that by definition are highly stable and have a strong influence in the way we think, feel and behave, may be some of the main perceiver's characteristics that moderate mental health literacy. However, few studies have addressed this relation.

Recently, Swami, Persaud & Furnham [12] explored personality factors related to general public's ability to recognise mental health disorders in a sample of 477 British subjects. They employed a measure of the Big Five personality factors to document that the traits labelled "agreeableness" (positively) and "openness to experience" (negatively) predicted mental health literacy, as indexed by the difference in ratings of real disorders and foils. According to these authors, the association between agreeableness and mental health literacy is explained as a function of the tendency for agreeable individuals to be more concerned with the well-being of others. On the other hand, the possible negative association between mental health literacy and openness is more difficult to explain. Open individuals are expected to be more intellectually curious and attentive to inner feelings. Thus, even the researchers themselves noted that in their study, the Big Five factors showed moderate internal consistency, and it is important to replicate these findings using more reliable scales.

However, this was the first study that investigated, with an overclaiming technique, the relationship between personality features and one of two main components of mental health literacy: *the ability to recognise mental disorders*. The other domain that should be addressed is the *knowledge and beliefs about their management*. Currently it is well accepted that the public have a poor opinion of psychiatry and psychological treatments for mental disorders [13, 14], preferring self-help interventions and alternative therapies.

Lauber et al [15] concentrate their efforts to explain personality influence on the attitude to compulsory admission, a relative common treatment aspect of severe mental disorders like schizophrenia. They found that "rigid personality" is a negative predictor of compulsory admission acceptance, suggesting that authoritarian people believe that rather the legal system than psychiatry must pay attention to mentally ill. Nevertheless, authors defined *rigid personality* as the presence of an extreme political orientation (leftists and rightists) and did not use a comprehensive instrument based on a conceptual framework of personality.

Taking these together, the main objective of the present work is to assess temperament and character features, based on Cloninger's biosocial model of personality, relating people's recognition and beliefs about schizophrenia. Additionally, we examined personality differences according to the subjects' belief about the most adequate treatment for symptoms, using the Cloninger's biopychosocial model of personality, a hierarchical conceptualization of both temperament and character that has been shown to have good predictive ability in many senses, but it has not been previously used to examine mental health literacy. Given the dearth of previous work in relation to Cloninger's personality model with illness recognition and treatment beliefs in general community, formulating explicit hypotheses in this instance was difficult.

METHOD

Subjects

Recruitment was performed by a convenience sampling approach with subjects from the general population of Mexico City. As the present study can be consider as a pilot testing, this type of sampling was the most useful as it only samples those who are available and willing to participate. All subjects gave verbal informed consent after receiving a comprehensive explanation of the nature of the study. The Ethics Review Board of the Instituto Nacional de Psiquiatría Ramón de la Fuente approved the study.

This community sample is not intended to be representative of Mexico City's population, since the methods of the present work include a nonprobabilistic sample approach and intentionally matched procedures for comparison purposes. In this way, a total of 203 subjects who recognized symptoms as part of a mental disorder and 203 age-gender-and educational level-matched subjects who did not recognize mental illness were included. From the 406 subjects included 53.2% (n=216) were men and 46.8% (n=190) were women with a mean age of 36.8 ± 10.6 years (18 – 59 years) and an educational level of 13.2 ± 3.2 years (5 – 20 years).

Assessment Procedures

A case vignette, constructed so that it met DSM-IV criteria for paranoid schizophrenia, was used, such as in many of the studies on factors influencing mental health literacy[16]. After presenting the vignette to the respondents, they were asked to assess their recognition of a mental disorder and their belief about treatment options. Recognition of a mental disorder was scored as present or absent and it was used as the variable to define comparison groups. Several treatment options were included: 1) non-psychiatric, non-restrictive interventions (e.g., the person does not need any intervention at all, talking to the person or closer observation), 2) psychiatric interventions (e.g., use of oral medications, injections or hospitalization), and 3) restrictive interventions (e.g., seclusion, use of restraints or treatment for injuries).

Personality was assessed using the Temperament and Character Inventory-Revised (TCI-R) which was released in 1999 by C. Robert Cloninger. The TCI-R differs from the original TCI [17, 18] in several aspects. First, the true-false scale was replaced by a 5-point Likert type scale. A total of 51 items from the 240 of the original TCI were rewritten and include 5 validity items. Also, the temperament dimensions Persistence and Reward Dependence are now composed of 4 subscales. Briefly the temperament and character dimensions are described as follows.

Novelty Seeking (NS) is defined as the tendency to respond impulsively to novel stimuli with active avoidance to frustration. The second temperament dimension, *Harm Avoidance* (HA) is the tendency to inhibit responses to aversive stimuli leading to avoidance of punishment. *Reward Dependence* (RD), the third temperament dimension, is the tendency for positive responses to signals of reward that maintain ongoing behaviors. The last temperament dimension, *Persistence* (PE), is viewed as a tendency to perseverance despite frustration and fatigue. The character dimension, *Self-directedness* (SD), refers to the ability of an individual to control, regulate and adapt behavior to fit the situation in accordance to personal goals. The second character dimension, *Cooperativeness* (CO), accounts for individual differences in the acceptance of other people and measures features related to agreeability vs. self-centered aggression and hostility. *Self-transcendence* (ST) is viewed as the identification with everything conceived as essential and consequential parts of a unified whole [17-19].

Statistical Analyses

Demographic and clinical characteristics description was done with frequencies and percentages for categorical variables and with means and standard deviations (S.D.) for continuous variables. Chi-squared (χ^2) analysis for contingency tables on categorical data and independent sample t-tests on continuous data were used for the comparison between subjects who recognize and don't recognize core symptoms of schizophrenia as a mental disorder.

In addition, personality dimensions were compared between the suggested treatment options using a covariance (ANCOVA) model which contained illness recognition status as covariate. The significance level for tests was established at $p \leq 0.05$ (2-tailed).

RESULTS

A) Personality Differences According to Illness Recognition

The mean scores of the four temperament dimensions and the three character dimensions of groups are shown in Table 1. As can be seen, most of the personality dimensions did not differ between illness recognition groups. Nevertheless, the temperament dimension PE was significantly higher in the group of subjects who recognize symptoms of schizophrenia as a mental illness.

B) Beliefs about Adequate Treatment for Symptoms

From the total sample, 77.6% (n=315) considered the use of non-psychiatric, non-restrictive interventions for the treatment of symptoms (talking or closer observation), while only 17.0% (n=69) considered psychiatric interventions (medications or hospitalization) as the most adequate treatment and 5.4% (n=22) reported restrictive interventions such as seclusion, use of restraints or treatment for injuries.

When we compared the reported treatment beliefs according to illness recognition, subjects who recognized mental illness more frequently considered psychiatric interventions as the most adequate treatment of symptoms (n=52, 25.6% vs. n=17, 8.4%) while non-psychiatric interventions were preferred by those who did not recognize symptoms of a mental illness (n=180, 88.7% vs. n=135, 66.5%) (χ^2=28.7, df 2, p<0.001).

C) Personality and Beliefs of Adequate Treatment for Symptoms of Schizophrenia

Temperament and character dimensions were compared in terms of the belief about the most adequate treatment for symptoms. Illness recognition status was included in the statistical model as a covariate.

Subjects who considered non-psychiatric, non-restrictive interventions exhibited higher scores on the temperament dimension RD and in the character dimension CO when compared to groups who considered psychiatric or restrictive interventions for symptoms management. No differences emerged between groups on other personality dimensions (Figure 1).

Table 1. Mean scores of the TCI-R dimensions between groups

TCI-R Dimension	Subjects recognizing mental illness (n=203)		Subjects non-recognizing mental illness (n=203)		Statistic
	Mean	SD	Mean	SD	
Temperament					
Novelty Seeking	100.0	13.3	99.4	10.9	t=-0.5, df 404, p=0.58
Harm Avoidance	86.1	16.9	88.8	15.8	t=1.2, df 404, p=0.20
Reward Dependence	97.3	13.8	96.9	12.2	t=-0.3, df 404, p=0.73
Persistence	125.5	17.4	122.0	17.4	t=-2.0, df 404, p=0.04
Character					
Self-directedness	146.5	20.0	147.4	20.1	t=0.4, df 404, p=0.62
Cooperativeness	130.9	17.7	131.1	17.3	t=0.1, df 404, p=0.89
Self-transcendence	76.0	15.1	76.4	14.9	t=0.2, df 404, p=0.79

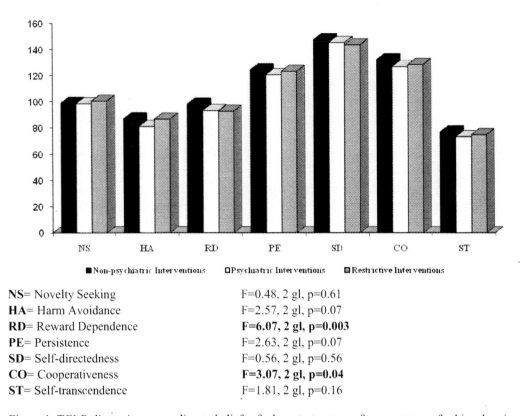

NS= Novelty Seeking	F=0.48, 2 gl, p=0.61
HA= Harm Avoidance	F=2.57, 2 gl, p=0.07
RD= Reward Dependence	**F=6.07, 2 gl, p=0.003**
PE= Persistence	F=2.63, 2 gl, p=0.07
SD= Self-directedness	F=0.56, 2 gl, p=0.56
CO= Cooperativeness	**F=3.07, 2 gl, p=0.04**
ST= Self-transcendence	F=1.81, 2 gl, p=0.16

Figure 1. TCI-R dimensions according to beliefs of adequate treatment for symptoms of schizophrenia

DISCUSSION

The aim of the present study was to determine the temperament and character traits differences between subjects who recognize core symptoms of schizophrenia as a mental disorder and according to subjects' belief about the most adequate treatment for these symptoms.We think that subjects who recognize mental illness have a different personality structure when compared to those who do not recognize it.

Recently, research efforts have been directed to the reduction of stigma toward psychiatric disorders, especially schizophrenia. As stigmatizing attitudes may be a reflection of the lack of knowledge or recognition of psychiatric disorders [20-22] we considered that an important question is how personality features may have a direct influence in the recognition of schizophrenia as a mental disorder. Recognition and management of core symptoms of schizophrenia in the general population has been rarely studied in terms of characteristics of the perceiver; nevertheless, some studies have found that sociodemographic factors such as gender, age, and educational level have a direct influence on mental illness stigma [9-11, 23]. Due to these previous results, we decided to use these variables to match our sample and avoid their probable influence in the comparison of personality features between subjects recognizing mental illness and those who do not recognize it.

Our results partially support the notion that personality differences may have a direct influence in the recognition of mental disorders, as the only significant difference found between illness recognition groups was in the PE scores. Persistence has been related to the ability to generate and maintain internal motivation in the absence of immediate external reward [24]. Perhaps people with high persistence seem more likely to intensify their efforts to the recognition of a mental disorder in the vignette in response to anticipated reward related to social desirability and may not reflect their real knowledge or attitudes toward mental disorders.

Another plausible explanation, may be that persistent persons are really more motivated to know about different others, even in the absence of evident social efforts or incentives to do it. Congruently, Swami el al [12] suggested that agreeableness individuals are more concerned with the well being of others. Then, these kinds of persons have in fact much more mental health literacy. This second explanation is supported by the fact that, in the present study, a greater number of subjects recognizing mental illness (that also exhibited higher scores in PE) considered psychiatric intervention – the use of medication and hospitalization – as the adequate treatment for the symptoms described in the vignette.

As in previous studies among different populations around the world [8, 13, 14], in this sample, more than half of the subjects, independently of their illness recognition' status, did not consider psychiatric interventions as the most adequate treatment for symptoms. It is not uncommon to believe that psychiatric symptoms are due to *weakness of character*[25], so that medications or psychiatric hospitalizations may be considered as extreme solutions. Our results in terms of higher RD and CO in subjects that preferred non-psychiatric, non-restrictive interventions for symptom management gives us an alternative explanation. It is plausible to think that their treatment selection was a consequence of these particular features since they exhibited higher rates of social empathy, tolerance, compassion and a sensation of being useful to others. Moreover, it's important to consider that these interventions in the management of symptoms include an active participation of the subjects by talking or having a close observation of the patients, which is in accordance with the areas measured by these personality dimensions.

Although additional studies of the impact of the perceiver's personality features in mental illness recognition in particular schizophrenia, are required, these results could have important implications for anti-stigma campaigns for schizophrenia, as it is possible that part of the knowledge, attitudes and behaviors related to stigmatization are deeply rooted in the subject's personality and may require an additional or different management in these campaigns. Previous research has identified three types of stigma change strategies [11, 26] which are: protest, education and contact. This last strategy has shown the best impact as it facilitates change by promoting exchange between the perceiver and the people with mental illness. For example, it has been reported that formal contact with patients promotes familiarity, improves empathy and decreases stigma [11, 26-28]. Assuming that future studies replicate our findings concerning different perceptions of mental illness and treatment according to personality features, and these results validate the importance of them as mediators of knowledge and stigma in schizophrenia, new directions for how to handle anti-stigma programs in the community can be developed.

REFERENCES

[1] Üstün, T; Rehm, J; Chatterji, S; Saxena, S; Trotter, R; Room, R; Bickenbach, J. WHO/NIH Joint Project CAR Study Group: Multiple-informant ranking of the disabling effects of different health conditions in 14 countries. *Lancet,* 1999, 354, 111-115.

[2] World Health Organization: The World Health Report 2001. *Mental Health: New Understanding, New Hope Geneva,* World Health Organization.; 2001.

[3] Apiquian, R; Fresan, A; Garcia-Anaya, M; Loyzaga, C; Nicolini, H. Impacto de la duración de la psicosis no tratada en pacientes con primer episodio psicótico. Estudio de seguimiento a un año. *Gaceta Médica de México,* 2006, 142, 113-120.

[4] Loebel, A; Lieberman, J; Alvir, J; Mayerhoff, D; Geisler, S; Szymanski, S. Duration of psychosis and outcome in first-episode schizophrenia. *American Journal of Psychiatry,* 1992, 149, 1183-1188.

[5] Johnstone, E; Crow, T; Johnson, A; MacMillan, J. The Northwick Park Study of first episodes of schizophrenia. I. Presentation of the illness and problems relating to admission. *British Journal of Psychiatry,* 1986, 148, 115-120.

[6] Jorm, A. Mental health literacy. Public knowledge and beliefs about mental disorders. *British Journal of Psychiatry,* 2000, 177, 396-401.

[7] Wright, A; Harris, M; Wiggers, J; Jorm, A; Cotton, S; Harrigan, S; Hurworth, R; McGorry, P. Recognition of depression and psychosis by young Australians and their beliefs about treatment. *Medical Journal of Australia,* 2005, 183, 18-23.

[8] Jorm, A; Korten, A; Jacomb, P; Christensen, H; Rodgers, B; Pollitt, P. "Mental health literacy": a survey of the public's ability to recognize mental disorders and their beliefs about the effectiveness of treatment. *Medical Journal of Australia,* 1997, 166, 182-186.

[9] Farina, A. Are women nicer people than men? Sex and the stigma of mental disorders. *Clinical Psychological Review,* 1981, 1, 223-243.

[10] Farina, A. Stigma. In *Handbook of social functioning in schizophrenia.* Edited by In: KT; Mueser, N. Tarrier, Needham Heights MA; Allyn & Bacon Inc; 1998, 247-279.

[11] Corrigan, P; Watson, A. The stigma of psychiatric disorders and the gender, ethnicity, and education of the perceiver. *Community Mental Health Journal,* 2007, 43, 439-458.

[12] Swami, V; Persaud, R; Furnham, A. The recognition of mental health disorders and its association with psychiatric skepticism, knowledge of psychiatry and the Big Five personality factors: an investigation using the overclaiming technique. *Social Psychiatry and Psychiatric Epidemiology,* 2010, DOI 10.1007/s00127-010-0193-3.

[13] Angermeyer, M; Brier, P; Dietrich, H; Kenzine, D; Matschinger, H. Public attitudes toward psychiatric treatment: an international comparison. *Social Psychiatry and Psychiatric Epidemiology,* 2005, 40, 855-864.

[14] Nakane, Y; Jorm, A; Yoshioka, K; Christensen, H; Nakane, H; Griffiths, K. Public beliefs about causes and risk factors for mental disorders: a comparison of Japan and Australia. *BMC Psychiatry,* 2005, 5, 33.

[15] Lauber, C; Nordt, C; Falcato, L; Rössler, W. Public attitude to compulsory admission of mentally ill people. *Acta Psychiatrica Scandinavica,* 2002, 105, 385-389.

[16] Lauber, C; Nord, C; Falcato, L; Rossler, W. Do people recognise mental illness? Factors influencing mental health literacy. *European Archives of Psychiatry and Clinical Neuroscience,* 2003, 253, 248-251.

[17] Cloninger, C; Przybeck, T; Svrakic, D; Wetzel, R. *The Temperament and Character Inventory (TCI): a guide to its development and use.* Washington University, Center for Psychobiology of Personality; 1994.

[18] Cloninger, C; Svrakic, D; Przybeck, T. A psychobiological model of temperament and character. *Archives of General Psychiatry,* 1993, 50(12), 975-990.

[19] Cloninger, C; Przybeck, T; Svrakic, D. The Tridimensional Personality Questionnaire: U.S. normative data. *Psychological Reports,* 1991, 69(3 Pt 1), 1047-1057.

[20] Thornicroft, G; Rose, D; Kassam, A; Sartorius, N. Stigma: ignorance, prejudice or discrimination? *British Journal of Psychiatry,* 2007, 190, 192-193.

[21] Corrigan, P. *On the stigma of mental illness.* Washington, D.C: American Psychological Association; 2005.

[22] Rose, D; Thornicroft, G; Pinfold, V; Kassam, A. 250 labels used to stigmatise people with mental illness. *BMC Health Services Research,* 2007, 7, 97.

[23] Holmes, E; Corrigan, P; Williams, P; Canar, J; Kubiak, M. Changing public attitudes about schizophrenia. *Schizophrenia Bulletin,* 1999, 25, 447-456.

[24] Gusnard, D; Ollinger, J; Shulman, G; Cloninger, C; Price, J; Van Essen, D; Raichle, M. Persistence and brain circuitry. *Proceedings of the National Academy of Sciences of the United States of America,* 2003, 100, 3479-3484.

[25] Jorm, A; Griffiths, K. The public's stigmatizing attitudes towards people with mental disorders: how important are biomedical conceptualizations? *Acta Psychiatrica Scandinavica,* 2008, 118, 315-321.

[26] Corrigan, P; River, L; Lundin, R; Penn, D; Uphoff-Wasowski, K; Campion, J; Mathisen, J; Gagnon, C; Bergman, M; Goldstein, H; *et al*: Three strategies for changing attributions about severe mental illness. *Schizophrenia Bulletin,* 2001, 27, 187-198.

[27] Corrigan, P; Rowan, D; Green, A; Lundin, R; River, P; Uphoff-Wasowski, K; White, K; Kubiak, M. Challenging two mental illness stigmas: personal responsibility and dangerousness. *Schizophrenia Bulletin,* 2002, 28, 293-309.

[28] Batson, C; Chang, J; Orr, R; Rowland, J. Empathy, attitudes and action: Can feeling for a member of a stigmatized group motivate one to help the group. *Personality & Social Psychology Bulletin,* 2002, 28, 1656-1666.

In: Personality Traits: Theory, Testing and Influences   ISBN: 978-1-61728-934-7
Editor: Melissa E. Jordan   © 2011Nova Science Publishers, Inc.

Chapter 9

IS DEVELOPMENTALLY INFORMED THERAPY FOR PERSONS WITH ID AND CRIMINAL PERSONALITY/OFFENSES RELEVANT?

*Lino Faccini**

Consulting Psychologist, Long Island, NY, USA

Initially, the "Reconstructive Therapy" of Dr. Jerome Schulte, focused on the treatment of the homicidal psychotic patient. After decades of treatment applying this model with a variety of offenses, Dr. Schulte believed that it could be applied to understand and treat the "Criminal Personality", various offenses as well as treating non-clinical populations of children, adolescents and adults. The goal of therapy became one of promoting personal growth and humanness through the positive resolution of Ericksonian stages. The question remains if the successful resolution of Erickson's Psychosocial stages is relevant to the functioning of a Person with an Intellectual Disability, and Criminal Offenses? A theoretical and initial exploratory analysis suggests that the Reconstructive Therapy model can be relevant to the treatment for Persons with Intellectual Disabilities (ID) and various offenses.

Dr. Schulte initially developed his model of "Reconstructive Therapy" while working with forensic psychiatric patients at Atascadero Forensic Hospital in California. According to Dr. Schulte [1], the homicidal psychotic patient can be "the most challenging and complex case(s) where you have a traumatic syndrome superimposed upon a psychotic process and possibly a personality disorder (maybe psychopathy)". Essentially, Dr. Schulte applied the Erickson stages of Psychosocial Development to inform how to conceptualize and treated these patients.

Dr. Schulte's Reconstructive Therapy encompassed an initial stage where the psychosis needed to be treated and be in remission before the patient could join group psychotherapy. While in therapy, the patient would then work to address such stages as developing Self-Value, Autonomy, Pride, Identity, Intimacy and then work on two Relapse Prevention phases. Within each phase of therapy, the individual is presented with contradictory "forces" that pull

---

* Email: Hfaccini@aol.com

at the person. The goal is to withstand, negotiate and positively resolve these contradictory forces towards personal growth. In regards to the first phase of developing Self-Value, Dr. Schulte [1] explains "one must begin with the assumption that there has been a lifelong deficiency of value which antedates the homicide and is at the core of the homicide". The aim of this phase is to "develop a sense of worth as a human being which is not contingent upon achievements, derived from the outside but is part of one's birthright".Once the patient develops this sense of worth then s/he can work to reconcile the contradictory forces of trust versus the mistrust of others involving "fulfilling the need for unconditional love...(and) to seek out of oneself this need from an adult position".Once this is done, then the therapy can progress to the second phase of developing a sense of autonomy. According to Dr. Schulte [1], "the dynamic force in all homicides equals the need to destroy or individuate oneself from the symbiotic, parasitic force that is engulfing oneself, that is preventing in achieving autonomy and the completion of the work of separation and individualization or an attempt through fusion with an object that it seen as capable of bestowing the feeling of autonomy. The ongoing, lifelong struggle is a need for a feeling of existence or survival-an absolute need for a satisfactory fulfillment of the need for autonomy that is the foundation of the resolving of the human potential for dangerousness". Within this phase, the contradictory forces involve dependency versus developing a sense of independence.

The third phase involves the development of a sense of pride. The 'battleground' in processing initiative versus guilt involves "each patient (taking) responsibility for all of their actions in life including all crimes and homicides-go through a process of accountability to oneself and the group as a representative of society which they learn that they are all part of, a step by step process of working through all of their feelings, and actions leading up to the homicide as well as the homicide itself"..."It is this pride that develops through the taking full responsibility of all of the actions that one initiates in life that is the determining criterion for the realization of the position of non-dangerousness"[1]. Subsequently, the fourth phase involves the development of a sense of identity. A positive and stable sense of identity is important to be able to function. If this sense of identity is fragile, continues to have threatening/aggressive aspects to it or it doesn't encompass the different roles that the person takes on, then identity diffusion occurs. Finally, the fifth stage of intimacy and sense of love involves now that the person has an identity, it can be shared it with someone else. Two relapse prevention phases are then addressed which include learning about one's risk factors for developing a psychosis, and backsliding on the psychosocial stages.

In subsequent communications with Dr. Schulte, he has found that not only can Psychotic-Homicidal offenses be treated, but the "Criminal Personality"/offenses can be understood as a failure in reconciling these psychosocial stages. According to Dr. Schulte[2], "I have been equally successful in applying the model to non-psychotic criminal offenders, regardless of the type of offense...it is the progressive cumulative effect of unresolved or failed stages that not only determine the eventual occurrence of the criminal personality but even ultimately dictates the type of criminal personality...the resolution of the first three stages is mandatory to reach a position of considering a state of non-dangerousness". Subsequently, Dr. Schulte's writings concentrated on the development of the "Socially Acceptable" or "Criminal Personality". According to Dr. Schulte, these two personality types are different sides of the same coin and that both of them strive for "mastery and need fulfillment". However, the successful resolution of the Ericksonian Psychosocial stages leads one towards the development of the "Socially Acceptible" Personality; however, the negative resolution of these same stages can lead one to seek self-worth and value through the control and manipulation of others, thus starting one down the path of the "Criminal Personality".

In regard to persons with an Intellectual Disability, it would appear to be reasonable that the psychosocial stages outlined here would help guide or at a minimum inform the remediation of one's functioning deficits and address the developmental delays within this population. However, the author is unaware of any such approach being used in treating persons with ID and criminal offenses. However, a current prominent treatment model for Persons with ID and sex offenses, the Old Me New Me model, essentially does incorporate many of the Ericksonian stages and issues in a different manner.

According to Jim Haaven [3], the "Old/New Me model, in its simplest form, presents a theory of positive psychology in that the offender identifies his or her present characteristics and behaviors (Old Me) associated with the offending lifestyle and then develops new characteristics and behaviors (New Me) of the non-offending lifestyle that he or she wants to lead. The New Me is the endorsement of positive approach goals to live one's life in healthy, fulfilling ways without sexual offending behavior. This model stresses humanistic values in addition to addressing dynamic risk factors for offending."

Essentially, there are many fundamental similarities and few differences between the Reconstructive and Old Me New Me models. For instance, Dr. Schulte talks about the "Socially Acceptable and Criminal Personalities", while Jim Haaven talks about the Old Me and New Me identities. The Criminal Personality is similar to the Old Me identity since it was the identity that was prominent when the person was committing their offenses. The Socially Acceptable Personality is similar to the New Me identity where the person has entered treatment, is motivated to change, and develops and assumes a success-oriented identity (New Me). Just as Dr. Schulte conceptualizes that these two personality types are two different sides of the same coin, Jim Haaven also states that within each person is an Old and a New Me who battle for control of the person. In addition, the tasks of resolving the psychosocial stages, although they aren't addressed in the same order, are also the focus of Old Me New Me treatment. For instance, self value can be explored within one's Old Me identity, in that the Person with ID may have experienced a sense of stigmatization due to the disability defining their identity. The process of developing and strengthening a success-oriented identity or New Me, is a validating process that the offender can be successful and create a Good Life. The core Treatment paradigm to the Old Me New Me model is identity change from a criminal/disability-defining identity towards a positive, empowering success identity. This identity development and shift is highly empowering for persons with ID especially due to their experience of stigmatization and possible past abuse, which is more prevalent in this population than in the non-disabled population. Subsequently, once the Old Me and New Me identities are defined and developed, then the beliefs and skills to develop initiative, competence, intimacy etc are addressed. However, the one stage that is addressed differently in the Old Me and New Me model, than the reconstructive model, is the issue of autonomy. Although the person with ID will come to understand that they alone are responsible for their choices and actions, and need to develop their own "individualized" identity; however their autonomy can be limited due to their support system. At times, this support system may impinge upon their sense of autonomy. Within Old Me and New Me Treatment, the person is taught how to ask for help from their support system, and the support system is designed to "wrap around" the individual. Although the autonomy of a person may be "facilitated" by his admission to secure services, his connection with family and his support system is further developed and strengthened.

A main difference in the models involves how much they rely on disclosure and accountability of their past actions and offenses. For Dr. Schulte, the person must work orderly through attaining self-value, autonomy and then take responsibility and accountability for all of their actions which can result in a sense of pride for having done so. Only until this is accomplished is the position of non-dangerousness attained. However, in Old Me New Me Treatment, since it is difficult to know about all of the person's past offenses, and since the person with ID is more vulnerable to shame (due to prior stigmatization, disability defining identity, and a less coherent identity), this process of disclosing about one's past sexual behavior is non-confrontational. The goal of this task is to have the person continue to rely on their empowering New Me identity, and courage, to share the difficult information. However, during the process of therapy sufficient disclosures are made especially since conceptualizing one's Old Me as the offending identity gives one a safe enough distance from which to disclose about one's sexual offenses, and then not be defined by them.

In addition, another model has been applied to the Person with ID and sex offenses, namely the Good Lives Model. The Good Lives Model developed by Ward and Mann [4] believes that the person tries to attain certain goods in their lives, such as excellence in work and play, relatedness to others, inner peace etc. However, due to a number of barriers and factors, the person may primarily be able to access these "goods" only through criminal or offending behaviors. However, it is possible that Schulte's model would argue that certain "goods" can only be attained in a certain order-thus possibly placing their attainment along a hierarchy rather than merely teaching self-management and a process or skills in how to attain these "goods" without the use of offending behaviors.

In essence, the Old Me New Me and Good Lives models have recognized that negotiating or resolving various psychosocial issues is important in the treatment of persons with ID and criminal offenses. Since these two different models, which emphasize different but related methods and psychosocial issues, are applicable to treating offenders with ID, perhaps the Reconstructive model of treatment may not only be relevant, but necessary. This model has been the only model that directly linked the resolution of structured psychosocial stages and issues with the clinical-forensic treatment of various dangerous offenses. Although the model has been applied in Dr. Schulte's clinical experience, the proof of its effectiveness should now be evaluated in clinical research.

In order to empirically evaluate the model with persons with ID, first, it was essential to identify a measure of the degree of resolution of the various Ericksonian stages. To this author's knowledge, the Measures of Psychosocial development (Hawley [5]) is the only measure to evaluates one's functioning in this manner. According to Dr. Hawley, "the Measures of Psychosocial Development (MPD), is a self-report inventory, based on the Ericksonian constructs, which assesses adolescent and adult personality development. The MPD was designed to translate the constructs of Erickson's theory into objective measures to facilitate the investigation and clinical application of Erickson's work. Specifically, the MPD provides: an index of the overall psychosocial health based on Erickson's criteria; measures the eight positive and eight negative stage attitudes, and estimates the degree of resolution for the stage conflicts. It consists of 112 self descriptive statements which are rated on a 5 point scale (from very much like me to not at all like me)." This measure can be used with a person with ID if the examiner reads the questions and a visual scale is constructed that visually depicts the various structured responses. According to Dr. Hawley [6], she suggested that a significantly unresolved ericksonian stage, for a person with ID, may fall below a T score of 30 at the 2nd percentile. Secondly, it was believed that negatively resolved stages are related or can be identified as meaningful in offenders with ID and violent and sex offenses. To further ascertain if the ID sex offender does have psychosocial development deficits a la Erickson, an ad hoc analysis of a small group (N=20) of Intellectually Disabled Sex Offenders, who had already been evaluated by way of a Comprehensive Sex Offender Evaluation, was reviewed. Since the analysis was ad hoc, and the sample size was small, the results are only exploratory and suggestive. The first procedure involved trying to determine the extent that significantly negatively resolved psychosocial stages were related to sex offense risk. Since these individuals already had completed Sex Offender Evaluations, there was archival data already available. In particular, for Moderate Low and Moderate High risk sex offenders, with using the Rapid Risk Assessment of Sex Offender Recidivism (Hansen [7]), a substantial number of offenders evidenced significantly negative resolution towards mistrust (44% of the small sample) and isolation (37% of the sample). The results of this ad hoc analysis suggests that for moderate risk ID sex offenders, significantly negatively resolved psychosocial issues towards mistrust and isolation may exist.

In order to ascertain if the significant negatively resolved psychosocial stages can be identified for a Person with Intellectual Disabilities and a violent offense, the MPD was used to both inform and measure progress in therapy for a female who attempted matricide when psychotic. In essence, she wanted to attack her mother with a hatchet but her mother may have found it, hid it, and as a result, this female used a knife and blooded her, but stopped when she saw that her mother was bleeding. Subsequently, she was placed within secure services. Prior to the intensive individual therapy, she evidenced significant deficits in self-value, autonomy, initiative and intimacy. After one-and-a-half years of intensive individual therapy (which was informed by reconstructive therapy), none of her psychosocial stages were significantly negative resolved; in addition, as a result, her risk for violence had decreased from a former high risk to a moderate risk, and she was supported to leave secure services.

In conclusion, the Reconstructive model of therapy of a psychotic homicidal person has been expanded to the treatment for non-psychotic offenders, and non-clinical populations. Since this model makes use of treating the unresolved stages of Erickson's Psychosocial stages, the apparently reasonable premise was advanced that since the Intellectually Disabled (ID) population already have deficits in their functioning, that this model of treatment, especially among ID offenders might be particularly relevant. There doesn't appear to be any prior studies evaluating the relationship between an ID offender and his/her functioning in regards to these psychosocial stages of development. An ad hoc analysis of a small group of ID sex offenders and a case study of a psychotic homicidal offender appears to suggest that Dr. Schulte's Reconstructive Therapy model may be relevant to understanding and treating persons with ID who commit various offenses.

REFERENCES

[1]   Schulte, J. (1987). "Study and Treatment of 46 Psychotic Patients with Convictions of Homicide". *American Journal of Forensic Psychiatry*, 8:3, 47-54.
[2]   Schulte, J. (2007). *Personal Communication*.
[3]   Haaven, J. (2006). Evolution of Old/New Me Model. In Blasingame, G (ED). *Practical Treatment Strategies for Forensic Clients with Severe and Sexual Behavior Problems among Persons with Developmental Disabilities.* Oklahoma City, Oklahoma: Wood 'N' Barnes Publishing.
[4]   Ward, T. & Mann, R. (2004). Good lives and the rehabilitation of offenders: A positive approach to treatment. In: P. A., Linley, & S. Joseph, (Eds.), *Positive psychology in practice* (598-616). New Jersey, NY: Wiley.
[5]   Hawley, Gwen. (1988) *"The Measures of Psychosocial Development"*. Psychological Assessment Resources: www.parinc.com.
[6]   Hawley, Gwen (2009). *Personal Communication*.
[7]   Hanson, R. Karl. (1997). *The Development of a Brief Actuarial Scale for Sex Offence Recidivism* (RRASOR). User Report 97-04). Department of the Solicitor General of Canada, Ottawa, ON, Canada.

In: Personality Traits: Theory, Testing and Influences
Editor: Melissa E. Jordan

ISBN: 978-1-61728-934-7
© 2011 Nova Science Publishers, Inc.

Chapter 10

PERSONALITY TRAITS:
REFLECTIONS IN THE BRAIN

Feryal Cam Celikel

Associate Professor of Psychiatry
Gaziosmanpasa University School of Medicine, Tokat, Turkey

ABSTRACT

New research suggests that the structure of human brain predicts core qualities of the individual's personality. One specific model of personality, developed by Cloninger, was based upon an association of specific personality traits to an underlying neurobiology. This seven-factor model consists of four dimensions of temperament (harm avoidance, novelty seeking, reward dependence, persistence) and three dimensions of character (self-directedness, cooperativeness, self-transcendence). Each dimension represents a specific stimulus-response sensitivity, the particular modes of behavior that resulted, and the specific neurotransmitters involved. Four dimensions of temperament are thought to be genetically independent traits and are moderately inheritable and stable throughout life. Novelty seeking is thought to be derived by the behavioral activation system. Harm avoidance is related to the behavioral inhibition system. It reflects the tendency of an individual to inhibit or interrupt behaviors. Reward dependence refers to the individual's tendency to respond intensely to signals of reward, and it involves maintaining or continuing behaviors that have been previously associated with reinforcement. Persistence is the individual's ability to generate and maintain arousal and motivation internally, in the absence of immediate external reward. It reflects perseverance in behavior despite frustration, fatigue, and lack of reward. In this model, neurotransmitters were hypothesized to be associated with behavioral manifestations: dopamine for novelty seeking (behavioral activation), serotonin for harm avoidance (behavioral inhibition), and noradrenaline for reward dependence (behavioral maintenance). Character reflects individual differences in self-concepts about goals and values in relation to experience. It is predominantly determined by socialization. Temperament provokes perception and emotion, character regulates the cognitive processes. Thus, character leads to the development of a mature self-concept. The three dimensions of character develop over the course of time, and influence personal and social effectiveness into adulthood. Self-directedness expresses individual's competence toward autonomy, reliability, and maturity. Cooperativeness is related to social skills, such as support, collaboration, and partnership. Self-transcendence refers to identification with a unity of all things in the world and it reflects a tendency toward spirituality and idealism. Findings suggest that an association exists between personality dimensions, neurotransmitters' function and regional brain metabolism. As morphometric studies have stated, regional variance in the neuronal volume of specific brain structures seem to underpin the observed range of individual differences in personality traits. In this chapter, I will particularly focus on recent work at the molecular genetic and functional imaging level with respect to specific personality traits.

INTRODUCTION

As Allport (1961) stated, personality, the dynamic organization of the psychological and physical systems, underlie a person's patterns of actions, thoughts, and feelings. Despite extensive literature and research on the subject, what makes everyone the same and what leads to unique differences is far from conclusive. Under the spectrum of broad theories, such as those of Freud, Erikson or Piaget, recent ones focused on neurobiological insights for explaining different components of personality (Cloninger, 2009).

New research suggests that the structure of human brain predicts core qualities of the individual's personality. One specific model of personality, developed by Cloninger, was explicitly based upon an association of specific personality traits to an underlying neurobiology (Cloninger, 1994). Cloninger suggested a psychobiological model of the structure and the development of personality that accounts for dimensions of both temperament and character. This seven-factor model consists of four dimensions of temperament (harm avoidance, novelty seeking, reward dependence, persistence) and three dimensions of character (self-directedness, cooperativeness, self-transcendence). Each dimension represents a specific stimulus-response sensitivity, the particular modes of behavior that resulted, and the specific neurotransmitters involved (Svrakic et al., 2002).

Cloninger's dimensional psychobiological model of personality accounts for normal and abnormal variations in two major personality components: temperament and character (Cloninger, 1987). This model was initially based on a synthesis of information from twin and family studies, studies regarding neuropharmacologic and neurobehavioral aspects of learning in humans and other animals, and psychometric studies of personality in individuals as well as in twin pairs (Kose et al., 2009).

Cloninger (1987) developed the model of personality traits and hypothesized that individual neuromodulator / neurotransmitter systems might be related uniquely to specific traits. In Cloninger's model, neurotransmitters were hypothesized to be associated with behavioral manifestations: dopamine for novelty seeking (behavioral activation), serotonin for harm avoidance (behavioral inhibition), and noradrenaline for reward dependence (behavioral maintenance) (Cloninger, 1987). Cloninger's model provides insight into human personality at multiple levels. It includes genetics of personality, neurobiological aspects of behavior, as well as the behavioral correlates of individual differences in personality dimensions (Cloninger et al., 1994, Cloninger, 2002).

Despite the fact that recent research has made the distinction between temperament and character not as clear as it had been stated previously, there are significant hypothetical differences in their definitions.

PERSONALITY: TEMPERAMENT AND CHARACTER

Temperament is considered as the 'emotional core' of personality (Cloninger et al., 1994; Svrakic et al., 2002). It refers to endogenous basic tendencies of thoughts, emotions, and behavior (Whittle et al., 2006). Rutter (1987) viewed temperament as simple, non-motivational and non-cognitive characteristics that represent meaningful ways of describing individual differences among people. It involves heritable neurobiological dispositions to early emotions, like fear, anger, and attachment. It is generally agreed upon that temperamental dimensions are observed in infancy. Temperament traits are genetically determined and are significantly preserved across lifespan (Svrakic et al., 2002; Whittle et al., 2006).

Temperament implies related automatic behavior reactions, like inhibition, activation, and maintenance of behavior in response to specific environmental stimuli, such as danger, novelty, and reward, respectively (Svrakic et al., 2002). In other words, temperament traits are heritable biases in procedural learning leading to such automatic behavior responses. The four temperament traits are relatively stable throughout life, and invariant across different cultures (Gutiérrez et al., 2001; Kose et al., 2009; Kazantseva et al., 2009).

Character involves individual differences in higher cognitive processes. These cognitive processes are logical thinking, formal construction, symbolic interpretation, and invention. The hippocampal formation and cerebral neocortex are the regions crucial for cognitive abilities (Svrakic et al., 2002). The character dimensions involve differences in social goals and values and seem to be moderately influenced by family environment (Cloninger et al., 1994). In contrast to temperament, character develops over the course of time and changes with age and maturation. As Constantino et al. (2002) states, in the seven-factor model, character development is operationalized as the extent to which an individual is self-directed, the extent to which he or she is capable of engaging cooperatively in self–other relationships, and the extent to which he or she is capable of 'transcending self' in arriving at an intuition of one's place or purpose in the larger social context.

Temperament traits, sociocultural pressures, life events experienced by the individual combine with the person's adaptation and make up the final character (Svrakic et al., 2002, Constantino et al., 2002). Thus, personality development is a function of interaction between genetic factors and the environment.

WHAT GENETICS BRINGS

Studies (Canli, 2008; Melke et al., 2003; Keltikangas-Jarvinen et al., 2003; Kim et al., 2006) have shown that interindividual variations in measures of personality are, to a great extent, heritable. Extensive research has been carried out with particular candidate genes, including polymorphisms related to the serotonin transporter, serotonin receptor, dopamine transporter, dopamine receptor, etc (Bond, 2001). Neurotransmitters, serotonin, dopamine and noradrenaline, are believed to influence at least three of the four temperament dimensions in the seven-factor model (harm avoidance, novelty seeking and reward dependence, respectively) (Constantino et al., 2002).

Research on the genetic background of Cloninger's temperament model has been most active in relation to novelty seeking. The dopamine D4 receptor gene polymorphism is identified as a candidate gene that may be associated with the novelty seeking trait (Kluger et al., 2002). In different genetic populations, different variants in the dopamine D4 receptor gene seemed to be responsible for the high and low novelty seeking scores (Munafo et al., 2008, Tsuchimine et al., 2009). The type 4 dopamine receptor gene is predominantly expressed in a restricted set of dopamine-rich limbic areas, which are involved in cognition and emotion. In additon to the dopamine D4 receptor gene, the dopamine transporter might also be a candidate gene for behavioral traits, and has crucial roles in terminating dopaminergic neurotransmission (Munafo et al., 2008).

Studies confirmed findings on the association between the type 4 dopamine receptor gene and novelty seeking, in particular exploratory excitability and impulsiveness (Keltikangas-Jarvinen et al., 2003; Ekelund et al., 1999). The authors state that considering the evidence on genetic factors and novelty seeking, excitability seems to be associated with different gene variants in different populations. The same gene variants were considered to be associated with different novelty-seeking subscales depending on cultural and other factors (Keltikangas-Jarvinen et al., 2003). Exploratory excitability is hypothesized to reflect the tendency to avoid or approach novel situations. This characteristic may be a core concept of several temperamental theories (Keltikangas-Jarvinen et al., 2003). However, failures to replicate this association have also been reported (Herbst et al., 2000; Kluger et al., 2002; Kim et al., 2006). Their data suggested that dopamine 4 receptor and dopamine transporter gene polymorphism may not be associated with personality traits. A possible explanation for these contradictory findings might be the variance in sample sizes, the heterogeneity among the studies; and these findings should be replicated in larger independent samples.

The results of studies regarding the possible association between harm avoidance and polymorphisms in the serotonin transporter gene are partly conflicting. Studies (Blairy et al., 2000; Kusumi et al. 2002) investigating this relationship in genes coding for the serotonin 5-HT2A and 5-HT2C receptors have yielded negative results. However, Melke et al. (2003) supported the notion that harm avoidance may be affected by serotonin and suggest that this effect may partly be mediated by serotonin 5-HT3 receptors.

Reward dependence have been found to be associated with polymorphisms of dopamine related genes such as the dopamine transporter gene (Wills et al., 2000).

Research has also shown that the character traits of self-directedness and cooperativeness are both associated with specific genes (Hamer et al., 1999, Kumakiri et al., 1999). This finding alters the distinction between the temperament and character traits as suggested by Cloninger et al. (1994).

Human personality is a complex phenotype in which both genetic and environmental factors play a role. Character modulates early perceptions and emotions regulated by temperament and thus optimizes adaptation of early temperament to the environment. In other words, temperament regulates what is noticed, and, in turn, character modifies its meaning (Svrakic et al., 2002). Temperament can be defined as the automatic associative responses to basic emotional stimuli (Cloninger et al., 1994). In contrast, character develops gradually as a function of social learning and maturation of interpersonal behavior. Thus, personality is conceptualized as a complex adaptive system. Multiple factors, such as biological, developmental, environmental, interact and finally develop into one outcome (Svrakic et al., 2002).

WHAT IMAGING SHOWS

For a better understading of personality and psychopathology, we need to characterise psychopathology accurately with its underlying neural circuitry. Studies investigated personality profiles within normal subjects (Sugiura et al., 2000; Turner et al., 2003) as well as subjects with personality disorders (Siever & Weinstein, 2009; Wingenfeld et al., 2010; Walterfang et al., 2010) using functional imaging techniques. Attempts have been made to relate temperament to specific brain regions and function (Johnson et al., 1999; Sugiura et al., 2000; Turner et al., 2003; Youn et al., 2002). In these studies, the dimensions seemed to correlate with the activity of several brain structures. Yet, results were not entirely consistent; increased or decreased activity levels were reported within the same brain structures.

Sugiura et al. (2000) were the first to investigate the Temperament and Character Inventory in relation to regional cerebral blood flow. Their results suggested a biological basis for the Temperament and Character model. They found significant relationships between regional cerebral blood flow and the three temperament traits, novelty seeking, harm avoidance, and reward dependence. In their study, Turner et al. (2003) showed a significant relationship in specific regions of the brain to persistence, self-directedness, cooperativeness, and self-transcendence.

In his review, Canli (2004) reports a series of functional magnetic resonance imaging which suggest that individual differences in personality traits may be key in modulating amygdala responses to affective stimuli. As morphometric studies have stated, regional variance in the neuronal volume of specific brain structures seem to underpin the observed range of individual differences in personality traits. Recent neuroimaging studies supported evidence for a neurobiological basis of personality traits (Deckersbach et al., 2006, Hakamata et al., 2006, Sugiura et al., 2000, Yamasue et al., 2008).

The final question is "Does the present evidence indicate that genotypically defined variability in regional brain morphology expresses itself phenotypically as individual differences in personality traits?". Yet, the answer and the evidence are still, far from conclusive.

TEMPERAMENT DIMENSIONS AND NEUROBIOLOGICAL UNDERPINNINGS

Findings suggest that an association exists between personality dimensions, neurotransmitters' function and regional brain metabolism. The range of individual differences in harm avoidance, novelty seeking, reward dependence and persistence observed in normal subjects reflects the structural variance in the regional morphology of human brain.

1) **Harm avoidance** is the individual's tendency to respond intensely to aversive stimuli, to inhibit behaviors and to learn to avoid punishment, novelty, and frustrating nonreward. Harm avoidance is related to the behavioral inhibition system. It reflects the tendency of an individual to inhibit or interrupt behaviors. It manifests as fear of uncertainty, shyness, and pessimistic worry in anticipation of future problems (Cloninger et al., 1994; Raeymaekers & Broeckhoven, 1998).

Individuals who score high in harm avoidance tend to be careful, fearful, tense, and cautious (Cloninger, 1994; Raeymaekers & Broeckhoven, 1998). They feel easily discouraged and pessimistic, even in situations which do not worry other people. Harm avoidance appeared linked to variability in the level of activity of the serotoninergic system. Studies, that indicated a negative correlation between harm avoidance scores and metabolism values in temporo-frontal regions, suggested that high scores on this dimension might reflect low levels of serotonin, which is a neurotransmitter linked to anxiety disorders (Sugiura et al., 2000; Tyler et al., 2005; Venneri et al., 2008; Youn et al., 2002).

In a study by Turner et al. (2003), increased levels of harm avoidance were associated with activations in the temporal and occipital lobes. Sugiura et al. (2000) displayed a negative correlation between harm avoidance and the medial prefrontal network, and besides suggested that these regions were associated with deactivations rather than activations. In a recent study, Gardini et al. (2009) found a negative correlation between harm avoidance and grey matter volume values in orbito-frontal and posterior occipital areas. Therefore, the authors suggested that, since orbito-frontal regions are functionally responsible for emotions, anxiety control and reward, the relatively lower level of grey matter volume in these regions might explain a degree of behavioral inhibition and the development of a highly harm avoidant personality phenotype.

2) **Novelty seeking**, represents the individual's tendency toward frequent exploratory activity and intense excitement in response to novel stimuli and active avoidance of monotony. Novelty seeking is thought to be derived by the behavioral activation system. Individuals high in novelty seeking tend to be enthusiastic, impulsive, quick-tempered, curious, and disorderly (Cloninger et al.,1994; Celikel et al., 2010).

Novelty seeking was found associated with variation in dopamine levels. The finding, which suggests a negative correlation between novelty seeking scores and metabolic activity in the substantia nigra, supported the hypothesis that individuals who have high novelty seeking scores might have low levels of dopamine (Gardini et al., 2009).

Novelty seeking is expected to be related to the amygdala, which is crucial for emotional memory. Amygdala influences drive-related behavior patterns and subjective feelings (Cloninger, 2002, Balleine et al., 2006). It was shown that novelty seeking was related to an activation in the precentral and postcentral gyri, which correspond to the motor cortex and the somatic sensory cortex (Turner et al., 2003). Sugiura et al. (2000) showed positive correlations between novelty seeking and the orbital prefrontal network, which in turn, sends information to the amygdaloid subdivision.

In their study, Gardini et al. (2009) showed that novelty seeking scores were positively correlated with grey matter volume in frontal and posterior cingulate areas. Overall, findings of these anatomical associations were consistent with the evidence that individuals who score high on novelty seeking tend to seek for active, and high-risk behaviors and rich stimuli.

3) **Reward dependence** refers to the individual's tendency to respond intensely to signals of reward, in particular to signals of social approval and support, and to maintain the behavior that has previously been rewarded or to resist to extinct it. Reward dependence involves maintaining or continuing behaviors that have been previously associated with reinforcement and is manifested as sensitivity, sentimentality, and dependency on the approval of others (Cloninger et al., 1994; Celikel et al., 2010). People who score high on reward dependence are in need of social contact and are open to communication with other people; they are sensitive, tender-hearted, dedicated and sociable (Raeymaekers & Broeckhoven, 1998).

Research, suggesting a positive correlation between reward dependence scores and metabolic activity in the orbito-frontal cortex, supported the hypothesis that high scores in reward dependence might signify high responsiveness of those structures involved with reward mechanisms (Hakamata et al., 2006; Gardini et al., 2009, Forbes et al., 2010).

Reward dependence is expected to be related to the circuit of Papez (Cloninger, 2002). This circuit involves the thalamocingulate subdivision of the limbic system. It loops from the hippocampal formation through the fornix, mammillary body, anterior thalamic nucleus, cingulate gyrus, part of the parahippocampal gyrus, and back to the hippocampal formation (Avila et al., 2008).

In their study, Sugiura et al. (2000) showed a relationship between reward dependence and a decrease in blood flow in the paralimbic regions. Turner et al.'s (2003) findings showed increased reward dependence related to activations in the frontal and temporal lobes and deactivations in the temporal and occipital lobes. They also found in the left middle frontal gyrus in the same region as a negative correlation, as previously reported by Sugiura.

In the study by Gardini et al. (2009), reward dependence scores were negatively correlated with grey matter volume values in fronto-striatal and limbic areas, including the caudate nucleus. The authors indicated that since fronto-striatal regions of the brain, which are associated with behavior control, emotional reward and motivation (Sinha et al., 2004) and are also rich in dopaminergic projections (Scott et al., 2006), striatal modifications in these regions might change the dopaminergic activity.

Variability in grey matter volume in fronto-striatal structures might therefore be suggested to result in different levels of dopaminergic functioning (Iversen & Iversen 2007), and expresses itself as a personality trait, that is highly dependent on reward. A positron emission tomography study found that novelty seeking, harm avoidance, reward dependence scores correlated significantly with cerebral glucose metabolism values in paralimbic and temporal regions (Youn et al., 2002).

4) **Persistence** is the individual's ability to generate and maintain arousal and motivation internally, in the absence of immediate external reward. Highly persistent individuals are hard-working, ambitious and perfectionist. They tend to persevere despite frustration, fatigue, and lack of reward. Persistence refers to eagerness of effort in response to signals of anticipated reward vs laziness, ambitious overachieving in response to intermittent frustrative nonreward vs underachieving (Cloninger et al., 1994; Kose et al., 2003).

In Turner et al.'s study (2003), persistence, like reward dependence, exhibited activations in the temporal lobe. However, unlike reward dependence, persistence displayed activations in the parietal, occipital, and limbic lobes; and deactivations in the parietal, temporal, and frontal lobes. In their functional magnetic resonance imaging study, Gusnard et al. (2003) found that individual variations in persistence were associated with differences in brain activation in lateral orbital and medial prefrontal cortex. The authors also demonstrated that individuals scoring high in persistence had increases in activation in orbitomedial prefrontal cortex and ventral striatum, while those scoring low in persistence had decreases in activation in these regions.

In their study, Gardini et al. (2009) has recently shown that persistence showed a positive correlation with posterior parietal and parahippocampal regions. Significant activation in these brain regions are involved in cognitive tasks, including visuo-spatial imagery, episodic memory, self-processing and consciousness (Cavanna & Trimble, 2006). The authors stated that the association between the persistence scores and the variance in posterior parietal and parahippocampal structures grey matter volume might possibly reflect the role that this structure plays in the process of self-representative memory, which takes place during the normal behavior of waiting for reward and learning (Gardini et al., 2009).

CHARACTER DIMENSIONS AND NEUROBIOLOGICAL UNDERPINNINGS

Character reflects individual differences in self-concepts about goals and values in relation to experience. It is predominantly determined by socialization. Temperament provokes perception and emotion, character regulates the cognitive processes. Thus, character leads to the development of a mature self-concept. The three dimensions of character mature over the course of time, and influence personal and social effectiveness into adulthood (Cloninger et al., 1994). The character traits are expected to be related to higher cognitive functions, and thus, the brain regions expected to be related to the character traits are the thalamoneocortical system and the prefrontal cortex (Cloninger, 2002).

1) **Self-directedness** refers to identification with the autonomous self and the confidence to deal with any situation in accordance with one's goals and values. It expresses individual's competence toward autonomy, reliability, and maturity. Self-directedness represents the individual's ability to regulate their behavior and to choose and commit goals (Cloninger et al., 1994; Kose et al., 2003). Individuals with low self-directedness show difficulties in taking responsibility; they lack long-term goals. In their functional brain imaging study, Turner et al. (2003) found that self-directedness showed activations in the frontal lobe only, with deactivations in the precentral gyrus, frontal lobe, temporal lobe, and occipital lobe.

2) **Cooperativeness** indicates the extent to which individuals view other people as a part of the self. It is related to social skills, such as support, collaboration, and partnership. Cooperativeness represents the ability to identify with and accept other people. Individuals with low cooperativeness have difficulty in tolerating others, and are generally not eager to help people (Cloninger et al., 1994; Bond, 2001). In Turner et al.'s study (2003), the activations were observed in the frontal lobes but also involved the limbic lobe, temporal lobe, and subcortical gray nuclei, whereas the deactivations were found mainly in the parietal lobe, central region, and occipital lobe with involvement also from the temporal lobe, middle frontal gyrus, and cerebellum.

3) **Self-transcendence** refers to identification with a unity of all things in the world. It reflects a tendency toward spirituality and idealism. It represents the ability to identify with being an integral part of the universe (Cloninger et al., 1994; Bond, 2001). Self-transcendence showed activations in the occipital lobe and optic radiation and deactivations in the temporal and parietal lobe (Turner et al., 2003). Although no causative link could be shown, a few neuroimaging studies suggest that neural activation of a large fronto-parieto-temporal network may underpin spiritual experiences. In their study, Urgesi et al. (2010) found that selective damage to left and right inferior posterior parietal regions induced a specific increase of self-transcendence, indicating an active role of left and right parietal systems in determining self-transcendence.

CONCLUSION

In a broad sense, personality is considered as the dynamic organization of the psychobiological systems that modulate adaptation to experience. The distinction between temperament and character traits, based on the underlying neurophysiological processes, provide a better understanding of personality disorder (Svrakic et al., 2002). The concepts of character and temperament help to distinguish the core symptoms of psycopathology. All types of personality disorder share poorly developed character traits at different levels. Low levels of self-directedness and cooperativeness were found strongly associated with clinical diagnoses of personality disorder (Svrakic et al., 2002). Low self-directedness, defined by difficulties in taking responsibility, planning and carrying out long-term goals, having low self-esteem and identity problems, are typical features of individuals with personality disorder. These individuals generally have low cooperativeness, as well. Self-transcendence correlated with borderline, narcissistic, and histrionic as well as schizotypal and paranoid symptoms. In contrast, when coupled with high self-directedness and cooperativeness, high self-transcendence indicates maturity, spirituality, and creativity rather then psychopathology (Cloninger & Svrakic, 1999).

As Svrakic et al. (2002) suggested, once character dimensions give the idea for a possible personality disorder, temperament traits can be used for differential diagnosis. In clinical studies of patients with personality disorders, Cloninger (1987) showed that an individual could be classified as 'high' or 'low' with respect to each of the four temperament dimensions (Constantino et al., 2002). The resulting profile accurately predicted the specific type of personality disorder with which the person was affected. As Constantino et al. (2002) stated, subsequent research (Cloninger & Svrakic, 1999) indicated that the condition of having a personality disorder was largely determined by level of character development, and the temperament profile predicted which of the various personality disorders an affected individual would have.

The authors defined each of the three Diagnostic and Statistical Manual of Mental Disorders clusters corresponds symptomatically to one of the underlying TCI temperament traits (Svrakic et al., 2002). The 'odd' Cluster A corresponds symptomatically by low reward dependence, the 'impulsive' Cluster B by high novelty seeking, and the 'fearful' Cluster C by high harm avoidance. Thus, patients with cluster A, B and C diagnoses according to the Diagnostic and Statistical Manual of Mental Disorders classifications were differentiated by low reward dependence, high novelty seeking, and high harm avoidance, respectively. Persistence predicted obsessive compulsive traits, especially when coupled with high levels of harm avoidance (Svrakic et al., 2002). Since the sample size was small and some of the categorical subtypes were represented by a relatively low number of symptoms, further work on a larger sample is needed to confirm these relationships.

Even though the underlying neurobiology of each specific personality trait cannot clearly be defined, evidence from recent studies indicates possible associations between personality and regional variances in brain structure and function. New research suggests that variations in the development of specific brain structures might lead to the individual variations within the normal range of personality. The ability to characterise psychopathologies on the basis of their underlying neurobiology improves our understanding of disorder etiology. Future research might focus on longitudinal magnetic resonance imaging studies from childhood to adulthood in order to understand the actual relationship between regional brain morphology and personality trait expression.

REFERENCES

Allport, GW. *Pattern and Growth in Personality*. New York: Holt, Rinehart & Winston; 1961.

Avila, C; Parcet, MA; Barros-Loscertales, A. A cognitive neuroscience approach to individual differences in sensitivity to reward. *Neurotoxicity Research*, 2008, 14(2,3):191-203.

Balleine, BW; Killcross, S. Parallel incentive processing: an integrated view of amygdala function. TRENDS in *Neurosciences*, 2006, 29(5):272-279.

Blairy, S; Masat, I; Staner, L; Le Bon, O; Van Gestel, S; Van Broeckhoven, C; Hilger, C; Hentges, F; Souery, D; Mendlewicz, J. 5-HT2a receptor polymorphism gene in bipolar disorder and harm avoidance personality trait. *Am J Med Genet*, 2000, 96:360-364.

Bond, AJ. Neurotransmitters, temperament and social functioning. *European Neuropsychopharmacology*, 2001, 11:261-274.

Canli T. Functional brain mapping of extraversion and neuroticism: Learning from individual differences in emotion processing. *Journal of Personality*, 2004, 72(6):1105-1132.

Canli, T. Toward a neurogenetic theory of neuroticism. *Ann N Y Acad Sci*, 2008, 1129:153-174.

Cavanna, AE; Trimble, MR. The precuneus: a review of its functional anatomy and behavioural correlates. *Brain*, 2006, 129:564-583.

Celikel, FC; Kose, S; Erkorkmaz, U; Sayar, K; Cumurcu, BE; Cloninger, CR. Alexithymia and temperament and character model of personality in patients with major depressive disorder. *Comprehensive Psychiatry*, 2010, 51:64-70.

Cloninger, CR. A systematic method for clinical description and classification of personality variants: a proposal. *Archives of General Psychiatry*, 1987, 44:573-585.

Cloninger, CR; Przybeck, TR; Svrakic, DM; Wetzel, R. *The Temperament and Character Inventory (TCI): a guide to its development and use*. St. Louis: Washington University School of Medicine, Department of Psychiatry; 1994.

Cloninger, CR; Svrakic, DM. Personality disorder, In:Sadock B & Kaplan H, eds. *Comprehensive Textbook of Psychiatry*, 7th edn. Williams & Wilkins; 1999: 1567-1588.

Cloninger, C. Functional Neuroanatomy and Brain Imaging of Personality and its Disorders. In: D'haenen, H; den Boer, J; Westenburg, H; Wilner, P. (Eds.), *Textbook of Biological Psychiatry*, Vol. 2, Chapter XXVI-6, New York: Wiley; 2002.

Cloninger, CR. Evolution of human brain fnctions: the functional structure of human consciousness. *Australian and New Zealand Journal of Psychiatry*, 2009, 43:994-1006.

Constantino, JN; Cloninger, CR; Clarke, AR; Hashemi, B; Przybeck, T. Application of the seven-factor model of personality to early childhood. *Psychiatry Research*, 2002, 109:229-243.

Deckersbach, T; Miller, KK; Klibanski, A; Fischman, A; Dougherty, DD; Blais, MA; Herzog, DB; Rauch, SL. Regional cerebral brain metabolism correlates of neuroticism and extraversion. *Depress Anxiety*, 2006, 23:133-138.

Ekelund, J; Lichtermann, D; Jarvelin, M-R; Peltonen, L. Association between novelty seeking and the type 4 dopamine receptor gene in a large Finnish cohort sample. *Am J Psychiatry*, 1999, 156:1453-1455.

Forbes, EE; Olino, TM; Ryan, ND; Birmaher, B; Axelson, D; Moyles, DL; Dahl, RE. Reward-related brain function as a predictor of treatment response in adolescents with major depressive disorder. *Cogn Affect Behav Neurosci*, 2010, 10(1):107-118.

Gardini, S; Cloninger, CR; Venneri, A. Individual differences in personality traits reflect structural variance in specific brain regions. *Brain Research Bulletin*, 2009, 79:265-270.

Gusnard, DA; Ollinger, JM; Shulman, GL; Cloninger, CR; Price, JL; Van Essen, DC; Raichle, ME. Persistence and brain circuitry. *Proc Natl Acad Sci*, 2003, 100:3479-3484.

Gutiérrez, F; Torrens, M; Boget, R; Martin-Santos, R; Sangorrin, J; Pérez, G; Salamero, M. Psychometric properties of TCI questionnaire in Spanish psychiatric populations. *Acta Psychiatrica Scand*, 2001, 103:143-147.

Hakamata, Y; Iwase, M; Iwata, H; Kobayashi, T; Tamaki, T; Nishio, M; Kawahara, K; Matsuda, H; Ozaki, N; Honjo, S; Inada, T. Regional brain cerebral glucose metabolism and temperament: a positron emission tomography study. *Neurosci Lett*, 2006, 396:33-37.

Hamer, DH; Greenberg, BD; Sabol, SZ; Murphy, DL. Role of the serotonin*J Pers Disord* 1999, 13(4):312-327.

Herbst, JH; Zonderman, AB; McCrae, RR; Costa, PT. Do the dimensions of the temperament and character inventory map a simple genetic architecture? Evidence from molecular genetics and factor analysis. *Am J Psychiatry*, 2000,157:1285-1290.

Iversen, SD; Iversen, LL. Dopamine: 50 years in perspective. *Trends Neurosci*, 2007, 30:188-193.

Johnson, DL; Wiebe, JS; Gold, SM; Andreasen, NC; Hichwa, RD; Watkins, GL; Boles; Ponto, LL. Cerebral blood flow and personality: a positron emission tomography study. *Am. J. Psychiatry*, 1999, 156:252-257.

Kazantseva, AV; Gaisina, DA; Malykh, SB; Khusnutdinova, EK. *Genetika*, 2009, 45(8):1110-1117 (abstract).

Keltikangas-Jarvinen, L; Elovainio, M; Kivimaki, M; Lichtermann, D; Ekelund, J; Peltonen, L. Association between the type 4 dopamine receptor gene polymorphism and novelty seeking. *Psychosomatic Medicine*, 2003, 65:471-476.

Kim, SJ; Kim, YS; Lee, HS; Kim, SY; Kim, CH. An interaction between the serotonin transporter promoter region and dopamine transporter polymorphisms contributes to harm avoidance and reward dependence traits in normal healthy subjects. *J. Neural Transm.*, 2006, 113:877-886.

Kluger, AN; Siegfried, Z; Ebstein, RP. A meta-analysis of the association between DRD4 polymorphism and novelty seeking. *Molecular Psychiatry*, 2002, 7:712-717.

Kose, S. A psychobiological model of temperament and character: TCI. *New Symp*, 2003, 41(2):86-97.

Kose, S; Sayar, K; Kalelioglu, U; Aydın, N; Celikel, FC; Gulec, H; Ak, I; Kırpınar, I; Cloninger, CR. Normative data and factorial structure of the Turkish version of the

Temperament and Character Inventory (TCI). *Comprehensive Psychiatry*, 2009, 50:361-368.

Kumakiri, C; Kodama, K; Shimizu, E; Yamanouchi, N; Okada, S; Noda, S; Okamoto, H; Sato, T; Shirasawa, H. Study of the association between the serotonin. *Neurosci Lett, 1999*, 26(263):205-207.

Kusumi, I; Suzuki, K; Sasaki Y; Kameda, K; Sasaki, T; Koyama, T. Serotonin 5-HT (2A) receptor gene polymorphism, 5-HT (2A) receptor function and personality traits in healthy subjects: a negative study. *J Affect Disord*, 2002, 68:235-241.

Melke, J; Westberg, L; Nilsson, S; Landén, M; Soderstrom, H; Baghaei, F; Rosmond, R; Holm, G; Björntorp, P; Nilsson, LG; Adolfsson, R; Eriksson, E. A polymorphism in the serotonin receptor 3A (HTR3A) gene and its association with harm avoidance in women. *Arch Gen Psychiatry*, 2003, 60:1017-1023.

Munafo, MR; Yalcin, B; Willis-Owen, SA; Flint, J. Association of the dopamine D4 receptor (DRD4) gene and approach-related personality traits: meta-analysis and new data. *Biol Psychiatry*, 2008, 63(2):197-206.

Raeymaekers, P; Broeckhoven, CV. Comment - Genes and temperament, a shortcut for unravelling the genetics of psychopathology? *International Journal of Neuropsychopharmacology*, 1998, 1:169-171.

Rutter, M. Temperament, personality and personality disorder. British Journal of Psychiatry 1987, 150:443-558.

Scott, DJ; Heitzeg, MM; Koeppe, RA; Stohler, CS; Zubieta, JK. Variations in the human pain stress experience mediated by ventral and dorsal basal ganglia dopamine activity. *J Neurosci*, 2006, 26: 10789-10795.

Siever, LJ; Weinstein LN. The neurobiology of personality disorders: Implications for psychoanalysis. *J Am Psychoanal Assoc*, 2009, 57:361-398.

Sinha, R; Lacadie, C; Skudlarski, P; Wexler, BE. Neural circuits underlying emotional distress in humans. *Ann N Y Acad Sci*, 2004, 1032:254-257.

Sugiura, M; Kawashima, R; Nakagawa, M; Okada, K; Sato, T; Goto, R; Sato, K; Ono, S; Schormann, T; Zilles, K; Fukuda, H. Correlation between human personality and neural activity in cerebral cortex. *Neuroimage*, 2000, 11:541-546.

Svrakic, DM; Draganic, S; Hill, K; Bayon, C; Przybeck, TR; Cloninger, CR. Temperament, character, and personality disorders: etiologic, diagnostic, treatment issues. *Acta Psychiatr Scand*, 2002, 106:189-195.

Tsuchimine, S; Yasui-Furukori, N; Kaneda, A; Saito, M; Sugawara, N; Kaneko, S. Minor genetic variants of the dopamine D4 receptor (DRD4) polymorphism are associated with novelty seeking in healthy Japanese subjects. *Prog Neuropsychopharmacol Biol Psychiatry*, 2009, 33(7):1232-1235.

Turner, RM; Hudson, IL; Butler, PII; Joyce, PR. Brain function and personality in normal males: a SPECT study using statistical parametric mapping. *NeuroImage*, 2003, 19:1145-1162.

Tyler, LK; Marslen-Wilson, W; Stamatakis, EA. Dissociating neuro-cognitive component processes: voxel-asedcorrelationalmethodology. *Neuropsychologia*, 2005, 43:771-778.

Urgesi, C; Aglioti, SM; Skrop, M; Fabbro, F. The spiritual brain: selective cortical lesions modulate human self-transcendence. *Neuron*, 2010, 65(3):309-319.

Venneri, A; McGeown, WJ; Hietanen, HM; Guerrini, C; Ellis, AW; Shanks, MF. The anatomical bases of semantic retrieval deficits in early Alzheimer's disease. *Neuropsychologia*, 2008, 46:497-510.

Walterfang, M; Chanen, AM; Barton, S; Wood, AG; Jones, S; Reuten, DC; Chen, J; Velakoulis, D; McGorry, PD; Pantelis, C. Corpus callosum morphology and relationship to orbitofrontal and lateral ventricular volume in teenagers with first-presentation borderline personality disorder. *Psychiatry Research: Neuroimaging*, 2010, 183:30-37.

Whittle, S; Allen, NB; Lubman, DI; Yücel, M. The neurobiological basis of temperament: Towards a better understanding of psychopathology. *Neuroscience and Biobehavioral Reviews*, 2006, 30:511-525.

Wills, TA; Sandy, JM; Yaeger, A. Temperament and adolescent substance use: an epigenetic approach to risk and protection. *J Pers*, 2000, 68:1127-1151.

Wingenfeld, K; Spitzer, C; Rullkötter, N; Bernd, L. Borderline personality disorder: Hypothalamus pituitary adrenal axis and findings from neuroimaging studies. *Psychoneuroendocrinology*, 2010, 35:154-170.

Yamasue, H; Abe, O; Suga, M; Yamada, H; Inoue, H; Tochigi, M; Rogers, M; Aoki, S; Kato, N; Kasai, K. Gender-common and -specific neuroanatomical basis of human anxiety-related personality traits. *Cereb Cortex*, 2008, 18:46-52.

Youn, T; Lyoo, IK; Kim, JK; Park, HJ; Ha, KS; Lee, DS; Abrams, KY; Lee, MC; Kwon, JS. Relationship between personality trait and regional cerebral glucose metabolism assessed with positron emission tomography. *Biol Psychol*, 2002, 60:109-120.

In: Personality Traits: Theory, Testing and Influences
Editor: Melissa E. Jordan
ISBN: 978-1-61728-934-7
© 2011 Nova Science Publishers, Inc.

Chapter 11

THE CAREGIVERS OF PERSONS WITH ALZHEIMER'S DISEASE: THE IMPACT OF PERSONALITY TRAITS ON OWN STRESS PERCEPTION AND IN EVALUATING COGNITIVE AND FUNCTIONAL IMPAIRMENT OF THEIR RELATIVES

Marco Vista, Lucia Picchi* and Monica Mazzoni
Alzheimer Diagnostic Unit, Section of Neurology, Campo
di Marte Hospital, Lucca, Italy; *Section of Neurology, Versilia Hospital, Lido di
Camaiore, Italy

ABSTRACT

Alzheimer's disease (AD) is a degenerative pathology of the brain, causing dementia. Caregivers of persons with AD (ADcg) have to cope with cognitive impairment, behavioral symptoms and incompetence in daily living and they experience heavy burden. Besides, ADcg are the most important referent for physicians in reporting information about patients with AD (ADp), because ADp show lack of awareness of their changes. The aims of our research were to examine the relationship between specific personality traits of ADcg and perceived stress; moreover, to highlight the caregivers' capacity to be "objective" in evaluating functional abilities of ADp. In the first study, 118 ADcg were assessed using Caregiver Burden Inventory (CBI) and 16 Personality Factors-C form questionnaires (16PF-C). In the second study, 40 ADp and their caregivers were assessed in order to measure awarness using the Deficit Identification Questionnaire (DIQ); ADcg were also administered 16PF-C. Data from the first sample show that Reasoning (B), Emotional Stability (C) and Rule-Consciousness (G) were more strongly associated with caregiver burden; each indicator seems to be significant, to a different extent, for objective, developmental, physical, social and emotional burden. Caregivers characterized by emotional unstability, unable to stand frustration, high self-demanding and with difficulty in self abstracting from concrete problem solving are going to

---

* Corresponding author: Marco Vista, MD, m.vista@usl2.toscana.it

perceive higher distress in caregiving ADp. In the second research, 26 of 40 ADp showed unawareness of their deficits, while 11 ADp were enough aware of their difficulties and only 3 ADp overvalued their impairment: the majority of ADp were unaware of their cognitive impairment and functional deficits in activities of daily living and overestimated their abilities compared to ADcg perception. ADcg DIQ correlated with four 16PF-C factors: Dominance (E), Liveliness (F), Social Boldness (H) and Privateness (N). This indicate an influence of personality on ADcg judgment: in fact, traits of personality such as being deeply involved in evaluating cognitive impairment and functional deficits, ability to perceive problems in daily living, especially for those aspects that could make them feel inadequate in social situations and that engage them emotionally, could influence ADcg judgment about their relatives. In conclusion,focusing on specific personality traits, which are predictive of caregivers' burden, might be helpful in planning psychological approach aimed to improve caregivers' quality of life. In order to evaluate functional abilities of ADp, even detailed scales of awareness provided by ADcg seem not to be objective means to assess ADp functional state, because they are influenced by ADcg personality.

INTRODUCTION

Alzheimer's Disease (AD) is a degenerative disorder of the Central Nervous System and is the most common cause of dementia among the elderly people in Europe, United States and Canada, affecting an estimated 50% - 80% of the population [1;2]. The ILSA (Italian Longitudinal Study on Aging) research [3] showed a prevalence of the illness in the Italian population, up to 6.4% over the age of 65: in particular, dementia affects 5.3% of men and 7.2% of women. The risk of dementia grows exponentially with the increasing of age, which is considered the most important risk factor and it seems to cause the doubling of the prevalence every five years between the age of 65 and 85 [1;2]. Incidence studies are less numerous owing to the difficulties and costs they imply [1;2]; data show that, as well as prevalence, also incidence grows exponentially between the age of 65 and 90, even if with rates that vary from study to study [4]: the rate of incidence has grown from 1.2 x 1000 individuals/year between the age of 65 and 69 up to 53. 5 x 1000 individuals/year for the over 90s [2].

Clinically, AD is an extremely heterogeneous illness whose symptoms arise and progress in different ways. Its typical onset is insidious and its course is characterized by a slow, progressive loss of cognitive functions such as memory, language, attention, praxis and executive functions; this global impairment gradually becomes so severe that it interferes with the normal carrying out of working and social activities, causing the loss of functional autonomy in daily life activities, compromising the relationship between the subjects and their surrounding environment [5].

In most AD cases (90%), a broad spectrum of 'non-cognitive', psychiatric features is associated to cognitive impairment, defined as Behavioral and Psychological Signs and Symptoms of Dementia (BPSSD), then shortened to BPSD [6]. With the aim of giving a brief and concise description, BPSD have been divided in clusters, such as apathy, agitation, irritability, psychotic symptoms, and depression [7]. The BPSD often represent the most disruptive clinical dimension of the illness because not only do they have a deep impact on the demented person, but also on the caregivers, engendering a stronger stress and becoming the most frequent cause of institutionalization [8]. Up to now, from the diagnostic and prognostic point of view, the 'non-cognitive' features represent a grey area in clinical practice [7]: this seems to be due both to the complexity with which biological, psycho-spiritual, environmental, and interpersonalis factors contribute to their onset, and to the lack of formal diagnostic criteria to define them, except for those designed for psychosis [9] and apathy [10]. The BPSD are unlikely to be standardized as different symptoms can show up simultaneously or in sequence in the same patient, with different rates of prevalence and incidence based on, the type and phase of dementia, but they also depend on evaluation tools, on thresholds of gravity, and on evaluation settings [11]. Currently, several studies agree to consider such symptoms as a primary demonstration of the neuropathologic and neurobiological abnormalities of dementia which, although unrelated to cognitive impairment [12;13], are strongly influenced by the socio-cultural environment and can be associated to the pre-morbid personality of the subject [14; 15]. The alterations of personality are the most common 'non-cognitive' symptoms [16] appearing in the mild phase of the illness [17]. Previous studies point out a more frequency of apathy, irritability, anxiety and depression [13; 18], starting from the early stages and increasing with the worsening of the illness; in the advanced phases, psychotic symptoms and agitation are very frequent [19]. The distinction among behavioral and psychic symptoms refers to the fact that, generally, the first ones are directly observable, while the second ones are reported by the people near to the patient.

The average duration of AD course covers about 10-12 years and is divided in the following phases of progressive gravity:

- Mild Phase, in which an impairment of episodic memory appears, especially affecting recent information, with a difficulty in learning and maintaing new information; the autobiographic memory is well preserved in this phase. Difficulties can be observed also in executive functions; moreover, first episodes of temporal and spatial disorientation in unfamiliar places might appear. The subjects might sometimes have word finding problems and their spontaneous speech might be less articulated, more confused and incoherent. In this phase, some subjects show a rather preserved awareness of their own deficits and this can provoke anxiety and bending of their mood, up to the development of real depressive symptoms among which are loss of initiative and motivation; they often show a great irritability which might lead to anger releases [2];
- Moderate Phase, in which the thought, the language, the attention, the ability of logical reasoning, of conceptualization, and of judgment, result impoverished; the autobiographic memory begins to become poor: the sense of uncertainty, which is typical of AD patients, defined by Spinnler [20] as "cognitive hesitancy", "emotional trepidation", grows. At the same time, patients show behavioral and psychic symptoms (BPSD);
- Severe Phase: the patients become completely dependent on others in their daily life activities: they need assistance to be dressed, washed, fed, and they are incontinent. The memory, also the remote one, is deteriorated, and the subjects become incapable of recognizing people, nor even themselves and their own relatives (prosopoagnosia-prosopoamnesia); disorientation is now complete and the subjects cannot distinguish day from night. Language deficits get more worse, spontaneous speech disappears, and the patients are unable to communicate or answer to oral commands. In the

Terminal Phase, ancient reflexes as suction or palmar prehension often appear. The patient progressively arrives to a complete *cachexia*, complicated by immunodepression with pulmonary, cutaneous, and urinary infections leading to death in few months [2].

Certainty of AD diagnosis is only possible by means of autoptic examination, but the introduction of international specific diagnostic criteria [5;21;22] allows a better clinical evaluation and a clearer differential diagnosis between the several types of dementia [23].

Moreover, differential diagnosis is extremely important to distinguish between various forms of dementia and "pseudodementia", a term which was defined by Kiloh in 1961 [24], to denote the cognitive symptoms which are secondary, and consequently reactive, to a depressive episode. Such concept, even if it's still embraced, has often been criticized as it underlines a dichotomy between depression and dementia. There are various forms of linkage relevant to these two pathologies; some authors think that depressive symptoms can sometimes precede a subsequent manifestation of dementia [25], others believe it appears during the course of dementia, and this brings on different complications concerning the course and the prognosis [2], and globally worsens the cognitive impairment which causes a significant reduction in autonomy [26].However, there is the evident datum that AD patients shows depressive symptoms in 30-50% of cases, not only in the early stages, when they are still aware and able to verbalize their own experiences, but also when such ability seems reduced or canceled by the gravity of cognitive impairment [27]. On this point, some authors remark that with the gradually increasing of AD, the depressive symptoms explicitly emerge: from the "mentalist" form, characteristic of Mild AD, to the behavioral one of the Moderate-to-Severe Phase [28].

The Disease Awareness

The evolution of AD involves the patients' progressive loss of ability to identify deficits resulting from their disease. These deficits concern the cognitive functions and the ability of managing oneself – inside and outside their homes –, as well as the presence of psychiatric symptoms (BPSD). In the last 15-20 years, several studies examined illness awareness in dementia, with particular reference to AD [29-34]. This increasing attention, both clinical and theoretical, is due to the fact that the loss of awareness of AD patients towards their own condition significantly affects their care and management [35]. Besides, poor awareness is a widely investigated argument as it represents a sort of loss of identity in subjects that do not recognize their own changes. The interest around this phenomenon originates from different scientific approaches, and this is why it's been so difficult to define it with just one single term. Actually, we can talk about Insight, Anosognosia and Awareness as if they were synonymous, but the truth is that we are dealing with different facets of a vast concept that originates from different areas of study. The term Insight, which derives from Gestaltic psychology, is commonly used for pointing out the ability of introspection in the psychiatric and psychoanalytic literature, while, with regards to neurological pathology, it refers to the generic awareness of some symptoms. Awareness refers to patients' acknowledgment or subjective perception of their particular condition: awareness of a change in progress, or of specific symptoms, and understanding of the meaning and consequences of those symptoms, up to the awareness of being affected by one particular illness [36]. Anosognosia comes from Neuropsychology and it refers to the condition of subjects that, subsequently to a focal lesion of cerebral areas, immediately show unawareness of that damage [37]. When associated to dementia, it points out the absence of awareness of neuropsychological deficits (cognitive anosognosia) [38], of behavioral symptoms and functional impairment [39]. In medical area, therefore, the word "awareness" does not so much refer to the "awareness of oneself", but, on the contrary, to the "awareness of the illness", and therefore to the awareness that patients have about their own present and future changes.

In dementia, anosognosia shows as: a) inadequate awareness of behavioral alterations, changes of personality, dishinibition, and affective deficit; b) wrong causal attribution of memory and cognitive deficits; c) underestimation of the limitations in daily living activities due to the illness, and proneness to maintain habits and behaviors without adopting compensatory strategies, with consequently adoption of risky behaviors; d) non-acknowledgement, explicitly and verbally, of being affected with a pathological process, and e) descriptions of an unchanged self compared with that before the illness. These are common characteristics of anosognosia which, however, manifests itself with distinctive and peculiar features according to the different forms of dementia. In AD, the deficit of awareness usually appears later and in a more gradually way, as the frontal lobes are damaged after the parietal lobes [40]. According to Gil et al. [41], illness awareness is the result of the convergence of different neural networks that are sparsely damaged in AD: information transit from the areas of memory, language, and visuo-spatial functions to the associative areas of the prefrontal cortex, resulting disturbed or compromised. In AD, the degree of impairment of illness awareness introduces therefore a wide individual variability, unrelated to the severity of the illness itself, implying the focal damage of associative areas in accordance with a neurodegenerative hypothesis of the deficit and with the finding of multiple senile plaques [42]. Anosognosia, has therefore been often interpreted as a symptom due to neurostructural modifications, detectable through its neuropsychological features. However, multiple aspects of that phenomenon can be described, leading to believe that different elements could affect it, such as the psychological and social ones [43;44]. Actually, different studies [33;42;43;45] underline the importance not only of some neurological aspects in the definition and understanding of anosognosia, but also of the characteristics of patients' and caregivers' personality, their coping strategies, and the impact of the illness on the patients' living environment.

The complexity of anosognosia is therefore clear, given the different aspects that have to be considered to reach an in-depth knowledge of it. Every patient might manifest a different type of anosognosia which appears like a web of traits of personality, coping strategies, and integration in a social context in which the illness operates and to which the primary caregiver pertains. It is essential to understand the anosognosia of each patient, especially in the early stages of the illness, because it introduces significant implications for clinicians, both in communicating and sharing the diagnosis with the patients and their relatives, and in planning the most appropriate type of intervention [43].

As far as illness unawareness is concerned, it is difficult to succeed in identifying the right tools to be used to objectively assess it and give it a measure. Within years, with the increasing interest about this AD feature, several questionnaires of awareness evaluation have been created, which include a double comparison: a) the comparison between the subjects' description of their own cognitive abilities and the objective performance on neuropsychological tests; b) the comparison between the subjects' description of themselves in multiple areas of their daily life (cognitive, functional, behavioral), and the caregivers' description of the patients [43]. In the first case, the comparison is between "subjective" – the patient's self-ratings – and "objective" – the neuropsychological tests scores – data, while in the second case, we have a comparison between two absolutely "subjective" data, affected by the personal characteristics both of the patients and of the caregivers [29;46;47]. On this point, the study of Perkins [33] shows the possibility, for patients with AD, to express a judgment about the quality of their life nearly up to the most advanced phases of the illness. However, that judgment results affected by the presence of some depressive symptoms that are underestimated by the patients themselves, and by their cognitive difficulties. Furthermore, the study of Perkins [33] shows the presence of many factors that might influence the caregivers' judgment about their relatives' health: the type of relationship between patients and caregivers, for instance, and the burden in terms of type of assistance and hours employed. Generally, the impairment of awareness attracted researchers' attention mainly because of its phenomenological evidence, but also because of its negative impact on treatment compliance, on prognosis, and on the quality of life both of the patient and the caregiver which is mostly implicated in the management of the demented individual (primary caregiver). Anosognosia actually determines an additional stress for patients' relatives [40].

The Caregiving Process

Assistance to a person with dementia is often a long-term burden, to such extent that some authors spoke about a "career of the caregiving" [48]. It is composed of three phases: 1) Acquisition of the role, 2) Recognition of the problem, 3) Abandonment of the role of caregiver after death of patient. At the beginning, the members of the patient's family tend to gradually remove the problem and break away from it, more and more delegating assistance to a single person, who becomes the "primary" caregiver [49]. This designation seems to be generally determined by the relationship between caregivers and elderly subjects, or from the "history of the caregiving" [50] which is governed by rules depending on gender, generation, culture, family dynamics, personality, and degree of patient impairment [51;52].

The burden of assistance and psychological involvement associated to the informal care of the patients with dementia is well documented. Historically, studies in this field tend to focus on patients' deficits and their negative consequences on relatives, hypothesizing a linear relationship, not sustained by scientific evidences, between the degree of the patient's impairment and the load of assistance [53-56]. Recently, the focus has been shifted on the context of caregiving and the proper characteristics of the caregivers that might affect the perception of the burden of assistance [57].

The Caregiver Burden

The Caregiver Burden refers to the involvement of the caregivers, the individuals that are strongly implicated in the management of a demented elderly relative, in terms of assistance.

The Caregiver Burden depends on the caregivers' acknowledgement of their relatives' cognitive and functional deficits. The subjective perception depends on how the clinical status of the patient has been introduced, from the type of symptoms to their gravity, to the degree of kinship and affection ties, and to factors that are peculiar to the caregiver, such as time devoted to the patient, psychological state, knowledge of the illness, cultural and professional characteristics [45].

Also, the level of awareness that the patients have about their own disease has important implications in the study of the caregiving process as it is shown by the fact that poor awareness seems to be associated to the perception of a more difficult assistance by the caregivers [58].

When the interaction with the environment becomes difficult or when there is a feeling that flexibility runs the risk of being exceeded, a particular condition comes about, which is named "stress" [59]. One of the last decade psychological research results about stress is the knowledge about the difference between the objective influences of the environment and their cognitive evaluation or interpretation (cognitive appraisal): the stress is not only caused by the objective influences of the environment, but also by the subjective evaluation of situation. This subjective evaluation seems to be connected with individual vulnerabilities and the suitability of his/her defense system, in other words, with his/her peculiar physiological and psychological structure [42].

Personality Traits of Caregivers

Personality is referred to as the whole set of faculties, attitudes, and qualities that allow to differentiate individuals among them [60]. In former literature, different theories tried to organize knowledge just relying on dispositions and individual behavioral strategies, as well as on the processes and mechanisms supporting them, giving continuity and stability to individual experience [61]. They can be divided according to the research method they used or the theoretical assumptions they are based on [60;62]. Caprara and Pastorelli [61] tried to systematize currents of thought and research trends into three main directions:

Theories of psychoanalytic and phenomenological-existential inspiration based on the clinical method.

Psychology of traits, including theories based on the co-relational method and trying to delineate the structure of personality through the identification of a limited number of traits or dispositions. The trait is shaped as a disposition to act, relatively independent of variations in the circumstances. Cattel [63], for instance, identified 16 correlate factors of personality; Eysenk [64] reduced them to three (neuroticism, psychoticism, introversion-extraversion).

Theories based on the experimental method associated to the learning theory, the behaviorism, and the cognitive-social approach, with the aim of finding general laws that might rule various aspects, processes and structures of personality.

Personality traits, apart from the theoretical orientation which defines them, assume an important role as far as the subjective perception of the stress is concerned. The definition of stress itself implies that, as it is meant to be the mechanism that connects subjective-internal elaboration and objective-external event.

If personality traits are implicated in the process of elaboration of the stressors and therefore in the level of stress, they also necessarily affect the state of health. Several studies about personality type A, characterized by negative emotional states such as hostility and anger, found that it predisposes to cardiovascular diseases [65-67].

Alzheimer's Disease undoubtedly represents, in the family context in which it becomes manifest, an important factor of stress, that reverts on primary caregivers. It is for this reason that it seems worthwhile to analyze the role of the personality of the caregivers, emerging during the process of caregiving; particularly, there have to be personality traits that are to some extent protective against stress or, contrarily, can make caregivers more vulnerable to it. Caregivers' personalities also play a primary role in the detection of their demented relatives' impairment. Everyone actually "reads" the reality external to his/her own self, inevitably filtering through his/her own "lens": metaphoric "lens" which represent the idiosyncratic peculiarities of everyone of us.

OBJECTIVES

In dealing with AD patients, primary caregivers must be always taken into account as they are the most important reporters of illness evolution. Therefore, we cannot help wondering if those reporters, that in the majority of cases are fond of or emotionally involved with patients, can really be impartial judges in describing what happens to their relatives, or rather, if they are inevitably influenced by their bond of affection, as well as by the caregiving burden required by their role and by their own personality traits.

So, this is why this study has a double purpose: 1) exploring existing relationships among the characteristics of the caregivers' personality, in terms of personality traits and stress perception, and 2) exploring the illness awareness of both patients and caregivers, and how much the awareness of the latter could be influenced by specific characteristics of personality.

METHOD

For the first part of the study, 118 subjects were recruited from the Alzheimer Diagnostic Unit of Lucca Hospital with diagnosis of probable Alzheimer's Disease according to NINCDS-ADRDA criteria [21]. The selection of the subjects was performed during the six-monthly outpatient visits, scheduled for the delivering of specific drugs. In such occasion, it was possible to personally talk with the patients' relatives to illustrate them this study and ask for their informed consent to participate. The people who gave their consent, once assured that they were the closest to the patients (the primary caregivers), were contacted to fix an individual interview during which they've been provided with the proper tests and questionnaires. The evaluation of the caregivers was carried out by means of a couple of tools in order to investigate the caregivers burdens and their personality profiles, respectively.

The CBI *(Caregiver Burden Inventory)* [68] was used to assess the caregiver burden, because it is specifically intended to assess caregivers of people with AD. It is a self-report questionnaire, a quick and easy form to fill out, which allows a multidimensional approach to evaluate 5 different aspects of the caregiver burden:

1. The time dependence burden, which refers to the time the assistance activities require, and the level of the patient dependence on the caregiver;
2. The developmental burden, meant as the perception of caregivers about feeling themselves estranged compared to the expectations and opportunities of their peers;
3. The physical burden, related to the repercussions on health and the feeling of fatigue;
4. The social burden, tied up with the conflicts of role, the experience of the caregiver compared to the relationships with other members of the family, and the work commitment ;
5. The emotional burden, which includes the variety of feelings experienced by the caregivers towards the patients.

The caregiver should assign to each item a value on a five-point Likert scale of increasing intensity, that value shall represent his/her perceived condition. The total score allows us to measure the stress through the 5 aforesaid dimensions.

In order to assess the personality profile, we used Cattel's *16 Personality Factors questionnaire* in the form C [63]. The 16 PF-C consists of 105 items and the Italian form has been adapted by Sirigatti and Stefanile in 2001 [69]. The 16 PF was realized within the field of trait psychology and gives measurements for 16 dimensions of personality, traditionally presented as bipolar and individualized by letters [70]: Factor A *Warmth* (schizothymia-affectothymia); Factor B *Reasoning* (lower-higher mental capacity); Factor C *Emotional stability* (lower-higher ego strength); Factor E *Dominance* (submissiveness-dominance); Factor F *Liveliness* (desurgency-surgency); Factor G *Rule-Consciousness* (low-High super ego strenght); Factor H *Social Boldness* (threctia-parmia); Factor I *Sensitivity* (harria-premsia); factor L *Vigilance* (alaxia-protension); Factor M *Abstractedness* (praxernia-autia); factor N *Privateness* (artlessness-shrewdness); Factor O *Apprehension* (untroubled-guilt proneness); Factor Q1 *Openness to Change* (conservatism-radicalism); Factor Q2 *Self-reliance* (group adherence- self-sufficency); Factor Q3 *Perfectionism* (low integration-high self-concept control); Factor Q4 *Tension* (low – high ergic tension). Between the sixteen dimensions of personality, 15 are assessed through the answers given to 6 items, while the scale of intelligence (factor B) consists of 8 items. A seven-items control scale (MD-motivational distortion) is also available, which allows to monitor potential fake attempts by the subjects. Every item of the questionnaire is formulated so that the subject can choose among three alternative options (one of which corresponding to uncertainty or middle course/compromise). The examiner suggests the subject to answer with sincerity, thinking about the answer he/she feels more consistent with his/her case, and to avoid choosing the "uncertainty" option. The answers scoring originates raw scores which are then converted into Sten points expressed on a 1-to-10 measurement scale with an average of 5.5; SD= 2.

Among the caregivers who took part in the research, we noticed consensus, and a good willingness to talk during their individual interviews. The meetings were often prolonged over the scheduled time as the relatives of AD patients showed the need to talk of their own difficulties and their interviews with the psychologist became a listening place where their doubts about the illness could be resolved.

The scores of the CBI and the 16 PF-C have been connected between them, and a linear regression has been created by considering the personality traits as an independent variable compared to the caregivers' perception and the resulting report of their burden.

As for the second object of our research, we selected a sample of 40 patients with diagnosis of probable AD according to NINCDS-ADRDA criteria [21] and their respective primary caregivers. The patients were recruited during the six-monthly outpatient visits at the Alzheimer Diagnostic Unit of Lucca Hospital. The inclusion criteria were the early stage of the disease and the absence of a compromised auditory verbal comprehension.

Therefore, the main inclusion criteria were:

Mini Mental State Examination (MMSE) [71] score $\geq$ 18, corrected per age and education, in order to quantify the severity of impairment, namely mild;

Token Test (TT) score [72] ranging between 1 and 4 equivalent scores, for assessing verbal auditory comprehension, namely in a normal range.

The illness awareness was evaluated through a method based on the discrepancy/agreement among the reports of the patient and the caregiver [34;40;73]: we chose the *DeficitsIdentification Questionnaire* (DIQ) [74; 75]. The DIQ consists of a total of 25 items, divided into the 5 investigated dimensions:

Memory deficits;
Functional difficulties;
Language impairment;
Difficulties in the executive functions;
Psycho-affective state.

The score for every item is on a 0-2 point Likert scale where it is possible to get a maximum score of 50, which is the maximum level of identification of the deficit.

The DIQ has been filled out both by patients (DIQ p) and their primary caregivers (DIQ cg) with the purpose to be able to compare the subjective perceptions of illness of the two affected groups. To make the comparison (DIQ ratio), we used the following mathematical formula:

$$DIQratio = \frac{DIQcg - DIQp \; x \; 100}{DIQcg + DIQp}$$

The more the DIQ ratio is closer to zero, the more the subjective perception of the patient is concordant with that of the caregiver. To avoid rigidity in considering the agreement between the two perceptions of illness, according to the literature [76], a range (range of agreement) has arbitrarily been fixed between -20 and +20: the scores which fell within this interval were considered concordant.

If DIQ ratio < 0, we have two possibilities, either tenable: the patients tend to exaggerate their own disabilities, or the caregivers minimize them. If DIQ ratio > 0: the patients tend to be unaware of their own state, or the caregivers tend to exaggerate the disability of their demented relatives.

To verify if and which factors of personality are implicated in the perception of illness of the caregivers, we used again the Cattel's *16 Personality Factors questionnaire* in form C [63].

Every patient have been required to estimate their own functional abilities by filling out two scales forms: *Activities of Daily Living* (ADL) [77] and *Instrumental Activities of Daily Living* (IADL) [78]. Caregivers were also asked to report on the functional autonomy of their relatives, using the aforesaid scales. For both scales, ADL and IADL, high scores pointed out the preservation of their abilities, while low scores mark a loss of autonomy in some specific areas.

During the six-monthly outpatient visits, the subjects were tested through MMSE and TT in order to verify if they could satisfy our inclusion criteria; to primary caregivers, we asked about their availability to come back after the tests to be interviewed.

Firstly, statistic analysis consisted in the calculation of the Student's T test for coupled data to detect any existing discrepancy between the perceptions of patients and caregivers as to the cognitive deficits and functional autonomy. Secondly, multiple regression analysis with the procedure of the backward elimination was performed with the aim to test the main effects of the factors of personality on the perception that caregivers had about the illness of their demented relatives.

RESULTS

As far as the first part of the study is concerned, 118 caregivers completed the study; the social-demographic and clinical characteristics were the followings: the caregiver group consisted of 47 men and 71 women ranging (in age) from 24 to 84 (with a mean age of 58 years; SD = 13 years). In the majority of cases, the role of the caregiver was performed by daughters/sons (n = 65); 38 spouses; 5 daughters-in-law/sons-in-law; 4 nephews; 3 sisters/brothers; 2 sisters-in-law and only 1 subject with a different degree of kinship compared to the others listed above. In most of cases, the caregivers were married (93/118), 12 were single, 8 were separated or divorced, and 5 were widows/widowers. The school-attendance rate ranged from 3 – primary school – to 18 – university – years, with an average of 9.78 years; SD = 4.17 years. From a professional point of view, it emerged that, approximately, the sample was fairly distributed among those having a job (workers, employees, professionals, executives,...) and those who already retired. A considered variable was the time spent assisting the patient by each caregiver (measured in hours/week), that ranged from a minimum of 5 hours/week to a maximum of 168 hours/week, in case of cohabitation with the patient (with a mean value of 116.31 hours/week; SD = 56.75 hours/week).

"Clinical characteristics" of the caregivers include the perception of the caregiver burden, measured through the CBI, and the personality profile of each caregiver. Table 1 shows the scores of CBI sub-scales for the caregivers sample.

Table 2 shows the mean and SD values for each factor which was identified through the 16 PF-C; the raw scores of every scale have been converted into Sten points (with a mean value of 5.5; SD = 2) within a "normality" range going from 4.5 to 6.5 Sten points; Table 3 shows the correlation coefficents (p<.05 and p<.01) between the CBI and the 16 PF-C.

Table 1. Description of CBI

	Mean	SD	Range
Time dependence	11.92	5.66	1-20
Developmental	11.14	6.37	0-20
Physical	6.69	5.22	0-16
Social	4.54	4.46	0-19
Emotional	4.56	4.4	0-19
Total	38.86	20.24	1-83

Table 2. Description of 16PF-form C

		Mean	SD
A	Warmth	4.34	1.8
B	Reasoning	4.19	1.87
C	Emotional stability	4.23	2.87
E	Dominance	4.19	1.99
F	Liveliness	5.87	2.39
G	Rule-Consciousness	6.47	1.99
H	Social Boldness	4.45	2.33
I	Sensitivity	7.5	1.98
L	Vigilance	5.57	2.3
M	Abstractedness	5.05	2.1
N	Privateness	6.62	2.58
O	Apprehension	7.17	2.04
Q1	Openness to Change	3.81	1.54
Q2	Self-Reliance	3.62	2.2
Q3	Perfectionism	4.92	2.26
Q4	Tension	7.32	2.25

Once the presence of numerous correlations between the personality traits of the caregiver and the perceived caregiving burden was identified, the next step was finding out which ones, among these personality traits, were the principal responsible for the perception of a certain level of burden. This was possible thanks to the model of the linear regression in which the CBI total score is considered a dependent variable, while its relevant personality traits are the independent variables. Through a series of passages (backward elimination), we've been able to eliminate statistically unimportant variables, and to identify, as the meaningful predictors of the perceived caregiver burden, the following factors of personality: B (Reasoning), C (Emotional Stability), and G (Rule-Consciousness), as shown in Table 4.

In the second part of our study, the selected sample (divided into two groups of patients and their relevant caregivers) was recruited by trying not to overlapping it with the former sample. In spite of this, some characteristics, especially those concerning the social-demographic variables of the caregivers, are similar, to show that the process of caregiving concerns a rather homogeneous population, even when assessed in different times and contexts.

Table 3. Correlation between CBI and 16PF-form C

		Time Dependent	Developmental	Physical	Social	Emotional	Total
A	Warmth	.159	-.007	.004	-.027	.105	.060
B	Reasoning	-.269**	-.271**	-.226*	-.125	-.247**	-.300**
C	Emotional stability	-.203*	-.369**	-.405**	-.158	-.099	-.344**
E	Dominance	-.081	-.041	-.060	.057	-.017	-.042
F	Liveliness	-.068	-.216*	-.143	-.161	-.091	-.179
G	Rule-Consciousness	-212*	-334**	.329**	.298*	.197*	.358**
H	Social Boldness	-.205*	-.243**	-.213*	-.116	-.116	-.240**
I	Sensitivity	.147	.066	.123	.034	.175	.139
L	Vigilance	.047	.166	.160	.160	-.097	.121
M	Abstractedness	.068	.002	.101	.013	-.049	.038
N	Privateness	.176	-.019	-.092	-.074	.026	.009
O	Apprehension	.062	.253**	.091	.192*	.117	.188*
Q1	Openness to Change	.030	.043	.109	.120	.080	.094
Q2	Self-Reliance	-.176	-.174	.261**	-.129	-.146	-.231*
Q3	Perfectionism	.055	-.008	.085	.014	-.222*	-.010
Q4	Tension	.233*	.287**	.283**	.135	.267**	.316**

* $p < .05$; ** $p < .01$

Table 4. Linear regression between CBI total scores and personality traits on 16PF- form C

	β	SE	βs	t	p
B Reasoning	-2.571	.889	-.232	-2.832	.005
C Emotional Stability	-1.592	.617	-.217	-2.581	.011
G Rule-Consciousness	2.821	.848	.277	3.327	.001

The sample of patients and caregivers for whom complete data were collected consisted of 40 dyads (patient/caregiver). In Table 5, the most important social-demographiccharacteristics of the sample are shown.

Table 6 shows the mean and SD values obtained through the evaluation of the perception of the cognitive symptoms of the illness carried out using two exact versions of the DIQ forms filled out by patients and caregivers.

The mean and SD values of the scores obtained by patients and caregivers within the evaluation scales of the functional state are reported in Table 7, showing how the ability of the AD patients in base (ADL) and instrumental (IADL) activities of daily living was perceived.

Clinical characteristics of the caregivers subgroup are shown by the profile of personality identified through the 16 PF-C. Table 8 shows the mean and SD values for each factor identified through the questionnaire.

Table 5. Social-demographic characteristics of the sample

	Patients	Caregivers
Gender	35 Women; 5 Men	27 Women; 13 Men
Age	Mean, 80.4 years; SD= 5.28	Mean, 56.47; SD= 15.16
Marital status	19 spouses 19 widows/widowers 2 singles	35 spouses 3 singles 1 partner 1 divorced
Kinship degree		27 sons/daughters 8 spouses 3 nice 2 daughter-in-law/sons-in-law
School-attendance	Mean, 5.75 years; SD = ± 3.23	Mean, 11 years; SD = 4.36
Job (or previous job if retired)	11 pz workers 11 pz housewives 4 artisans 3 domestic helps 11 with other jobs: professionals, teachers, nurses, social workers, dealers/shopkeepers	8 employees 7 housewives 6 teachers 3 nurses 16 with other jobs: professionals, workers, social workers, dealers/shopkeepers

Table 6. Description of the DIQ scores

	Mean	SD	Range
DIQ p	14.3	6.7	3-31
DIQ cg	24.37	7.62	3-36

Table 7. Description of the ADL and IADL scores

	Mean	SD	Range
ADLp	5.45	0.87	3-6
IADLp	4.95	2.33	0-8
ADLcg	4.72	1.39	1-6
IADLcg	3.07	2.11	0-7

Once the descriptive variables of the sample were obtained, a discrepancy among the reports of the patients and those of the caregivers regarding the symptomatology of the disease has been detected. This discrepancy was shown by a value ranging from a minimum of -100 to a maximum of +100 on DIQ ratio. In Fig.1, one can see that only 3 cases are positioned below -20 (7.5%); 11 cases (27.5%) fall within the range of agreement (+20 /-20), while most of the patients (n= 26; 65%) are positioned above it.

We can deduce from this that in most of cases the caregivers more seriously perceived the impairment of the patients, or the patients tend to perceive their own cognitive and functional difficulties to a lesser extent.

Table 8. Description of 16PF form C

		Mean	SD
A	Warmth	4.3	2
B	Reasoning	3.6	1.89
C	Emotional stability	4.7	2.78
E	Dominance	4.77	2.14
F	Liveliness	6	1.95
G	Rule-Consciousness	6.37	1.99
H	Social Boldness	4.45	2.58
I	Sensitivity	7.15	1.9
L	Vigilance	5.7	2.23
M	Abstractedness	5.9	2
N	Privateness	5.87	2.28
O	Apprehension	7	1.87
Q1	Openness to Change	4.1	1.85
Q2	Self-Reliance	4.37	2.52
Q3	Perfectionism	4.47	2.33
Q4	Tension	6.65	2.5

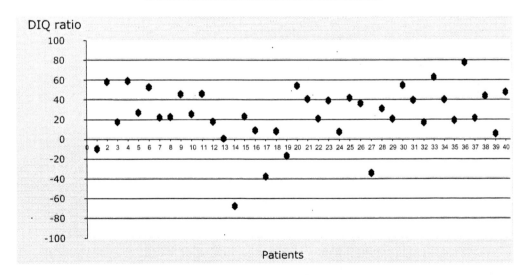

Figure 1. Distribution of Deficit Identification Questionnaire ratio of each patient

**Table 9. Statistical comparison between ADL, IADL, and
DIQ of patients and caregivers**

	Patients	Caregivers	T	p
ADL	Mean, 5.45; SD= 0.87	Mean, 4.72; SD= 1.39	-3.70	.001
IADL	Mean, 4.95; SD= 2.33	Mean, 3.07; SD= 2.11	-4.35	.0001
DIQ	Mean, 14.37; SD= 6.7	Mean 24.37; SD= 7.6	5.93	.0001

**Table 10. Correlation between personality traits and perception
of the illness of the caregivers**

			SE	p
	MMSE		n.s.	
16PF-C	E Dominance *"Docile-Dominant"*	-1.61	.40	.0005
	F Liveliness *"Serious-Happy"*	-1.69	.49	.0021
	HSocial Boldness *"Shy-Bold"*	1.98	.48	.0003
	N Privateness *"Open-Shrewd "*	0.36	.08	.0002

As shown in Table 9, the discrepancy between the subjective perception of patients and caregivers was confirmed by the Student's T test for coupled data that showed a significant difference (p <.001) between the perception of patients and caregivers compared to the carrying out of the base activities of daily living (ADL p/cg) and (p<.0001) both for the instrumental activities of daily living (IADL p/cg), and for the perception of cognitive symptoms (DIQ p/cg).

By using this model of multiple regression together with applying the procedure of the backward elimination to get some good hints on the influence of personality traits of caregivers on their perception of the illness (DIQ cg), statistically important interactions were obtained, as shown in Table 10.

DISCUSSION

In the first part of the study, the social-demographic and clinical characteristics of the selected caregivers are substantially representatives of the population of caregivers, according to data reported in previous literature. Particularly, it has been proved that assistance is carried out mainly by women (60% women vs 40% men) [79-82]. Besides, the caregivers are generally adults, married and, in 50% of cases, still professionally active. An essential role in the welfare net is performed by intergenerational solidarity, as underlined by the Italian Censis survey [79]. Also, this datum is confirmed for the present sample, as the role of primary caregiver is mostly performed by daughters/sons, as in 50% of cases patients are widows/widowers.

The duration of the caring service, measured in hours of assistance per week, is definitely important if we consider that the mean value is 116 hours/week. In confirmation of many previous studies [83-85], also in the present sample women report higher levels of stress, not only for the overall burden, but also in terms of time dependent, developmental, and physical burden. These sub-scales underline how women are more involved in practical assistance of the patients and, compared to men, show more depression symptoms and physical repercussions [86-91].

If we consider the kinship degree, we can notice that daughters/sons are the ones to have a stronger feeling of what the CBI identifies as the social burden, a scale related to role conflicts and to a joint effort within the family. We can gather that the spouses play their role of assistants more serenely and in a more tolerant way [49;92-94], without feeling any particular resentment towards other relatives.

Some authors found an inverse proportionality between the quality of the relationship with the patient before the illness and the perceived stress [95-99]. Our results might confirm these studies, nevertheless, the elements we have to define the quality of the relationship are not enough, especially where it is necessary to distinguish between spouses and daughters/sons. It is possible, however, to assume that the interviewed people have been reserved and discreet in talking about their private questions such as these family matters, which have a strong emotional connotation and might even show some hostile feelings towards the affected relatives [79]; this is mostly the case of spouses, who are generally elderly people inclined to justify the nonsupport of their relatives, especially when they are their sons and daughters.

No doubt then that the caregivers' reports about their involvement in the assistance activities and their stress in providing care for their relatives depend on the aforesaid social-demographic factors, but also on their specific personality traits. Particularly, with the use of the 16 PF-C questionnaire, in this study, three traits have been identified which are useful in predicting the perception of the caregiver burden. It's a case of factors concerning the ability of reasoning (B), the emotional stability (C), and the consciousness (G).

Factor B – Reasoning, which is predictive of high scores in each of the five sub-scales of the CBI, is characterized by the propensity to concrete thought, to a superficial interpretation of the reality, and to face problems in a too practical way, showing great difficulties to find alternative strategies of problem solving. The caregivers with personality traits like these result more involved in the daily assistance of their demented relatives, more "emotionally exhausted" by circumstances, more physically tired and with a higher level of resentment towards their demented relative. This resentment may derive from a difficulty in deeply understanding the disease, which gradually takes away from the patient each intellectual, functional, motor ability that he possessed before the illness, forcing him to perform actions that often result hardly comprehensible. If individuals do not succeed in attributing the change of their own relative to a pathological process in progress, facing cohabitation and performing the assistance activities may seem very difficult.

Also, a poor emotional stability and the incapability of bearing frustration, typical in subjects with a weak self (factor C Emotional Stability), seem to determine greater levels of time dependent, developmental and physical burden. Dementia is, in itself, an event that causes troubles both to the patients and to the people around them; while the demented gradually lose awareness of their own deficits, their relatives see their decline from the outside, grieve for that, and find it difficult to accept it. If we add to all that a vulnerability of trait and a propensity to escape the claims of their reality, it will be particularly difficult to take care of a patient with Alzheimer's Disease. An Italian study [100] underlined a negative correlation between this trait and the burnout in formal caregivers measured with the Maslach Burnout Inventory (MBI) [101] or with an analogous questionnaire [102;103]. Particularly, the highlighted correlation is with the scale of the "emotional exhaustion" related to the caregivers' feeling of being emotionally dried up and exhausted by their job [104]. That scale may have some aspects in common with the developmental burden of the CBI, the dimension assessing the "emotional drainage" and that, in our sample, showed a significant relationship with factor C. That same factor, being for the level of emotional stability, has been confirmed as a good predictor of caregivers' stress. It may also be interpreted as a component of neuroticism, a dimension that many authors considered potentially able to condition the wellbeing of people [105-107]. During the process of caregiving demented patients, the neuroticism seems to foretell depressive symptoms [108;109]: it is connected to the caregiving burden and, according to previous studies, it may condition the bodily health of caregivers [110;111]. In confirmation of this, in our sample, a relationship between a low emotional stability and the physical burden of the caregivers appeared: the subjects with that personality trait tend to somatize their frustrations to a greater extent.

Finally, being too hard on and expecting the utmost from oneself (Factor G – Rule-Consciousness) correlates to every sub-scales of the CBI and explains the high distress of the caregivers. Dementia is a disease that completely takes up the people around you, both during the first phases, in which the relatives realize they have to watch patients that do not show a complete judgment ability anymore, and the last ones, when the demented is completely dependent on others. Basically conscientious caregivers, who have a sense of duty, proved to be persevering also in the assistance of their own relative: this characteristic of their personality results to predict high levels of stress that actually appear for every dimension evaluated by the CBI.

In the second part of our study, even if the sample consisted of different subjects, some characteristics of the caregivers showed again: in this subgroup, women were more often represented and most of them were daughters. In the majority of cases, they were adults, with an extra-domestic job, and married.

From the analysis of the results obtained comparing the answers of the patients with those of their caregivers, a general discrepancy can be observed in the way they perceive the symptoms of the AD. This discrepancy seems to be confirmed by the results emerged from the Student's T test comparison: there is a statistically significant difference between the two groups in the perception of cognitive symptoms and functional characteristics of the illness; particularly, the caregivers reported a greater presence of cognitive deficit compared to the patients. Also, as regards the perception of the functional state, the caregivers showed low scores compared to the patients. This shows that the caregivers perceived that the ability of the patients to perform their base and instrumental activities of daily living was significantly more compromised. What emerged from the data of our study is in accord with most of the former literature that highlighted a different perception of the cognitive and functional impairment between patients and caregivers [45;58;112-114], and particularly, the frequent propensity of the patients to bring a smaller presence of symptoms compared to their caregivers. The research of the determinants of this discrepancy has been generally focused on the patient, probably because the evaluation method based on the comparison between the patients' and caregivers' perceptions of the illness assumed, sometimes also implicitly, the good accuracy and objectivity of what was reported by the caregivers [73]. Fewer studies focused on investigation of predictors for the caregivers' perception of illness. Actually, although considering in a different way the cognitive and functional deficits might well reflect a (real or apparent) lack of awareness of the patients compared to their own condition, some authors suggested that this can also depend on the propensity of the caregivers to report a higher impairment of the same dimensions compared to what reported by the patient, also in an initial phase of the illness [74;115]. It follows that, to understand the real nature of the discrepancy between patients' and caregivers' evaluations of the illness, we need to direct our studies also towards the search of those factors that could really interfere with subjective perceptions. The debate on the reliability of the reports of the caregivers is, to this day, still open and controversial, also considering the contradictory results of several studies. Some authors emphasized the fact that the perception of the caregivers can be influenced by numerous factors of subjective nature, therefore losing its implied character of objectivity [58;116-118].

Starting from the suggestions given by these studies, we tried to find, by means of a multiple regression, the personality traits that might have an influence on the perception of the caregivers about the disease of their relatives. The personal dimensions that significantly show an interference with the perception of the illness (E- Dominance; H- Social Boldness; N- Privateness, and F- Liveliness) have been individually interpreted.

People positioned in the negative polarity of Factor E (Dominance) tend to be indulgent with others, to depend on their judgment, to conform and often to be brought towards precision and correctness in an obsessive manner. In this case, the perception of the deficits of their demented relatives shall be as strong as their propensity to be the victim of other people's judgment and their willingness of being and feeling suitable in every social context. The cognitive and behavioral impairment characterizing an AD patient inevitably interferes with social relationships. As a result, the caregivers which are the most respectful of conventional social norms may find it difficult to face social situations and can be induced to pay particular attention to the impairments of the patient, to such a degree that they would consider them more severe than they actually are.

The negative polarity of Factor F (Liveliness) shows a propensity to avoid sharing one's own thoughts and facing with other people; these individuals, unlike the others, have a propensity to excessive thinking and "to brood over" their problems in life. Before the impairments which results from the different stages of the disease, the caregivers with this kind of personality trait might be inclined to an excessive thinking about the changes characterizing the actual state of the patients compared to their pre-morbid condition. These continuous thinking, unshared with anyone else, might induce the caregiver to assess a worse degree of patients' deficits and of their pathological state as a whole.

Similarly, people prone to socializing and seeking contacts with others (Factor H- Social Boldness), but not really willing to share their own thoughts or lives (Factor F- Liveliness), and never getting deeply involved, seem to get an exaggerative perception of their relative's state of health. As it has been observed in a recent study [80], by spending a lot of time in taking care of their patients, caregivers tend to progressively isolate themselves. In this situation, people prone to socialization, no matter how superficial they are, might, sooner than others, preceive a sense of isolation and loneliness; as a result, their relatives state of health might appear worse than it really is to them.

Caregivers who got a higher score in Factor N (Privateness), usually have a propensity to obstinately seek solutions to tangible problems and, in their relationships with other people, they seem to emphasize the presence of the deficits the illness implies. Face to face with the stress induced by the AD, the constant search for solutions to the problems they have to face during their caregiving activities might cause them a sense of frustration since a pathology which is, by definition, "degenerative" as the AD, does not allow caregivers to definitively solve any problem.

We cannot take for granted that all the caregivers with a propensity to report more severe symptoms of the illness are characterized by these four personality traits, but, when detected, they result predictive of the perception of illness and show the "non-objectivity" of caregivers reports; this "non-objectivity" depends on the inevitable subjectivity of those same reports.

CONCLUSION

The two studies we carried out and described in this paper show how specific personality traits, which are the subjective characteristics of the caregivers, can influence the perception of stress associated to the caregiving of a patient affected by AD, and how, in the same way, they might significantly condition the perception of illness, making the caregivers lose their assumed objectivity in their reports.

For clinicians, the support of demented persons often includes both patients and their primary caregivers, which experience high levels of burden and ask for a pharmacological support intervention. Pharmacological therapy appears to be the fastest and easiest way to resolve the depressive-anxious problems which affect the caregivers. Actually, understanding the fact that specific personality traits may condition the caregivers' approach to their relatives' illness, allows us to propose a psychological intervention aimed to the improvement of the quality of life without using drugs.

Besides, the individualization of some specific characteristics of the caregivers personality can be a useful additional evaluation tool for clinicians, allowing them to assess the reliability of the caregivers, as they're the only source of information about the functionality of patients in their environmental context; important decisions of medical nature are based on those information. In those terms, the caregivers appear as a "second voice" within the illness diagnostic and management process [33].

It is therefore desirable that qualitative research shall be taken into account in order to understand the various aspects of the caregivers subjectivity, as they might determine their way of perceiving their own as well as their patients' state of health, and make their perceptions less objective or accurate, since "what is being observed is built by an observer in his own living routine" [119].

REFERENCES

[1] Baldereschi, M., Di Carlo, A., Maggi, S. & Inzitari, D. (2005). Le demenze: epidemiologia e fattori di rischio. In: Trabucchi M. (Ed.), *Le demenze* (IV ed., 13-36). Torino: UTET.

[2] Mecocci, P., Cherubini, A. & Senin, U. (2002). *Invecchiamento cerebrale, declino cognitivo, demenza, un continuum?* Roma: Critical Medicine Publishing.

[3] Maggi, S., Zucchetto, M., Grigoletto, F., Baldareschi, M., Candeline, L., Scarpini, E., Scarlato, G. & Amaducci, L. (1994). The Italian Longitudinal Study on Aging (ILSA): design and method. *Aging Clinical and Experimental Research*, 6, 464.

[4] Jorm, A. F. & Jolley, D. (2000). The incidence of dementia: a meta-analysis. *Neurology, 51(3)*, 728-733

[5] American Psychiatric Association (1994). *DSM-IV. Diagnostic and Statistic Manual of Mental Disorders*, 4 [th] ed. Washington, DC

[6] Finkel, S. I. (1996). Behavioural and Psychological Signs and Symptoms of Dementia: Implication for research and treatment. *International Psychogeriatrics*, 8 (suppl.3).

[7] De Vreese, L. P. (2004). La demenza nell'anziano: dalla diagnosi alla gestione. *Torino:UTET*.

[8]   Bernabei, R., Caltagirone, C., Govoni, S., Provinciali, L., Scapicchio, P. L. & Trabucchi, M. (2002). Il concetto di BPSD e la realtà clinica. In: R., Bernabei, C., Caltagirone, S., Govoni, L. Provinciali, & P. L. Scapicchio, (Eds), Razionale del trattamento con risperidone dei disturbi comportamentali e psichici. Milano: NextHealth

[9]   Jeste, D. V. & Finckel, S. I. (2000). Psychosis of Alzheimer's disease and related dementias. Diagnostic criteria for a distinct syndrome. *American Journal of GeriatricPsychiatry*, *8*, 29-34.

[10] Starkstein, S. E., Petracca, G., Chemrinski, E. & Kremer, J. (2001). Syndromic validity of apathy in Alzheimer's disease. *American Journal of Psychiaty*, *158*, 872-877.

[11] Brodaty, H., Draper, B. M. & Low, L. F. (2003). Behavioral and Psychological Symptoms of Dementia: a seven-tired model of service delivery. *Medical Journal ofAustralia*, *178*, 231-234.

[12] Spalletta, G., Baldinetti, F., Buccione, I., Fadda, L., Perri, R., Scalmana, S., Serra, L. & Caltagirone, C. (2004). Cognition and behaviour are independent and heterogeneous dimensions in Alzheimer's disease. *Journal of Neurology*, *251(6)*, 688-695.

[13] Toledo, M., Bermelo-Pareja, F., Vega-Quiroga, S. & Munoz-Garcia, D. (2004). Behavioural disorders in Alzheimer's disease. Data from a populational study. *Revue Neurologique*, 16-31, *38(10)*, 901-905.

[14] Cummings, J. (1997b). Changes in neuropsychiatic symptoms as outcome measures in clinical trials with cholinergic therapies for Alzheimer disease. *Alzheimer Disease and Associated Disorders*, *11(4)*, S1-S9.

[15] Woods B. (2003). Evidence-based practice in psychosocial intervention in early dementia: how can it be achieved? *Aging and Mental Health*, 7, 5-6

[16] Siegler, I. C., Dawson, D. V. & Welsh, K. A. (1994). Caregiver ratings of personality change in Alzheimer's disease patients: a replication. *Psychology and Aging*, *9(3)*, 464-466

[17] Bianchetti, A. & Trabucchi, M. (2005). *La valutazione clinica del demente*. In: Trabucchi M. (Ed.), Le demenze (IV ed., pp.37-102). Torino: UTET

[18] Piccinini, M., Di Carlo, A., Baldareschi, M., Zaccara, G. & Inzitari, D. (2005). Behavioral and psychological symptoms in Alzheimer's disease: frequency and relationship with duration and severity of the disease. *Dementia and Geriatric Cognitive Disorders*, *18*, 19(5-6), 276-281

[19] Lyketsos, C. G., Lopez, O., Jones, B., Fitzpatrick, A. L., Breitner, J. & Dekosky, S. (2002). Prevalence of neuropsychiatric symptoms in dementia and mild cognitive impairment. *Journal of American Medical Association*, *288*, 1475-1483.

[20] Spinnler H. (1990). Il deterioramento demenziale. In Denes G., Pizzamiglio L. (Eds.), Manuale di Neuropsicologia (I ed., pp. 867-873). Bologna: Zanichelli.

[21] Mc Khann, G., Drachman, D., Folstein, M., Katzman, R., Price, D. & Stadlan, E. M. (1984). Clinical diagnosis of Alzheimer's disease: report of the NINCDS-ADRDA Work Group under the auspices of *Department of Health and Human Services Task Force onAlzheimer'sDisease.Neurology*, *34(7)*, 939-944.

[22] Dubois, B., Feldman, H., Jacova, C., DeKosky, S. T., Barberger-Gateau, P. & Cummings, J. et al. (2007). Research criteria for the diagnosis of Alzheimer's disease: revising the NINCDS-ADRDA criteria. *Lancet Neurology*, *6(8)*, 734-746.

[23] Aguglia, E. & Carmignani, M. (2000). Nosografia, fattori di rischio ed epidemiologia delle demenza di Alzheimer. In Pancheri P., Ravizza L. (Eds.), *Demenza degenerativa primaria e disturbi depressivi* (1-26). Pisa: Pacini.

[24] Kiloh, L. G. (1961). Pseudodementia. *Acta Psychiatrica Scandinavica, 37,* 336-351.

[25] Alexopoulos, G. S., Young, R. C. & Meyers, B. S. (1993). Geriatric depression: age of onset of dementia. Biological Psychiatry, *34,* 141-145.

[26] Torta, R., Caltagirone, C., Scalabrino, A. & Spalletta, G. (2006). *Depressione e Demenza.* Torino: UTET.

[27] Chemerinski, E., Petracca, G. & Sabe, L. et al. (2001). The specificità of depressive symptoms in patient with Alzheimer's disease. *American Journal of Psychiatry, 158,* 68-72.

[28] Ritchie, K., Gilham, C., Ledesert, B., Touchon, J. & Kotzki, P. O. (1999). Depressive illness, depressive symptomatology and regional cerebral blood flow in elderly people with sub-clinical cognitive impairment. *Age and Aging, 28(4),* 385-391.

[29] Clare, L. (2002). Awareness in Dementia: new directions. *Dementia, 1˙(3),* 275-278.

[30] Klein, S. B., Cosmides, L. & Costabile, K. (2003). Preserved knowledge of self in a case of Alzheimer's dementia. *Social Cognition, 21(2),* 157-165.

[31] Ecklund-Johnson, E. & Torres, I. (2005). Unawareness of deficits in Alzheimer's disease and other Dementias: Operational definitions and Empirical findings. *Neuropsychology Review, 15(3),* 147-166.

[32] Hardy, R. M., Oyebode, J. R. & Clare, L. (2006). Measuring awareness in people with mild to moderate Alzheimer's disease: development of the memory awareness rating scale-adjusted. *Neuropsychological Rehabilitation, 16(2),* 178-193.

[33] Perkins, E. A. (2007). Self and Proxy reports across three population: older adults, persons with Alzheimer's disease and persons with intellectual disabilities. *Journal of Policy and Practice in Intellectual Disabilities, 4(1),* 1-10.

[34] Robertsson, B., Nordstrom, M. & Wijk, H. (2007). Investigating poor insight in Alzheimer's disease. *Dementia, 6(1),* 45-61.

[35] Aalten, P., Van Valen, E., Clare, L., Kenny, G. & Verhey, F. (2005). Awareness in dementia: in the eye of the beholder. *Aging and Menthal Health, 9(5),* 414-422.

[36] Markovà, I. S. & Berrios, G. E. (1995). Insight in the clinical psychiatry: a new model. *Journal of Nervous and Mental Disease, 183,* 743-751.

[37] Babinsky, J. (1914). Contribution à l'étude des troubles mentaux dans l'hémiplegie organique cérébrale (anosognosie). *Revue Neurologique, 22,* 845-848.

[38] Barret, A., Eslinger, P., Ballentine, N. & Heilman, M. (2005). Unawareness of cognitive deficit (cognitive anosognosia) in probable AD and control subjects. *Neurology, 2,* 693-699.

[39] Defanti, C. A., Tiezzi, A., Gasparini, M., Gasperini, M. & Congedo, M. et al. (2007). Problemi Etici nella cura della persona con Demenza. Parte I: il rispetto dell'autonomia: consapevolezza, capacità e disturbi del comportamento. *Neurological Science, 28,* 216-231.

[40] Orfei, M. D., Spalletta, G. & Caltagirone, C. (2007). I disturbi della consapevolezza nelle demenze: rilevanza clinica e ipotesi patogenetiche. *Psicogeriatria, 3,* 32-38.

[41] Gil, R., Arroyo-Anllo, E. M., Ingrand P., Gil, M., Neau, J. P. & Ornon, C. et al. (2001). Self-consciusness and Alzheimer's disease. *Acta Neurologica Scandinavica, 104(5),* 296-300.

[42] De Vanna, M., Carlino, D. & Aguglia, E. (2005). Aspetti concettuali ed interpretativi dell'insight nella Malattia di Alzheimer. *Italian Journal of Psychopathology*, *11*, 62-73.

[43] Seiffer, A., Clare, L. & Harvey, R. (2005). The role of personality and coping style in relation to awareness of current functioning in early-stage dementia. *Aging and MentalHealth*, *9(6)*, 535-541.

[44] Zanetti, O. & Calabria, M. (2006). La consapevolezza di malattia nella demenza. *Neurological Sciences*, *27*, XXXVII Congresso SIN.

[45] Onor, M. L., Trevisiol, M., Negro, C. & Aguglia, E. (2006). Different perception of cognitive impairment, behavioral disturbaces and functional disabilities between persons with mild cognitive impairment and mild Alzheimer's disease and their caregivers. American Journal of Alzheimer' *Disease and other dementias*, *21(5)*, 1-6.

[46] Clare, L. (2004a). The construction of awareness in early-stage Alzheimer's disease: A review of concepts and models. *British Journal of Clinical Psychology*, *43*, 155-175.

[47] Clare L. (2004b). Awareness in early-stage Alzheimer's disease: a review of methods and evidence. *British Journal of Clinical Psychology*, *43*, 177-196.

[48] Aneshensel, C. S., Pearlin, L., Mullan, J., Zarit, S. H. & Whitlatch, C. J. (1995). Profiles in caregiving: the unexpected career. San Diego, CA: Academic Press.

[49] Catalano, D. J. & Johnson, C. L. (1983). A longitudinal study of family support to impaired elderly. *Gerontologist*, *23*, 612-618.

[50] Pearlin, L. J., Mullan, J. T., Semple, S. S. & Skaff, M. N. (1990). Caregiving and the stress process: an overview of the concepts and their measures. *The Gerontologist*, *30*, 583-594.

[51] Pruchno, R. A., Burant, C. J. & Petres, N. D. (1997). Typologies of caregiving families: family congruence and individual well-being. *Gerontologist*, *37(2)*, 157-167.

[52] Pyke, K. D. & Bengston, V. L. (1996). Caring more or less: individualistic and collectivist system of family eldercare. *Journal of marriage and thefamily*, *58(2)*, 379-393.

[53] George, L. K. & Gwyther, L. P. (1986). Caregiver well-being: a multidimensional examination of family caregiver of demented adults. *The Gerontologist*, *26*, 253-259.

[54] Haley, W. E., Levine, E. G., Brown, S. L., Berry, J. W. & Hughes, G. H. (1987). Psychological, social and health consequences of caring for a relative with senile dementia. *Journal of the American geriatrics society*, *35*, 405-411.

[55] Pagel, M. D., Becker, J. & Coppel, D. B. (1985). Loss of control, self-blame and depression: an investigation of spouse caregivers of Alzheimer's disease patients. *Journal of Abnormal Psychology*, *94*, 169-182.

[56] Vitaliano, P. P., Young, H. M. & Russo, J. (1991). Burden: a review of measures used among caregivers of individuals with dementia. *Gerontologist*, *31*, 67-75.

[57] Tamanza, G. (1998). La malattia del riconoscimento. *L'Alzheimer, le relazioni familiari, il processo di cura.*Milano: Unicopli.

[58] De Bettignies, B., Mahurin, R. K. & Pirozzolo, F. J. (1990). Insight for impairment in independent living skills in Alzheimer's disease and multi-infarct dementia. *Journal of Clinical and Experimental Neuropsychology*, *12*, 355-363.

[59] Lazarus, R. S. & Folkman, S. (1984). *Stress, appraisal and coping*. New York: Spinger.

[60] Granieri, A. (2002). Teorie, metodi, strumenti e loro interrelazione. In: Granieri A. (Ed.), *I test di personalità: quantità e qualità* (3-24). Torino: UTET.

[61] Caprara, G. V. & Pastorelli, C. (2001). Personalità. In: Moderato P. e Rovetto F. (Eds), Psicologo: verso la professione (435-448). Milano: Mc Graw-Hill.

[62] Sirigatti, S. (1978). *La personalità*. Firenze: Le Monnier.

[63] Cattel, R. B. (1956). *Handbook supplement for Form C of the Sixteen Personality Factor Questionnaire* (16 PF), Champaign, III, Institute for Personality and Ability Testing; trad. it. 16 PF: I sedici fattori della personalità. Forma C. Manuale. Firenze: Organizzazioni Speciali, 1978.

[64] Eysenk , H. J. & Eysenck, M. W. (1985). *Personality and individual differences*. New York: Plenum.

[65] Barefoot, J. C., Dahlstrom, W. C. & Williams, R. B. (1987). Hostility, CHD incidence and total mortality: a 25-years follow-up study of 255 physicians. *Psychosomatic Medicine, 49,* 450-457.

[66] Friedman, H. S. & Booth-Kewley, S. (1987). The "disease-prone personality". A meta-analytic view of the construct. *American Psychologist, 42,* 539-555.

[67] Pruneti, C. A. (2002). *Stress, disturbi dell'integrazione mente-corpo e loro valutazione.*Pisa: ETS.

[68] Novak, M. & Guest, C. (1989). Application of a Multidimensional Caregiver Burden Inventory. *Gerontologist, 9,* 169-186.

[69] Sirigatti, S. & Stefanile, C. (Eds) (2001). 16 PF-5. Manuale. Firenze: Organizzazioni Speciali.

[70] Sanavio, E. & Sica, C. (1999). *I test di personalità. Inventari e questionari.* Bologna: Il Mulino.

[71] Folstein, M. F., Folstein, S. E. & McHugh, P. R. (1975). "Mini Mental State": a practical method for grading the cognitive state of patient for the clinicians. *Journal of Psychiatric Research, 12,* 189.

[72] Spinnler, H. & Tognoni, G. (1987). Standardizzazione e taratura italiana di test neuropsicologici. The Italian *Journal of Neurological Sciences* (suppl. 8).

[73] Marcovà, I. S. & Berrios, G. E. (2006). Approaches to the assessment of awareness: Conceptual issues. *Neuropsychological Rehabilitation, 16(4),* 439-455.

[74] Smyth, K. A., Neundorfer, M. M., Koss, E., Geldmacher, D. S., Ogrocki, P. K. & Withehouse, P. J. (2002). Quality of life and deficit identification in dementia. *Dementia, 1(3),* 345-358.

[75] Sacco, L. (2007). La consapevolezza del paziente con demenza. *Traduzione ed adattamento del Questionario di Identificazione dei Deficit.* Congresso Nazionale FERB, 1 giugno 2007, Bergamo.

[76] Migliorelli, R., Teson, A., Sabe, L., Petracca, G., Petracchi, M., Leiguarda, R. & Starskein, S. E. (1995). Anosognosia in Alzheimer's disease: a study of associated factors. *Journal of Neuropsychiatry and Clinical* Sciences, *7,* 388-344.

[77] Katz, S., Ford, A. B., Moscowitz, R., Jackson, B. A. & Jaffe, M. W. (1963). The index of ADL: a standardized measure of biological and psychosocial function. *Journal of the American Medical Association, 185,* 914-919.

[78] Lawton, M. P. & Brody, E. M. (1969). Assessment of older people: Self-maintaining and instrumental activities of daily living. *Gerontologist, 9,*179-186 .

[79] Censis, (1999). *La mente rubata.* Bisogni e costi sociali della malattia di Alzheimer. Milano: Franco Angeli.

[80] Manigrasso, L., Liperoti, R. & Bernabei, R. (2005). La famiglia del demente e la rete dei servizi. In Trabucchi M. (Ed.), *Le Demenze* (IV ed., pp. 681-694). Torino: UTET.

[81] Nobili, A., Ricci, A., Merli, M. R., Fasolino, A., Cassinesi, N. & Tettamanti, M. (2001). Assessment of the relationship between health persons and caregivers caring for dementia patients. Assistenza infermieristica e ricerca: *AIR, 20(4),* 211-219.

[82] Onishi, J., Suzuki, Y., Umegaki, H., Nakamura, A., Endo, H. & Iguchi, A. (2005). Influence of behavioral and psychological symptoms of dementia (BPSD) and environment of care on caregivers' burden. *Archives of Gerontology and Geriatrics, 41,* 159-168.

[83] Schultz, R., O'Brien, A. T., Bookwala, J. & Fleissner, K. (1995). Psychiatric and physical morbidity effects of dementia caregiving: prevalence, correlates and causes. *Gerontologist, 35,* 771-791.

[84] Colvez, A., Joel, M. E., Ponton-Sanchez, A. & Royer, A. C. (2002). Health status and work burden of Alzheimer patients informal caregiver. Comparisons of five different care programs in the European Union. *HealthPolicy, 60,* 219-233.

[85] Argimon, J. M., Limon, E., Vila, J. & Cabezas, C. (2004). Health-related quality of life in carers of patients with dementia. *Family Practice, 21(4),* 454-457.

[86] Donaldson, C., Tarrier, N. & Burns, A. (1997). The impact of symptoms of dementia on caregivers. *British Journal of Psychiatry, 170,* 62-68.

[87] Montgomery, R. J. W. (1999). The Family role in the context of long term care. *Journal of Aging andHealth, 11(3),* 383-416.

[88] Merril, D. (1997). *Caring for elderly parents: juggling work, family and caregiving in middle and working class families.* Westport: Auburn House.

[89] Thommessenn, B, Aarsland, D., Brackus, A., Oksengaard, A. R., Engedal, K. & Laake, K. (2002). The psychosocial burden on spouses of the elderly with stroke, dementia and Parkinson's disease. *International Journal of Geriatric Psychiatry, 17(1),* 78-84.

[90] Thompson, R. L., Lewis, S. L., Murphy, M. R., Hale, J. M., Blackwell, P. H., Acton, G. J., Clogh, D. H., Patrick, G. J. & Bonner, P. M. (2004). Are there sex differences in emotional and biological responses in spousal caregivers of patients with Alzheimer disease? *Biological Research Nurses, 5(4),* 319-330.

[91] Winslow, B. W. & Carter, P. (1999). Patterns of burden in wifes who care for husbands with dementia. *Nursing Clinics of North America, 34(2),* 275-287.

[92] Archbold, P. G. (1983). The impact of parent-caring on women. *Family Relations, 32,* 39-45.

[93] Cantor, M. H. (1983). Strain among caregiver: a study of experience in the United States. *The Gerontologist, 23,* 597-604.

[94] Soldo, B. & Myllyluoma, J. (1983). Caregivers who live with dependent elderly. *The Gerontologist, 23,* 605-611.

[95] Connell, C. & Gibson, G. (1997). Racial, ethic and cultural differences in dementia caregiving: review and analysis. *Gerontologist, 37,* 355-364.

[96] Miller, B., Campbell, R., Farran, C., Kaufinan, J. & Davis, L. (1995). Race, control, mastery and caregiver distress. *Journal of Geriatric, 50,* S374-S382.

[97] Pushkar, G. D., Reis, M., Markiewicz, D. & Andres, D. (1995). When home caregiving ends: a longitudinal study of outcomes for caregivers of relatives with dementia. *Journal of American Geriatric Society, 43,* 10-16.

[98]   Given, C. W., Collins, C. E. & Given, B. A. (1988). Sources of stress among family caring for relatives with Alzheimer's disease. *Nursing Clinics of North America, 23,* 69-82.

[99]   Williamson, G. M. & Schultz, R. (1990). Relationship orientation, quality of prior relationship and distress among caregivers of Alzheimer's patients. *Psychology and Aging, 5 (4),* 502-509.

[100] Belloni Sonzogni, A., Fiorucci, G., Floridia, L. & Fumagalli, A. (1997). Aspetti organizzativi, relazionali e di personalità nella sindrome di burnout tra gli operatori di una unità di cur palliative. *Ricerche di Psicologia, 4(21),* 135-148.

[101] Sirigatti, S. & Stefanile, C. (1993). The Maslach Burnout Inventory. Adattamento e taratura per l'Italia. Firenze: *Organizzazioni Speciali.*

[102] Sirigatti, S., Stefanile, C. & Menoni, E. (1988a). *Aspetti psicologici della formazione infermieristica: iscrizione, frequenza, abbandono.*Roma: La Nuova Italia Scientifica.

[103] Sirigatti, S., Stefanile, C. & Menoni, E. (1988b). Sindrome di burnout e caratteristiche di personalità. *Bollettino di Psicologia Applicata,* 187-188, 55-63.

[104] Maslach, C. & Jackson, S. E. (1984). Patterns of burnout among National sample of public contract workers. *Journal of Health and Human Resources Administration, 7,* 189-212.

[105] Bolger, N. (1990). Coping as a personality process: a prospective study. *Journal of Personality and Social Psychology, 59 (3),* 525-537.

[106] Bromberger, J. T. & Matthews, K. A. (1996). A longitudinal study of the effects of pessimism, trai anxiety and life stress on depressive symptoms in middle-aged women. *Psychologist and Aging, 11,* 207-213.

[107] Endler, N. S. & Edward, J. (1982). Stress and personality. In: Goldenberg L., Breznitz S. (Eds.), Handbook of stress: theoretical and clinical aspects (36-48). New York: Free Press.

[108] Gallant, M. & Connell, C. (2003). Neuroticism and depressive symptoms among spouse caregivers: do health behaviors mediate this relationship? *Psychology and Aging, 18 (3),* 587-592.

[109] Jang, Y., Clay, O., Roth, D., Haley, W. & Mittelman, M. S. (2004). Neuroticism and Longitudinal Change in Caregiver Depression: Impact of a Spouse-Caregiver Intervention Program. *Gerontologist, 44(3),* 311-317.

[110] Hooker, K., Monahan, D. J., Bowman, S. R., Frazier, L. D. & Shifren, K. (1998). Personality counts for a lot: predictors of mental and physical health of spouse caregivers in two disease groups. *The Journal of Gerontology Series B,* Psychological *Sciences and Social Sciences, 53(2),* P73-P85.

[111] Laschever, R. E. (2004). The impact of caregiver personality styles on help-seeking in Alzheimer's disease. Dissertation Abstracts International: Section B: *The Sciences of Engineering,* 65(1-B), 444.

[112] Correa, D. D., Graves, R. E. & Costa, L. (1996). Awareness of memory deficits in Alzheimer's disease patients and memory.impaired older adults. *Aging, neuropsychology and cognition, 3,* 215-228.

[113] Feher, E. P., Mahurin, R. K., Inbody, S. B., Crook, T. H. & Pirozzolo, F. J. (1991). Anosognosia in Alzheimer's disease. *Neuropsychiatry, neuropsychology and behavioral neurology,4,*136-146.

[114] Mc Glone, J., Gupta, S., Humphrey, D., Oppenhaimer, S., Mirsen, T. & Evans, D. R. (1990). Screening foe early dementia using memory complaints from patients and relatives. *Archives of Neurology*, *47*, 1189-1193

[115] Trosset, M. V. & Kaszniak, A. W. (1996). Measures of deficit unawareness in for predicted performance experiments. *Journal of the International NeuropsychologicalSociety*, *2*, 315-322.

[116] Jorm, A. F., Christensen, H., Henderson, A. S., Korten, S., Mackinnon, A. E. & Scott, R. (1994). Complaints of cognitive decline in the elderly: a comparison of reports by subjects and informants in a community survey. *Psychological Medicine*, *24*, 365-374.

[117] Zanetti, O., Geroldi, C., Frisoni, G. B., Bianchetti, A. & Trabucchi, M. (1999). Contrasting results between caregiver's report and direct assessment of activities of daily living in patients affected by mild and very mild dementia: the contribution of the caregiver's personal characteristics. *Journal American of Geriatric Society*, *47(2)*, 196-202.

[118] Snow, A. L., Cook, K., Lin, P. S., Morgan, R. O. & Magaziner, J. (2005). Proxies and other external raters: methodological considerations. *Health Service Research*, 40 (5 pt 2), 1676-1693.

[119] Maturana, H. (1997). *Autocoscienza e realtà* (V ed.). Milano: Raffaello Cortina Editore.

In: Personality Traits: Theory, Testing and Influences
Editor: Melissa E. Jordan

ISBN: 978-1-61728-934-7
© 2011 Nova Science Publishers, Inc.

Commentary

HOW "TO BE OR NOT TO BE": THE ANSWER IS IN IDENTITY

*Lino Faccini**

Consulting Psychologist, Long Island, NY, USA

According to the Merriam-Webster dictionary, "Identity" is defined as "the sameness of essential or generic character in different instances". Essentially, how a person views oneself, is different from his personality, namely the totality of the characteristics that make up that person. The importance of identity change in treatment has been identified for well over 40 years, however it continues to be limited in its application to clinical disorders or populations. The nature and importance of identity change will be highlighted, and the recommendation made that it be expanded to treat different offending patterns, and even dysfunctional patterns of "normal" individuals.

In the 1960's, William Glasser stressed the importance of identity in the change process. He believed that every individual had an inborn need for growth (as well as other needs such as being loved and feeling worthwhile) towards a "success identity". The success identity helped a person bring their external reality closer to their internal world of expectations, and perceptions of what they wanted their lives to be. Glasser believed that if one didn't experience love, feeling significant to others, being meaningfully connected to others, and have a positive self worth, than instead of a success identity they would have a "failure identity". A failure identity was associated with a maladjusted personality and a sense of not being in control of one's life. As a result, one might then use inappropriate means to fulfill the same needs, such as manipulating and coercing others as a way to feel a semblance of worth or connect etc. Therefore, the goal of therapy was to help one develop a successful identity, to obtain a good life, with a sense of connection, love, and positive self worth.

The importance of one's self-identity was later stressed by Jim Haaven and Emily Coleman in the 1990s. They believed that the goal of becoming the sort of person, or having the identity, that would lead one to be successful, and become a "somebody" was important for persons with intellectual disabilities (ID) who committed sex offenses. The central tenet of

---

* Corresponding author: Hfaccini@aol.com

their model is that real change can be possible if the person develops a success identity (New Me), they learn to not allow the old identity/patterns (Old Me) to take control, and they persist in implementing their New Me coping skills and living their Good Life. The Old Me can be defined as the person, or identity, that engaged in the dysfunctional patterns and lifestyle and then offended, while the New Me is the person who is currently in treatment and trying to change. The goal of treatment is to live one's "Good Life", a lifestyle that is successful and functional for the person while being a New Me every day.

Another concept that is paramount in this treatment model is the reliance on self efficacy. Self efficacy or hanging in is defined as the individual having the belief and skills to hang in (or persist) and do the task and that that task will make a positive difference in their life.

Faccini [1] summarized "the Old Me New Me Model of treatment as a comprehensive model in that it addresses self-management via identity change, enhancing motivation, skill development and lifestyle enhancements. At the core of the treatment is the identification of the Old and New Me's identities, thoughts, feelings, behaviors, and situations. The utility of using the Old Me identity is that it allows enough of a personal distance from the past lifestyle and offenses that disclosures and acceptance of responsibility, and heightened levels of motivation are facilitated. The New Me, or success-oriented identity, is especially meaningful to the individual since he/she may have had to live with the stigma of their problems, and have possibly even had this come to define their identity; the New Me identity, goals and Good Life provides powerful motivation to progress through treatment. However, the relationship between a person's Old and New Me is dynamic and always present. The two "identities" are always battling for control of the person, namely the Old Me is probably stronger and smarter when therapy is initiated. One goal of therapy is for the New Me (the person who is now in treatment), to "hang in" (persist in coping) to become stronger and learn the tricks of the Old Me so that the person can further approach who they want to become (i.e. the New Me identity), and approach their "good life". Rather than a unidirectional relationship, the relationship that exists between the Old Me and New Me is transactional and dynamic."

The treatment model has four different phases, namely "Getting Ready, Learning theNew Me, Making the New Me Smarter and Stronger and New Me Every Day" (Haaven [2]. The first phase of "Getting Ready" involves such tasks as developing a support Plan learning how to be a good group member and getting to know the other group members, telling one's autobiography in group, and getting to learn about feelings and treatment concepts and terms. The second phase in treatment, "Learning the New Me", involves teaching and engaging each group member in meaningful and empowering personal projects to identify the Old and then New Me's identities, thoughts, behaviors, and situations. Other tasks during this second stage include developing a simple timeline discussing Good and Bad experiences during the person's life, who was in control during these times (i.e. Old Me or New Me), the disclosure of their Old Me's past sexual offending and its consequences, and the losses involved. Subsequently, a relationship development plan, goals and characteristics of their New Me and Good Life, and different coping skills are worked on. The third phase in therapy involves "Making the New Me Smarter and Stronger" such as seeking help skills, problem solving, and emotional control. Also, one particular New Me coping skill, is identified, practiced and strengthened on a daily basis. Other essential tasks, during this phase, involve identifying 'barriers" to one's New Life, learning thoughts, behaviors and situations that could lead one to reoffend, and how to cope with them (i.e. avoidance strategies, cognitive and arousalcontrol). The last phase of therapy, *New Me Every Day*, involves maintaining a realistic idea of one's risk level for reoffense, and to maintain relationships, openness, hanging in behaviors, seeking help when necessary and working on short and long term goals." One particular advantage of this model is that developing a New Me identity allows for a "base" for the skills to take hold and the necessary motivation for using them. This approach is different from other approaches that basically identify patterns and pathways, or means towards attaining "goods" and then teach alternative methods of attaining them and/or the necessary skills for better self-management.

This therapist has been able to apply the Old Me New Me model of sex offender treatment to both sex offenders with an intellectual disability (from the Moderate Mentally Retarded range through to Borderline IQ) as well as mentally ill sex offenders (who have average to high average IQs) who have been found by a court to be Not Guilty By Reason of Mental Disease or Defect (NGRI). It was surprising how quickly and easily even mentally ill psychopathic offenders admitted past sadistic and predatory patterns in treatment with the hope that they could learn to not identify with that "Old" identity and develop a new more empowering one. This reflects an ever growing trend that this efficacious model is being applied in Prison and Civil Commitment programs for person's with and without ID. The model is easily understood by most, and highly motivating and engaging for all in treatment. An example of an Old and New Me involves the case of an individual, with Mild Mental Retardation, who has been involved in Old Me New Me treatment for about 4 months and who had diagnoses of Depersonalization Disorder, Gender Identity Disorder, Pedophilia and Schizoid Personality Traits; this individual has been in treatment for many years with some progress.This person's Old Me was identified as "Peter Pan" since the person didn't want to grow up, and be like a baby or young child. The problem with this "identity" was that lived a child-oriented lifestyle, that contributed to and continued to put him at risk for pedophilia. His New Me, that of being a Man who valued having choices, helped motivate him to give up his imaginary friends (3 of whom"controlled" him to commit various sex offenses) and engage in Manly activities. He was so motivated by assuming his New Me identity that he also tried to help others. He mistakenly believed that another peer, who experienced command auditory hallucinations, was also talking to imaginary friends, like he used to. One day he approached this individual, and stated "don't talk to your imaginary friend, talk to real people like me". Proud that he had not only shared what had worked for himself, but that he was also practicing talking to real people instead of to his imaginary friends, he met with the response "Shut up, and go away" from his peer. After we both laughed about this in his individual session, he was praised regarding the changes that he was showing, and reminded that not all interactions will be positive nor like the one with his peer (who he knew for many years). Amazingly, with all of the co-morbid disorders that this person was diagnosed with, in about five months his levels of depersonalization, gender confusion, depression, anxiety, and child-oriented lifestyle, because of the Old Me and New Me Treatment (while not being on any psychotropic medications) were all at a minimal level.

Since many risky behaviors involve dysfunctional patterns etc. that need changing, it is believed that the Old Me New Me model can be applied with any offending pattern, and probably applied with most longstanding dysfunctional patterns of normal individuals. The basic power of the model involves the person examining his past identity, behaviors and patterns (Old Me) and learning that it is connected with unpleasant experiences in one's life, then purging oneself of this identity and developing a New identity and patterns that are successful. This core part of the process is similar to that which Scrooge goes through in *A Christmas Carol*. Basically, Scrooge in his examination of his past, present and future, comes to learn about the critical events that shaped who he became (an Old Me who loved money and nothing else), the losses and dysfunctional lifestyle and patterns that he developed, and how he still had a chance to develop a new identity (a New Me that valued caring and sociability) and lead a good life.

The Old Me New Me model of treatment has been ever expanding to the treatment of new populations. However, it is believed that this Old Me New Me treatment model could be used with other types of offending patterns such as in treating fire setting, aggression, violence and other criminal patterns especially when the patterns come to define the person. As more practitioners learn and apply the model they too will be astonished at the degree of engagement, involvement and disclosures of the participants, and the amount of change, not just progress, that can be attained.

REFERENCES

[1]   Faccini, L. (2009). Lost in the Shadow of the Crowd: Will I Be Healed? Choosing Treatment Targets and Approaches. *Sexuality and Disability,* (in press).
[2]   Haaven, J. (2006). *Personal Communication.* Jhaaven@comcast.net.

INDEX

E

F

G